Y. V. Koh
Royal Autobiography in the Book of Qoheleth

Beihefte zur Zeitschrift für die alttestamentliche Wissenschaft

Herausgegeben von
John Barton · Reinhard G. Kratz
Choon-Leong Seow · Markus Witte

Band 369

Walter de Gruyter · Berlin · New York

Y. V. Koh

Royal Autobiography
in the Book of Qoheleth

W
DE
G

Walter de Gruyter · Berlin · New York

♾ Printed on acid-free paper which falls within the guidelines of the ANSI
to ensure permanence and durability.

ISBN-13: 978-3-11-019228-5
ISBN-10: 3-11-019228-4
ISSN 0934-2575

Library of Congress Cataloging-in-Publication Data

A CIP catalogue record for this book is available from the Library of Congress.

Bibliographic information published by the Deutsche Nationalbibliothek

Die Deutsche Nationalbibliothek lists this publication in the Deutsche Nationalbibliografie;
detailed bibliographic data are available in the Internet at http://dnb.d-nb.de.

Printed in Germany
Cover design: Christopher Schneider, Berlin

To Revd. Professor John A. Emerton

In gratitude for his support and encouragement, and friendship.

Table of Contents

Abbreviations

General

col.	column
ET	English translation
l. , ll.	line , lines
LXX	Septuagint
MT	Masoretic text
PN	personal name
RN	royal name
v. , vv.	verse , verses

Publications cited by initials and short titles of works forming part of a series

AB	Anchor Bible
ABD	*Anchor Bible Dictionary*. Edited by D. N. Freedman. 6 vols. New York: Doubleday, 1992.
ACP	Archaeological Center Publication
AEL	*Ancient Egyptian Literature*. M. Lichtheim. 3 vols. Berkeley: University of California Press, 1973-1980.
AfO	Archiv für Orientforschung
ANET	*Ancient Near Eastern Texts Relating to the Old Testament*. J. B. Pritchard. 3rd edn. Princeton: Princeton University Press, 1969.
ANETS	Ancient Near Eastern Texts and Studies
Annals	*The Annals of Sennacherib*. D. D. Luckenbill. Chicago: University of Chicago Press, 1924.
AnSt	*Anatolian Studies*

APEANES   Athlone Publications in Egyptology and Ancient
            Near Eastern Studies
ARAB   *Ancient Records of Assyria and Babylonia.* D. D. Luc-
            kenbill. 2 vols. Chicago: University of Chicago
            Press, 1926-1927.
ARI   *Assyrian Royal Inscriptions.* A. K. Grayson. 2 vols.
            RANE. Wiesbaden: Harrassowitz, 1972-1976.
AS   Assyriological Studies
ASOR   American Schools of Oriental Research
ASOR DS   American Schools of Oriental Research Dissertati-
            on Series
ATAT   Arbeiten zu Text und Sprache im Alten Testament
ATD   Das Alte Testament Deutsch
ATM   *Altes Testament und Moderne*
AUK   Arbeiten und Untersuchungen zur Keilschrift-
            kunde
BASOR   Bulletin of the American Schools of Oriental Re-
            search
BBB   Bonner biblische Beiträge
BDB   F. Brown, S. R. Driver and C. A. Briggs. *A Hebrew*
            and English Lexicon of the Old Testament. Oxford:
            Clarendon, 1907.
BETL   Bibliotheca Ephemeridum theologicarum Lova-
            niensium
BHS   *Biblia Hebraica Stuttgartensia.* K. Elliger and W.
            Rudolph. Stuttgart: Deutsche Bibelgesellschaft,
            1984.
BHT   Beiträge zur historischen Theologie
Bib   *Biblica*
BibInt   *Biblical Interpretation: A Journal of Contemporary*
            Approaches
BiOr   Bibliotheca Orientalis
BKAT   Biblischer Kommentar, Altes Testament
BLS   Bible and Literature Series
BR   Biblische Reihe
BTB   Biblical Theology Bulletin
BZAW   Beihefte zur ZAW
CANE   *Civilizations of the Ancient Near East.* Edited by J.
            Sasson. 4 vols. New York: Simon & Schuster
            Macmillan, 1995.
CBQ   *Catholic Biblical Quarterly*
CBQMS   Catholic Biblical Quarterly Monograph Series

CBSC	Cambridge Bible for Schools and Colleges
CGFTD	Cahiers du Groupe François-Thureau-Dangin
ConBOT	Coniectanea biblica: Old Testament Series
COS	*The Context of Scripture.* 3 vols. Edited by W. W. Hallo and K. L. Younger, Jr. Leiden: Brill, 1997-2000.
CRRAI	Compte rendu de la Rencontre Assyriologique Internationale
EB	Études bibliques
EF	Erträge der Forschung
EI	*Eretz Israel*
EQ	*Evangelical Quarterly*
EvT	*Evangelische Theologie*
FC	Fathers of the Church
FOTL	The Forms of the Old Testament Literature
FSCS	Faith and Scholarship Colloquies Series
GKC	*Gesenius' Hebrew Grammar.* Edited by E. Kautzsch. Translated by A. E. Cowley. 2nd edn. [=28th German edn.] Oxford: Clarendon, 1910.
HAHL	*Handbook of Ancient Hebrew Letters.* D. Pardee, S. D. Sperling, J. D. Whitehead, and P. E. Dion. SBLSBS 15. California: Scholars Press, 1982.
HAL	L. Koehler, W. Baumgartner, and J. J. Stamm. *Hebräisches und aramäisches Lexikon zum Alten Testament.* 2 vols. 3rd edn. Leiden: Brill, 1995. [ET: *HALOT*]
HALOT	L. Koehler, W. Baumgartner, and J. J. Stamm. *The Hebrew and Aramaic Lexicon of the Old Testament.* Translated and edited under the supervision of M. E. J. Richardson. 4 vols. Leiden: Brill, 1994-1999. [=3rd German edn. *HAL*]
HAT	Handbuch zum Alten Testament
HBS	Herders biblische Studien
HKAT	Handkommentar zum Alten Testament
HOE	Handbuch der Orientalistik Ergänzungsband
HUCA	*Hebrew Union College Annual*
IBC	*Interpretation: A Bible Commentary for Teaching and Preaching*
ICC	International Critical Commentary
ILSSR	*International Library of Sociology and Social Reconstruction*
Int	Interpretation

ISBL	*Indiana Studies in Biblical Literature*
IT	Issues in Theology
ITC	International Theological Commentary
JAAR	*Journal of the American Academy of Religion*
JBL	*Journal of Biblical Literature*
JDS	Judean Desert Studies
JNES	*Journal of Near Eastern Studies*
Joüon	Joüon, P. *A Grammar of Biblical Hebrew*. Translated and revised by T. Muraoka. 2 vols. Subsidia biblica 14/1-2. Rome: Editrice Pontifio Istituto Biblico, 1991.
JSOT	*Journal for the Study of the Old Testament*
JSOTSup	Journal for the Study of the Old Testament Supplement Series
JSS	*Journal of Semitic Studies*
JTS	*Journal of Theological Studies*
KA	Kunst und Altertum
KAH1	*Keilschrifttexte aus Assur, historischen Inhalts*. L. Messerschmidt. Vol. 1. WVDOG 16. Leipzig: J. C. Hinrichs, 1911.
KAH2	*Keilschrifttexte aus Assur, historischen Inhalts*. O. Schroeder. Vol. 2. WVDOG 37. Leipzig: J. C. Hinrichs, 1922.
KAI	*Kanaanäische und aramäische Inschriften*. H. Donner and W. Röllig. 2d ed. Wiesbaden: Harrassowitz, 1966-1969.
KAT	Kommentar zum Alten Testament
KHC	Kurzer Handkommentar zum Alten Testament
LBS	Library of Biblical Studies
MBPS	Mellen Biblical Press Series
MC	Mesopotamian Civilizations
MCSA	Mesopotamia.Copenhagen Studies in Assyriology.
NAC	New American Commentary
NCBC	New Century Bible Commentary
NEB	Neue Echter Bibel
NICOT	New International Commentary on the Old Testament
NIV	New International Version
NJPS	*Tanakh: The Holy Scriptures: The New JPS Translation according to the Traditional Hebrew Text.*
NRSV	New Revised Standard Version
OBO	Orbis biblicus et orientalis

OLA	Orientalia lovaniensia analecta
OLP	Orientalia lovaniensia periodica
Or	Orientalia
OTE	*Old Testament Essays*
OTL	Old Testament Library
RA	*Revue l'assyriologie et d'archéologie orientale*
RANE	Records of the Ancient Near East
RdSO	Rivista degli Studi Orientali
RGG¹	*Die Religion in Geschichte und Gegenwart.* Edited by O. Scheel, L. Zscharnack and H. Gunkel. 5 vols. Tübingen: Mohr, 1909-1914.
RGG³	*Die Religion in Geschichte und Gegenwart.* Edited by K. Galling and H. F. Campenhausen. 7 vols. 3rd edn. Tübingen: Mohr, 1957-1965.
RIMA	*The Royal Inscriptions of Mesopotamia, Assyrian Periods.* 3 vols. A. K. Grayson. Toronto: University of Toronto Press, 1987-1996.
SAAS	State Archives of Assyria Studies
SBLDS	Society of Biblical Literature Dissertation Series
SBLSBS	Society of Biblical Literature Sources for Biblical Studies
SBLSCS	Society of Biblical Literature: Septuagint and Cognate Studies
SBTh	*Studia Biblica et Theologica*
SGV	Sammlung gemeinverständlicher Vorträge und Schriften
SJT	*Scottish Journal of Theology*
SQAW	Schriften und Quellen der Alten Welt
SSI	*Textbook of Syrian Semitic Inscriptions.* 3 vols. J. C. L. Gibson. Oxford: Clarendon, 1973-1979.
SSU	Studia Semitica Upsaliensia
SVT	Supplements to Vetus Testamentum
TB	Tyndale Bulletin
TCESSHRS	Travaux du Centre d'Etudes Supérieures Spécialisé d'Histoire des Religions de Strasbourg
TJ	*Trinity Journal*
TSJTSA	Texts and studies of the Jewish Theological Seminary of America
TV	*Theologische Versuche*
TZ	*Theologische Zeitschrift*
UF	*Ugarit-Forschungen*

UMS.SS	University of Missouri Studies: Social Science Series
VAB	Vorderasiatische Bibliothek
VF	*Verkündigung und Forschung*
VT	*Vetus Testamentum*
WBC	Word Biblical Commentary
WO	*Welt des Orients*
WUNT	Wissenschaftliche Untersuchungen zum Neuen Testament
WVDOG	Wissenschaftliche Veröffentlichungen der deutschen Orientgesellschaft
ZA	*Zeitschrift für Assyriologie*
ZAW	*Zeitschrift für die alttestamentliche Wissenschaft*

Sigla

Sigla used in transcribing and transliterating the ancient Semitic inscriptions

[ ]	in Semitic text denotes restored element(s)
< >	in Semitic text denotes element(s) omitted in error by the stone mason or scribe
[ ]	in English text denotes translation of restored element(s)
( )	in English text denotes additions to improve the sense
–	denotes the presence of an undecipherable letter
…	denotes the omission of a few words

Chapter 1

Introduction

From being described as the "black sheep"[1] and the "strangest"[2] book of the Old Testament to having its author depicted as a neurotic bureaucrat with homosexual tendencies[3], the book of *Qoheleth*[4] continues to mesmerize its readers and attract a myriad of eclectic interpretations of its enigmatic text. In fact, up until today, there is still no majority consensus on many of its literary details, including the more basic aspects such as its provenance, authorship, literary structure, and integrity. As Newsome aptly describes the situation, "every scholarly conversation with the book of *Qoheleth* is characterized by a set of perennial problems of a basic nature that are never completely resolved or transcended by a shift of paradigm".[5] Taking up Qoheleth's call for assertive achievement and joining in the interpretative fray, this present study seeks to offer a fresh approach to the interpretation of *Qoheleth* which focuses on the royal voice. Specifically, this study seeks to argue that the royal voice plays a more positive and integral role in the composition than is generally thought by the majority of commentators today. This approach also comes in response to growing sceptical views of *Qoheleth* which see the book as satirical, subversive, and anti-wisdom.

I shall begin with a brief survey of the history behind the arguments about authorship and the perceived contradictions in the work as a means to introducing key issues which I shall later

---

1   Wright 1946, 18.
2   Scott 1965, 191.
3   Zimmerman (1973).
4   In this monograph I shall use italics to indicate the book of *Qoheleth* and Roman script when I am referring to Qoheleth the character.
5   Newsome 1995, 183.

take up in my discussion of my proposed approach to interpreting *Qoheleth*.

I. A Survey of the History of Interpretation of *Qoheleth*

A. Pre-critical Interpretations of *Qoheleth*

1. Early Jewish Interpretations

The early rabbis accepted, from the start, a Solomonic authorship to the work on the basis of the identification of Qoheleth as the "son of David" (1:1) and "king over Israel in Jerusalem" (1:12) in the beginning verses of the book. This assumption, which stood as the main guiding exegetical presupposition for most of the book's early history of interpretation, found further support in Qoheleth's description of his grand achievements and lavish lifestyle which many saw as closely reflecting those of Solomon in his glory days. The presence of large portions of didactic material in the book further hinted at Israel's chief patron of wisdom as the author of the enigmatic book.

The tradition of the Solomonic authorship, however, appears not to have been firmly held as generally assumed for there were clearly some questioning of it within the rabbinic circles due to the inconsistencies of thought found in the book, which in turn led to questions about its suitability for public instruction and circulation. The rabbis discussed and debated at length over the issue of whether the work was to be considered divinely inspired. To be sure, the discussions on whether the book "defiles the hands" had no bearing on the canonicity of the book for this matter was already accepted early on.[6] The focus of the

---

6   Delitzsch, McNeile and Wright have all called attention to three Talmudic stories found in y. Ber. 11b (vii, 2), B. Bat. 4a and Šabb. 30b, which have characters that are set in the first century A.D. and who appear to be quoting the texts of *Qoheleth*. If these are anything to go by, they at least indicate that Qoheleth's place in the canon was already accepted early on. By the second century, its canonical authority appears to have been widely recognized as it featured in several canonical lists, the clearest of which belongs to Melito of Sardis (c. A. D. 170) which records the books of Proverbs, *Qoheleth*, and Canticles in this very order (Eus. *Hist. eccl.* iv. 26); McNeile (1904, 8); Audet

discussions and debates was rather on whether *Qoheleth* was to be regarded as sacred material, a product of divine inspiration, or merely an outcome of Solomon's "natural" wisdom. Leiman emphasizes this distinction, arguing that the rabbis were only concerned with the issue of *Qoheleth's* inspired origin and never with the presence of the book in the canon because the criteria for entry into the Hebrew canon did not necessarily require divine inspiration behind the composition but was instead based on three other principles. These are, according to Leiman, that first, the book was deemed to make a good authoritative guide for Jewish practice and belief; secondly, it was suitably binding for all time; and thirdly, it was appropriate for both private and public study.[7] Although Leiman's suggested criteria for entrance to the canon are debatable, his argument for the distinction between the issues of canonicity and divine inspiration is likely to be correct since by the first century A. D., at the discussion in Jamnia, it was not the issue of the canonicity of *Qoheleth* which was the focus of a particular session of the rabbinic gathering, but rather the issue of its inspired origin which was debated between the rival schools of Shammai and Hillel (m. Yad 3:5; m. 'Ed 5:3; b. Meg 7a). In the discussions of the divine inspiration of the book as well as of its contradictory nature, the assumption of Solomonic authorship was held by certain quarters in the rabbinic community to provide the justification for promoting its universal acceptance. This is seen, for example, in the Talmud (b. Meg. 7a), which records the ongoing debate among the early

---

(1950, 143); Murphy (1992, xxiii). If Josephus's description of the four books of "hymns to God and precepts for the conduct of human life" does refer to the books of Psalms, Proverbs, *Qoheleth*, and Canticles (*C. Ap.* 1.38-41) this would be additional evidence for its early canonical status. That there is a remarkable absence of Midrashim on all of the biblical wisdom books during the rabbinic period of the first to the sixth century A. D. might also indicate a long-standing acceptance of the book's canonicity by the Jewish community.

7   Leiman (1976, 115, 119-28). Wright (1883) and Barton (1908) similarly saw the rabbinic debates over the nature of the book to be for the purpose of deciding on its promotion rather than on the issue of canonicity. Beckwith likewise asks, "is it not possible that the disputes were about books long acknowledged as canonical... and all of them privately studied as Scripture, before and during the period of the disputes, no less than afterwards?" (Beckwith 1985, 276).

rabbis over *Qoheleth* and its perceived heresy and their attempts at deciding whether it "defiles the hands ritually".[8]

> R. Meir says that [the scroll of] Koheleth does not render the hands unclean, and that about the Song of Songs there is a difference of opinion. R. Jose says that the Song of Songs renders the hands unclean, and about Koheleth there is a difference of opinion. R. Simeon says that Koheleth is one of those matters in regard to which Beth Shammai were more lenient and Beth Hillel more stringent, but Ruth and the Song of Songs and Esther [certainly] make the hands unclean! – Samuel concurred with R. Joshua. It has been taught: R. Simeon b. Menasia said: Koheleth does not render the hands unclean because it contains only the wisdom of Solomon. They said to him, Was this then all that he composed? Is it not stated elsewhere, *And he spoke three thousand proverbs,* and it further says, *Add thou not unto his words?* Why this further quotation! – In case you might object that he composed very much, and what it pleased him to write he wrote and what it did not please him he did not write. Therefore it says, *Add thou not his words.*[9]

It is likely that the early rabbis saw the assumed Solomonic authorship of the book as responsible for the book's place in the canon with which, together with its orthodox epilogue, the contradictions could be eventually harmonized. Although the Solomonic assumption might have been thought to be the reason behind the book's canonization and hence treated austerely, not all of the early rabbis appear to have been fully convinced of the book's connection with Solomon. B. Šabb. 30b, for example, mentions how the contradictions in the book almost resulted in its withdrawal, but that it was eventually accepted because of its religious framing – that the words of the Torah were found in its opening (1:3) and closing passages (12:13) – which in some ways validated their presence, so that in the end, it was the orthodoxy of the epilogue, and not its assumed Solomonic authorship which helped to bring about the justification for its promotion.[10]

---

8   A similar record of this debate over the sacred character of *Qoheleth* is found in the earlier m. Yad. 3:5, and also m. 'Ed. 5:3, t. Yad. 2:13, b. Meg. 7a, 'Abot R. Nat. A, ch. 1, b. Šabb. 30b, and Qoh. Rab. 1:3.

9   Simon 1938, 36.

10   There are clear and observable tensions in the rabbinic texts which suggest that the debates and discussions were not always settled clearly and decisively. Sandberg points out, for example, that m. Yad. 3:5 is confusing and does not inform the readers about the reasons behind the decisions of both parties. She remarks, "what makes this passage so discordant is the fact that the earlier second-generation tannaim decided that Qohelet was definitely inspired

The early rabbinic treatments of *Qoheleth* were largely homogeneous as the interpreters found themselves constrained by the assumption of Solomonic authorship and their concern for the promotion of the primacy of the Torah. As such, the contradictions would almost always be reconciled to either one of these two major interpretative concerns. Hence, Qoheleth would often be pictured as a Solomonic sage with a manifest interest in the Torah. In dealing with the contradictions, many of the rabbis resorted to radical forms of reinterpretation to remove any heterodox overtones which might be seen to challenge the pietism of the Jewish traditions and the Torah. The methods used to overcome the problems raised by the texts were often extreme. However, there were also the more sober approaches such as the suggestion that Solomon gave himself freedom in airing a few disconcerting thoughts before eventually returning to qualify them with moral exhortations,[11] or for the more difficult passages, these were described as Solomon quoting the words of fools.[12] The Targumist went further to ascribe the spirit of prophecy to the Solomonic Qoheleth, explaining that the pessimism behind the words of 2:18 reflected Solomon's despair over the forthcoming tragedies which were to unfold upon his kingdom during the reign of Rehoboam. In attributing the spirit of prophecy to Qoheleth, the Targumist was also indirectly

---

scripture, and yet the later, third-generation tannaim appear to ignore this ruling and continue to debate the book's status. This lack of acceptance of Qohelet as divinely inspired by the third generation of tannaim may indicate the on-going difficulty the rabbis have with the contents of the book. The opening statement of this mishnah was probably added at a later, undesignated time, when for some unknown reason, the debate finally ceased and both books [i.e. *Qoheleth* and Canticles] were at last accepted as inspired" (1999, 21-2).

11   Qoh. Rab. 11:9. This strategy was also used by the Targumists.

12   The Zohar (the Talmud of the Kabbala), for example, interprets the "heretical" passages as Solomon quoting the words of the "worldly fool" to expose their folly. The commentary on 3:19 explains, "Solomon did not say this for himself, as the other words, but he repeats here the words of the worldly fool, who says so. And what do they say? That 'the destiny of man and the destiny of beasts,' ... They are fools, because they know not, nor do they enquire into wisdom; they say that this world goes on by chance, and the Holy One, blessed be He, takes no cognizance of it; but that 'the destiny of man and the destiny of the beast is the same, and the same destiny happens to all.' And as Solomon knew these fools who spoke in this manner, he called them beasts, for they degraded themselves into mere beasts by uttering such sentiments" Ginsburg (1861, 59). See modern discussion on the use of quotations on pp. 164-168.

seeking to affirm the divine inspiration and authority of the book.[13]

In the medieval period, the rabbis did apply stricter methods of interpretation as seen in their willingness to recognize the contradictory nature of the book, although there remained the tendency to use imaginative homiletic interpretations to overcome problems raised by the text. During this period, Rashbam notably suggested the presence of editorial activity in the book, arguing that the original work was possibly couched in a framework consisting of a prologue (1:1-2) and epilogue (12:8-14) added later by an editor.[14] Rashbam further offered the theory that there were two kinds of wisdom expressed in the book: the common or superficial wisdom, and the profound wisdom which lies beyond human comprehension. This distinction provided a way to account for some of the seeming contradictions in the book (e.g. 1:16 in relation to 7:23-24, and 2:13 in relation to 2:15-16) whilst simultaneously affirming its authority and suitability for public instruction. Throughout the rabbinic period of interpreting *Qoheleth*, the assumption of Solomonic authorship remained an interpretative enigma alongside the contradictions and inconsistencies that were found in the book.

2. Early Church Interpretations

Like the Jewish rabbis, the early Christian exegetes accepted *Qoheleth* as the work of Solomon without much questioning. Jerome, though aware of the divided opinions of the rabbis on the authority and purpose of the book, viewed *Qoheleth* as belonging to a trilogy of Solomon's poetic writings composed to instruct its readers in the three stages of their spiritual life:

---

13 In his comment on the part the rabbis played in helping the book gain a wider acceptance, Gordis writes, "That all these doubts were brushed aside and a place given the book in Holy Writ is surely to be credited to the August authority of Solomon... The homiletic interpretations of 'difficult passages' as embodied in the Targum and Midrash, did the rest" (1968, 41-2).

14 Japhthet believes that Rashbam is possibly the earliest known scholar to suggest evidence of editorial work in the book (1985, 34).

Proverbs, for instructing the young to fulfil their duties and live righteously; *Qoheleth*, to teach the more promising students to despise the things of the world that are perishing; and for the more mature, Canticles, a mystical song of the love of God which is the crown of life's teaching.[15] Like Rashbam, Jerome also spoke of the two different levels of meaning in the text, that is, the literal (*haec juxta litteram*) and spiritual (*secundum intellegentiam spiritalem*), in his explaination of the purported contradictions and inconsistencies in the book. Jerome was further guided in his interpretation by his view that "Ecclesiastes noster est Christus".[16] This latter principle, which was also held by other early Christian interpreters, meant that the words and message of the book were deemed authoritative and was therefore to be heard and obeyed by Christians.

The early Christian exegetes were not short in finding novel ways of "smoothening" the problematic texts as many were keen to transform what was seen as a contradictory and heretical book into a work which could be appreciated as Solomon's "sermon" to the whole assembly (ἐκκλησία) of God. Allegorical and mystical modes of interpretation were frequently relied upon to solve the inconsistencies and contradictions. Thus, for example, Qoheleth's admonition to eat, drink, and enjoy life (e.g. 2:26, 3:12-13, etc.) was spiritualized and read as an invitation to partake of Christ's body and blood, the true bread and drink, and the exhortation to "enjoy life" was interpreted as a call to exercise spiritual discipline in one's life. Where a spiritual interpretation was impossible, the difficult passages were assigned to the mouths of "fools", a euphemism for the opponents of ecclesiastical dogma.

Some of the early Jewish interpretations, which worked on the assumption of Solomonic authorship, reemerged in the early Christian circles. Gregory Thaumaturgos, for example, sub-scribed to the theory of Solomon rethinking his thoughts, positing that at the beginning Solomon did say such and such but in the end gave a dogmatically correct interpretation, or that the foolish words were those of Solomon spoken in his younger

---

15 Smalley 1986, 40.
16 Migne 1845, col. 1013.

days.[17] Gregory also explained a few of the contradictions and inconsistencies as Solomon's temporary loss of his gift of wisdom (e.g. 2:9-12, 17-21; 7:15, 23; 8:15-17; 12:10), or that Solomon was quoting those with whom he consequently showed disagreement.[18] Another popular interpretation in the Early Church was that Solomon in *Qoheleth* was acting as an orator and impersonating various characters having different opinions. This interpretative strategy was used, for example, by Gregory the Great who commented, "This book, then, is called 'the preacher' because in it Solomon makes the feelings of the disorganized people his own in order to search into and give expression to the thoughts that come to their untutored minds...".[19]

It is clear that, like the early Jewish interpreters, the Early Church had difficulties with the apparent contradictions in the book and its perceived challenge against religious dogma, but managed to overcome these by providing translations and paraphrases which removed much of its enigmatic character whilst shaping it into a composition clearly suitable for the edification of the Christian community. Against the assumption of Solomonic authorship of the book, which the early Christian interpreters accepted without criticism, the contradictions and heterodox passages were reinterpreted so as to ensure that these could eventually be seen as originating from the lips of Israel's chief patron of wisdom and suitable for providing moral guidance and instruction in the church. The methods employed to smoothen out the difficulties were extreme in many instances. They included blatant forms of modification such as the adding, removing, or overall changing of expressions and concepts which occasionally contradicted the original text in order that the book might be found to be "in unison with the general Christian tradition".[20] Thus, whilst Gregory Thaumaturgos freely rendered the scepticism of *Qoheleth* (e.g. on the shared fate of human beings and animals in 3:19-21), the repeated call to man to eat,

---

17   Holm-Nielsen 1974, 175-6.
18   Jarick 1990, 314, 359 n. 41.
19   Zimmerman 1959, 193.
20   Jarick 1990, 315.

drink, and find enjoyment for himself (e.g. 2:24; 3:12-13, 22; 5:17[ET v.18]) was rejected as the error of "men of vanity" with a further comment that "the perfect good does not lie in eating and drinking, and that enjoyment is only granted by God to those people who act righteously".[21] On Qoheleth's remark in 9:1-3 about the moral indifference of death in choosing its victims, Gregory comments, "I know now that these are fools' arguments – errors and deceits!"[22] Another strategy which Gregory frequently employed to remove the perceived heterodoxy in *Qoheleth* was to omit the word "God" from those texts which appear to blame divinity for human suffering and moral injustice (e.g. 1:13; 3:10).[23]

3. The Reformation

During the Reformation many of the exegetical assumptions and arguments belonging to earlier traditions were subjected to serious questioning for the first time as the language of *Qoheleth* was put under increasing critical analysis. The assumption that Solomon was the author of the book, in particular, began to draw increasing doubts. Luther who had, at first, viewed *Qoheleth* as a collection of Solomon's casual speech to his court retinue during dinner, assembled by those present and transmitted by the leaders of the church (like Luther's own "table talk"), changed his mind and later expressed doubt over the book's connection with Solomon. He remarked, "This book wants more completeness; it is too abrupt... Solomon himself has not written the book of Ecclesiastes, it was compiled by Sirach at the time of the Maccabees... It is like the Talmud, made up of many books, which perhaps belonged to the library of King Ptolemy Euergetes in Egypt."[24] Grotius likewise queried the traditional assumption of Solomonic authorship, arguing instead that the

---

21 Jarick (1990, 311). For a description of the other main "tactics" employed by Gregory Thaumaturgos, see (ibid., 309-316).

22 Ibid., 226.

23 Ibid., 313.

24 Förstemann and Bindseil (1844-48, 400-1) as translated by Ginsburg (1861, 113) cf. Luther (1972, 12).

book was a collection of opinions by different sages originally
spoken to different people. Grotius's doubts over the Solomonic
authorship were based on arguments to do with the language of
the book. He wrote, in his 1644 commentary, "I believe that the
book is not the production of Solomon, but was written in the
name of this king, as being led by repentance to do it. For it
contains many words which cannot be found except in Ezra,
Daniel and the Chaldee paraphrasts."[25]

B. Modern Critical Scholarship on *Qoheleth*

From the mid-eighteenth through to the nineteenth century,
along with the rise of literary criticism, there was an increasing
recognition that the language and message of the book spoke
against Solomon as its author. Bishop Lowth, for example,
observed that the style and the language of the work could not
support a Solomonic authorship but rather "the vanity of the
world was exemplified by the experience of Solomon, who is
introduced in the character of the person investigating a very
difficult question".[26] Delitzsch drew a list of a hundred words,
forms, and meanings which he argued *Qoheleth* shared with the
post-exilic books of the Old Testament and Mishnaic Aramaic.
This led him to make his classic remark, "If the Book of Koheleth
be of old Solomonic origin, then there is no history of the
Hebrew language."[27] As the notion of Solomon as author of the
book became untenable discussions on its authorship shifted
from Solomon to Qoheleth (as a word denoting an office – from
the Qal feminine participle קֹהֶלֶת – assembler, and by extension,
teacher, preacher). In a complete change in direction, literary
source critics took to solving the tensions by ascribing the more
orthodox and edifying texts to the work of pietistic interpolators.
Many held that the book in its final form had been subjected to
extensive additions and interpolations by enthusiastic editors
who were keen to curb the "heretical" tendencies of the original

---

25   As cited by Ginsburg 1861, 146.
26   Lowth 1815, xxiv, Lecture 24.
27   Delitzsch 1891, 190.

underlying text. Many also viewed the work, in its original form, to be essentially pessimistic and sceptical in character, and belonging to Qoheleth who perhaps had an Epicurean nature. Those verses which reflected the values and truths of conventional wisdom were ascribed to the hands of pietistic and wise interpolators and glossators who supposedly found it necessary to scatter orthodox maxims throughout the text to counter Qoheleth's negative teachings.

Haupt's interpretation is one such example of the theory of massive interpolation and gloss. Haupt argued that the "genuine" portions of the work, which reflected Sadducean and Epicurean values, were possibly left in a confusing state by the author himself, which was later made worse when, upon his death, it was edited by his friends who added many Pharisaic interpolations drawn from Stoic doctrines.[28] Siegfried posited a more sober version of the theory, suggesting that there were at least seven, if not more, interpolators and glossators who took the task of countering Qoheleth's heterodoxy.[29] McNeile preferred a more refined version, believing that the extent of the interpolations was much smaller and the process much simpler.[30] Jastrow, in the extreme, purportedly noted 120 instances of "orthodox" interpolations and maxims (which, he argued, were added to give the book a didactic character like Proverbs and Sirach), along with other miscellaneous comments, glosses, and minor changes.[31]

The theory of massive interpolation and gloss eventually fell out of favour as modern commentators came to doubt its plausibility; not because it was possible to imagine that a book may not have any editorial addition at all, but because the multiplicity of redactions posited by the majority of the proponents of this theory beggared belief. In particular, the theory drew a further question of why the glossators would have wanted to correct the book to such an extent when it would have

---

28   Haupt (1905).
29   Siegfried (1898).   Interestingly Siegfried observed a uniformity of style throughout the book which, he admitted, weakened his argument.
30   McNeile (1904)
31   Jastrow 1919, 245-55.

been easier to remove it altogether or to write another book to refute its arguments instead.[32] Moreover, upon closer look, the suggested glosses with their pious interventions had not been effective in their purpose of alleviating Qoheleth's pessimism and heterodoxy.[33] Scholars soon came to view the book as essentially the work of a single author, and that Qoheleth might be using material other than his own in the form of quotations in order to offer his critique. Thus Gordis later argued against Podechard that, rather than suggesting that a later Hasid was responsible for adding in some "orthodox" passages, it could be that Qoheleth was quoting traditional wisdom for the purpose of providing a text for his own commentary.[34] This theory of quotation had of course been suggested before by the early interpreters, though in relation to the assumption of a Solomonic authorship.

For most of the twentieth century, commentators continued to focus on the issues of unity and integrity of composition and discussions of authorship began to shift from Solomon to the character of Qoheleth. There were two reasons for this. First, the language of *Qoheleth* precluded a Solomonic date, and secondly, commentators found it easier to argue for the unity of the work by ascribing the contradictions to the character of Qoheleth. Galling, for example, suggested that the contradictions and the disparate thoughts found in the text were due to the single author's "dynamic process" of composition. He remarked:[35]

---

32   Whybray (1989, 24-5, n.7). Gordis writes, "That a passage here and there might have been added in Koheleth is at least a possible view. But that the book was subjected to thoroughgoing elaboration in order to make it fit into the Biblical canon is an assumption for which no real analogy exists, indeed is contradicted by the history of the Apocrypha and the Pseudepigrapha after their composition." (1968, 71-2).

33   As Fox points out, the "eliminated" sentences often appear to belong to the original work (e.g. 2:13-14a if excised would leave a gap which 2:12a anticipates), the glosses do not fulfil the purposes of the ascribed authors as Qoheleth's painful doubts have the last word (e.g. 8:11-12a and 14 do not effectively dispel Qoheleth's scepticism about God's justice), the sceptical and pessimistic character of the book remains blatant even after all the suggested additions are incorporated, and the putative additions do not result in consistency (1989, 24-5).

34   Gordis (1968, 71-4); Podechard (1912).

35   Galling 1932, 281.

Erweist sich der Versuch, das Buch Qohelet vom Thema und Aufbau her zu erfassen, als undurchführbar und in gleicher Weise der Weg der Umstellungen, Streichungen und Quellenaufteilung, so muß von den einzelnen Aphorismen ausgegangen werden. Ihre Einheit - nicht Einheitlichkeit – muß in der Einheit des Menschen Kohelet, ihre Widersprüche, Spannungen und Gebrochenheiten müssen in eben diesem Widerspruch, der Spannung und Gebrochenheit des Menschen Kohelet geschaut werden. Es gilt, die Kräfte des dynamischen Schaffensprozesses abzutasten, um ohne Nivellierung, Addition und Subtraktion die ganze Fülle der Lebensschau und Lebenshaltung in diesem Menschen und seinem Werk zu erkennen.

Galling argued that the book (besides its epilogues) was a collection of loose sayings, divided into 27 unconnected units of "sentenzen", bearing no organic connection to each other except that they belonged to Qoheleth. Galling further explained that the contradictions were due to Qoheleth's debate with traditional wisdom schools. Scholars soon took to the view that the contradictions were part of Qoheleth's peculiar literary technique and not the work of later redactors and that the "tensions" in the text reflected Qoheleth's examination and interaction with conventional wisdom. Earlier theories of Qoheleth being in debate with other parties were here revived in a modern version. Rather than being in debate with external associates, commentators began to view Qoheleth as being in debate with himself over the value and validity of traditional wisdom. Thus Loader, for example, posited that the contradictions in the book reflected Qoheleth's polemical debate with conventional wisdom, taking the form of counter-arguments occurring in a polar-opposite manner, all of which were held in the author's mind.[36] Loader argued further that this internal debate continued throughout the work without arriving at a resolution. Hertzberg also suggested that Qoheleth's self-debate reflected a "zwar-aber" style, whereby the author would assert or state a particular wisdom truth before proceeding to qualify it with another opposing statement or observation.[37] Hertzberg and Loader's theories sought to defend the integrity and unity of the work by attributing the contradictions and inconsistencies to Qoheleth's

---

36   Loader (1979). See later discussion in pp. 174-177.
37   Hertzberg (1963). See later discussion in pp. 178-184.

peculiar style of thought. The boldest argument yet for the unity of *Qoheleth* belongs to Fox who has suggested that the entire book, save its superscription (1:1), is the work of a single author who is writing about a story within a story. He explains that the work (i.e. 1:2-12:14) belongs to a "frame-narrator" who is telling the story of Qoheleth telling his own story.[38] According to Fox, the contradictions in the texts were deliberately created as is the tension between the epilogue and the main body of text – "both express the author's views, but with different tones and emphases".[39] Fox adds further, "Qohe-let's contradictions state the problems rather than resolving them, and the interpreter likewise must leave many of the observations in tension."[40]

C. Current Sceptical Interpretations of *Qoheleth*

In the discussions on the integrity and unity of the text, the interpretation of the royal elements (notably in 1:12-2:26 which is commonly described as Qoheleth's introduction) did not take center stage. The royal references were seen to belong to the fictitious guise which the author was using to help gain authority for his heterodox message. This widespread view was complemented by a corresponding argument that *Qoheleth* was essentially anti-wisdom.[41] In an interesting reversal of interpretation, rather than treating the more traditional "quo-tations" of wisdom as pious glosses, the unified view of the book led to views about Qoheleth's own rejection of traditional wisdom.

For a number of scholars today, *Qoheleth* represents a "crisis" in Israel's wisdom tradition in that the work is seen as a protest and ultimately a rejection of wisdom and its worth. Some have gone further to suggest that *Qoheleth* is essentially a subversive composition written to attack the dogma of wisdom tradition, the institution of monarchy, and also God.[42] Crenshaw, for

---

38 Fox (1977).
39 Fox 1989, 319.
40 Ibid., 11.
41 E.g. Gese (1963); Schmid (1966); Hengel (1974); Müller (1978); Crüsemann (1984); Crenshaw (1988).
42 Crenshaw (1988); Perdue (1996).

example, depicts Qoheleth as a disillusioned sage who is ambivalent about God's sense of justice and who, in response to his observations of the moral chaos that surrounds him, preaches a radical message to have pleasure in drinking and eating, urging others to throw away one's inhibitions and conscience because God has already approved such activities.[43] Crenshaw argues that the royal guise is only a temporary one and that "Qoheleth adopts this literary fiction for the moment, discarding it as soon as it has served its purpose", which is to establish authority for the work.[44] Reflecting this increasingly widespread view today, Crenshaw states that "except for the royal experiment in 1:12-2:26 the book does not adopt a royal perspective".[45] Crenshaw further argues that the image of the royal personage in Qoheleth's introduction is of a "self-indulgent monarch".[46]

Others who are also of the view that the royal fiction functions as a mask for what is essentially a piece of subversive literature include Seow who argues that the temporary Solomonic guise is used by Qoheleth "to show that even kings can have no real control over matters that are beyond the human grasp, and in some ways, even the wisest of kings is no better off than the ordinary fool".[47] Seow further contends that Qoheleth's observation of the absence of justice (3:16; 4:1-2; 5:7 [ET v.8]) reflects the work of a critic of the royal court rather than a king. Furthermore, the description of the king appears to be at a distance in passages such as 8:2-4, 10:4, 10:16-17, and 10:20, which appear to be words spoken by a subject rather than a monarch.[48] Seow argues that the purpose behind Qoheleth's use of the royal fiction, which he sees as limited to Qoheleth's self-introduction in 1:12-2:11, is for enhancing the element of irony in his ensuing message, namely that no one, not even kings or wise rulers, is spared from life's absurdities.[49] A similar argument is

---

43 Ibid., 27.
44 Ibid., 71.
45 Ibid., 55.
46 Ibid., 25.
47 Seow 1997, 98.
48 Ibid.
49 Ibid., 144.

forwarded by Brown who holds that the Solomonic fiction
functions both as a guise and a foil. He writes "As soon as the
sage dons the Solomonic mantle (1:12-2:12), he disposes it in
order to convey his harsh judgments about the futility of
"gainful" living."[50]

One of the most radical and negative views of Qoheleth's
royal guise belongs to Perdue who argues that Qoheleth's
message is essentially an attack on both the monarchy and God.
Perdue argues that Qoheleth's observation of the oppression of
victims by the "power elite" directly implicates the king and God
for their neglect of social duty.[51] He writes, "The monarchy for
Qoheleth, however, is grounded in an order of tyranny (kōaḥ,
"power"), which includes oppressive rule. And standing behind
the oppressive rule of kings is God."[52] Perdue adds, "for
Qoheleth, the 'fear of God' is not humble recognition that the
deity is the creator and sustainer of the cosmos who rules the
world in justice, as it is confessed elsewhere in the wisdom
corpus. Rather, the 'fear of God' is terror before the powerful,
divine tyrant who is able to destroy one's work and to take one's
life at his discretion, even caprice".[53]

More recently, Vinel has forwarded the argument that the
book Qoheleth was written as a "critical relecture" of the history
of the Israelite kings.[54] To support his thesis, Vinel points to a
number of allegedly "anti-royal" passages in the text (e.g. 1:2;
5:5, 7-8; 8:2-4; 9:1-14; 10:20) which, he argues, alludes to the
erroneous actions of the past kings of Israel as recorded in the
historical books of the Old Testament. Vinel contends that the
text of Eccl. 5:5, for example, echoes the incident in 1 Sam. 14:24

---

50   Brown 2000, 11.
51   Perdue (1994, 221). Perdue writes, "the royal voice of Solomon makes itself
     heard in new and startling fashion... The greatest patron of the sages and
     wisest of all of the Israelite and Jewish kings engages in a rather stunning
     critique of royal rule, undermining the theological basis for the legitimation of
     the monarchy" (ibid., 220).
52   Ibid.
53   Ibid., 224.
54   Vinel (1997). Vinel's interpretation is based on the LXX version of the book. He
     argues that the language of the Greek text (in particular, the vocabulary)
     displays a close affinity with the language of the narratives in the books of
     Reigns (i.e. 1, 2 Sam. and 1, 2 Kgs.), namely those that offer critiques of Israel's
     past kings.

where Saul, in the midst of waging a battle and based on his poor understanding of the Law, forbids his men to eat which consequently leads to their defeat. Similarly, Eccl. 9:14, might be a reference to the incident of Jeroboam's siege which is recorded in 1 Kgs. 12:24f. and 12:12; and perhaps even to Isa. 37:33-35 which describes Sennacherib's siege of Jerusalem, all of which, according to Vinel, the author of *Qoheleth* hints at to remind readers of the limits of the power of the king. Vinel further argues that 10:20 harks back to the incident of Shimei, whose cursing of David (2 Sam. 16:5-13) eventually costs him his life as Solomon exacted punishment for the offence (1 Kgs. 2:8, 43-46). Vinel's argument, that there are passages in *Qoheleth* which would readily evoke in the reader's memory the historical incidences to do with the mistakes of Israelite kings, shares in the increasingly common view that *Qoheleth* represents a critique of the Israelite institution of kingship and its wisdom tradition.

II. Purpose of This Study

Therefore, in contrast to the early traditional interpretations of *Qoheleth* where the Solomonic authorship of the book was strictly held for a relatively long period of its interpretative history, the majority of commentators today reject a Solomonic authorship and express a sceptical view of Qoheleth's self-representation as a king (let alone King Solomon) in the book. Commentators today generally take the view that the royal references in the book are part of a literary guise which is used by Qoheleth to gain authority for a work which is essentially protesting against the wisdom tradition and the institution of monarchy. It is argued that because of the unorthodox and heretical views found in the book, a royal guise was necessary in order to mask its true subversive intent.[55] Some commentators have gone further to interpret the work as a royal parody written in the form of a confession by a king who is indulging in self-criticism. The reason for adopting this view is that Qoheleth's sceptical attitude towards conventional wisdom (e.g. in his repeated

---

55   E.g. Crenshaw (1988); Perdue (1994); Seow (1997); Salyer (2000).

remarks about the futility of wisdom e.g. 1:18; 6:8; 7:23; 8:16-17)
and his encouragement of the pursuit of pleasure (e.g. "eat,
drink, and be happy" e.g. 2:24; 3:12-13, 22; 5:17 [ET v.18]) are
incongruent to the responsibility of a royal personage, and
perhaps even ironic for a wisdom composition. Furthermore,
Qoheleth's observation of moral injustice and social chaos is seen
as being incompatible with a royal voice.

It is against this prevalent sceptical interpretation of the royal
voice in *Qoheleth* that I wish to argue in this study. In particular,
this study seeks to demonstrate the limitations of such views
which assume that Qoheleth's self-representation as king is but a
temporary literary artifice, confined to the first two chapters and
used to disguise the author's true intentions in parodic or
satirical mode. I shall argue that the royal voice in *Qoheleth* plays
a more important role in the work than has been previously
recognized. I will seek to demonstrate that the royal voice is
much more pervasive and integral to the entire work and that,
rather than attacking the institution of monarchy by use of a
guise, the author is deliberately taking on a royal persona in
order to strengthen the book's royal connections. I shall further
suggest that Qoheleth's narrative is written in the form of a royal
autobiography and that the author's use of this motif – which is a
well-recognized conventional wisdom form – is deliberate and
affirms an essential continuity with a past tradition where
wisdom was once associated with the king and court. I shall
argue further that the motif of royal autobiography gives the
work its unity and helps explain the contradictions traditionally
found in the book.

III. Outline of This Study

This study will commence in Chapter 2 with the examination of
the main evidence for the royal voice in 1:12-2:26. This is
followed by an investigation of two recent arguments suggesting
that the royal voice is maintained throughout the work. Eight
passages of texts, which are commonly regarded as being "anti-
royal" in content and sentiment, will then be examined to see if
they are indeed incompatible with a royal voice (which I will

demonstrate they are not). In Chapter 3, I shall test the argument for the pervasiveness of the royal voice by investigating the language, style, and form of comparable texts from the ancient Near East in order to draw out parallel characteristics which might indicate that Qoheleth was using common forms which were well known in the ancient literary world. In Chapter 4, I shall give a more focused assessment of the characterization of the royal voice and suggest how the identification of the royal autobiography motif in *Qoheleth* can help us appreciate better the literary artistry and message of the book. In the final chapter, I shall discuss the implications arising from the conclusions of this study particularly in relation to the issue of Qoheleth's relationship to and place in the history of the wisdom tradition.

IV. Scope of This Study

The scope of my investigation and examination of the royal voice of Qoheleth will be limited to what is commonly referred to as the "main body of text" or "Qoheleth's narrative", that is, 1:12-11:6. There is an observable chiastic structure to the book of *Qoheleth* which separates this core body of text from two outer layers of framework. The first and inner framework consists of two sustained poems with the "vanity" refrains, whilst the second and outer framework, comprises the superscription and epilogue:

Superscription (1:1)
        Summary theme of "vanity of vanities" (1:2)
          Cosmological poem (1:3-11)

          Poem on old age and death (11:7-12:7)[56]
        Summary theme of "vanity of vanities" (12:8)
Epilogue (12:9-14)

---

56 Those supporting these limits to the passage include Witzenrath (1979); Crenshaw (1988, 181-2); Lauha (1978, 204-16); Murphy (1992, 114); Gilbert (1980, 97); Ogden (1984, 193-4); Fox (1989, 277); Backhaus (1993a, 303-17); Seow (1997, 368-9).

It is often said that these double frameworks are the only clearly
delineated sections of the book. The stylistic arrangement of
these frameworks with their clear limits are seen by many to
suggest that they may be the work of someone other than the
author of the inner body of text which, in contrast, is notorious
for its lack of logical order and structure.[57] Thus, Lauha, for
example, argues that the superscription (1:1), the "foreword" and
"concluding word" (1:2; 12:8), and the "colophon" of 12:9-11, are
from the hand of a first redactor and the epilogue of 12:12-14 a
second pietistic glossator.[58] Lauha, however, sees the opening
and closing poems as belonging to Qoheleth, although he adds
that these passages were likely "reorganized" by a later editor.[59]
Longman, in contrast, has suggested that the poems are the work
of another author.[60]

The argument that the location of Qoheleth's self-
introduction at 1:12 hints at a reorganization of the original text
finds support in the superscription of 1:1 in that it is possible to
imagine that the original work, having been rearranged in such a
manner that Qoheleth's self-introduction was moved away from
its original position at the start, now required a further
introduction by way of a superscription. This would help explain
the presence of 1:1 (which gives more details about Qoheleth
than he does of himself in his introduction[61]), and possibly even
the interjection of 7:27. The presence of a double introduction,
the first (arguably by the editor redactor) in 1:1, and the second
(and original) by Qoheleth himself in 1:12, does suggest that
some kind of editorial rearrangement of the text may have taken
place. Fox, however, views the issue of the presence of the
superscription (1:1) differently. Ignoring 1:1, Fox contends that
the rest of the work did not originally have a title, hence the
קֹהֶלֶת אָמַר in 1:2 was inserted by the editor as a temporary

---

57   Many scholars such as Galling, Loretz, Ellermeier, Whybray see the thematic
     refrains of 1:2 and 12:8 as not belonging to Qoheleth, remarking that they are
     "misleading" (Whybray 1989, 23).
58   Lauha 1978, 6-7.
59   Ibid., 32.
60   Longman 1998, 21.
61   The author of the superscription adds a further epithet of בֶּן־דָּוִד "son of
     David".

introduction for the benefit of its readers who would otherwise have to wait until 1:12 to hear of its author Qoheleth. Lohfink, however, raises the issue of the ambiguity and awkwardness of 1:2-3 at the start of the book which, without the presence of the superscription (1:1), would be more puzzling to its readers. He writes,[62]

> After 1:1 we would expect Qoheleth to be the speaker. But an unidentified authorial person speaks, and he cites Qoheleth. Without 1:1 we would have to say: "he is citing a leader of the assembly." It is as though we had turned on the radio in the middle of a program – the quoted text puts the reader in the middle of a speech, or even at the last sentence. One does not know to what the "all" refers.

There are many other theories of editorial arrangement and redaction which have in consideration the book's title, epilogue(s), and the sustained poems marking the ends of Qoheleth's main narrative. Loretz's particular argument of an editorial rearrangement of the original work, like that of Lauha, is especially interesting and holds further relevance to our purpose as he approaches the issue from the perspective of Qoheleth's opening speech which is royal in character.

Loretz and the Argument of Qoheleth's Royal Introduction

Loretz argues that Qoheleth's self-representation in 1:12 must be the original start of the author's work since self-introductions in first-person narratives, particularly those with a royal voice, typically occur at the beginning of their text, as is commonly attested in ancient Near Eastern royal inscriptions. Loretz contends that it is in fact natural to expect the narrator in a first-person narrative, especially if he is a king, to introduce himself at the beginning of a text.[63] To support his argument, Loretz refers to ancient Near Eastern royal inscriptions and the self-revelatory

---

62 Lohfink 2003, 36.
63 "So wird man als ursprunglichen Anfang des Buches die Selbsteinfuhrung: ‚Ich, Qoheleth, bin König...' (1:12) ansehen müssen. Dies ist der gegebene Anfang eines Buches, in dem ein König auftritt. Die handelnde und sprechende Person hat sich zu Beginn vorzustellen." (1964, 144).

speeches of God in Gen. 28:13 and Exod. 20:2.[64] Loretz's allusion
to ancient Near Eastern royal texts is interesting, especially in
regard to ancient Semitic royal inscriptions which, as we shall
see in Chapter 3, form an important parallel to *Qoheleth*. Loretz
gives two reasons for his view that 1:12 marks the original start
of Qoheleth's work. First, Loretz argues that it is commonly
expected that the speaker and protagonist of a narrative,
especially one with a royal voice, would introduce himself at the
beginning of the work, even if the work is a literary composition.
Furthermore, the opening passage which precedes 1:12 is unlike
the other prose passages of the book in terms of its poetic form.
Moreover, it is located outside Qoheleth's narration and is
without any first-person reference to tie it back to the main
narrative. Loretz's suggestion has come under the strong
criticism of Fox who argues that, in the absence of any formal
rules on literary forms with which Qoheleth's work may be
compared for evidence of possible editorial rearrangement of its
original composition, Loretz's suggestion of the original order of
the book is at best speculative.[65] Fox comments, "of course an
editor may rearrange an author's original order for his own
purposes, but unless we can discern the editor's activity by some
other criteria and discover his purpose in making the changes,
we cannot a priori attribute apparent disorder to him".[66] Fox's
argument about the lack of structural clues to its original form
and order is a valid one, and the missing criterion to which he
points is the similarities to ancient royal literature. Loretz's
argument, if it is to be judged truly persuasive, needs to be tested
further and this will be done in Chapter 3.

Other scholars who have expressed surprise at the "late"
appearance of Qoheleth's royal self-introduction include
Zimmerli and Ellermeier.[67] Ellermeier argues that the *Gattung* of

---

64   Ibid., 144 n.41.
65   Fox 1977, 87.
66   Ibid., 88 n.13. Ironically, Fox's own theory of a single authorship to the entire
      book of *Qoheleth*, based on the perceived parallel with ancient Egyptian didactic
      writings, is equally guilty of this same charge.
67   Whybray similarly spoke of the "displacement" of the royal introduction from
      the beginning of the work, attributing this and the two end poems to the work
      of a later editor (ibid., 22).

royal fiction is only used temporary in the book, that is, in 1:12-2:11, for the royal representations would have appeared at the beginning if the author had intended the entire work to be a royal fiction.[68] Zimmerli similarly raises the question whether the correspondence between *Qoheleth* and the Egyptian didactic literature of Ptahhotep, Kagemni, King Amenemhet, and Meri-kare is strictly correct since Qoheleth's introduction comes only in 1:12. Zimmerli comments:[69]

> In all den genannten Vorbildern steht die einführende Erzählung, welche den Zeitpunkt der Übermittlung der Weisheitslehre nennt, am Eingang des Buches. Es wird danach auffallen, daß diese Angabe im Predigerbuch in 1,12 erst im Anschluß an den Spruch 1,2 und das breit ausgeführte Wort in 1,3-11 erfolgt. Man wird sich danach fragen, ob nicht eine frühere Gestalt der Wortsammlung Kohelets mit 1,12 begonnen hat.

The arguments of those who speak of Qoheleth's narrative as possibly being "displaced" are interesting in that they see Qoheleth's royal self-representations in 1:12f. as having the appropriate characteristics of a true introduction, thus implicitly suggesting that there is more at work than a single layer of primary text between 1:1 to 12:14.

A proper investigation into this issue, which is beyond the scope of this study, would require the consideration of the relationship of the cosmological poem (1:4-11) and the extended poem on old age and dying (11:7-12:7) to this "main body of text". These poems could have been written by Qoheleth but at a different time and incorporated by a later editor. At present there is no majority consensus view on the matter of their authorship, and arguments for and against the originality of the poems are not conclusive. Because of the limits and the particular focus of my study, and without denying that there may be several other possibilities for interpreting the organization and composition of these passages of texts, I shall confine my discussion to the main body of the book, which is also the most relevant to my purpose

---

68 Ellermeier (1967, 42-44). Crenshaw similarly comments that in line with Qoheleth's "abandonment of the fiction of royal authorship after the second chapter... The royal fiction does not begin the book, as one would expect" (1988, 29).

69 Zimmerli 1962, 152.

and argument, that is to Qoheleth's narrative which I shall take, following the well-accepted arguments as to its limits, to be 1:12-11:6.

Chapter 2

The Royal Voice of Qoheleth

In this chapter, I shall investigate the pervasiveness of the royal voice in *Qoheleth* and this will be done in three parts. First, I shall examine the main evidence for the royal voice, which is usually said to be limited to the first two chapters of *Qoheleth*. Secondly, I shall investigate whether there is good evidence to suggest that the royal voice can be heard beyond the first two chapters of the book. The arguments of Perdue and Christianson are relevant in this regard and will be examined to identify their paucity, strengths, and weaknesses. Finally, I shall analyse eight passages of texts, which are often said to reflect "anti-royal" sentiment and perspective, to see whether this description given is indeed correct and justifiable or whether they might also reflect the thoughts and words of a royal persona.

I. Examination of the Main Evidence for the Royal Voice in 1:12–2:26

It is widely held that most, if not all, of the royal allusions in *Qoheleth* are contained in the first two chapters of the book.[70] In particular, scholars argue that the "royal fiction"[71] – where the

---

70 As mentioned in Chapter 1, the reference to Qoheleth's royal status first appears in the superscription (1:1) which falls outside Qoheleth's narration proper and which is commonly interpreted as belonging to the hand of a later editor.

71 The use of the term "fiction" recognizes the fact that the Solomonic references found in the text cannot be taken to be factual or historical and that the use of the royal guise is purely to serve a literary end. As Seow writes, "The pretense of Solomonic kingship was prompted by the author's desire to be perceived as sage-king par excellence, who, having observed and experienced wisdom, pleasure, and toil firsthand, as it were, is able to offer advice with sufficient credibility" (1995, 275). Similarly, Fox (1999, 159-60).

author is speaking in the first person under the guise of a king –
is limited to the passage of 1:12-2:26.[72] Some scholars have
suggested a narrower limit, that is, 1:12-2:11, arguing that
Qoheleth's self-identification with Solomon only extends to
Qoheleth's experiments with wisdom (1:12-18) and pleasure (2:1-
11).[73] However, such an argument is found wanting for, as
Whybray points out, given that the literary form of "first-person
narration" characterizes the entire work, "it is impossible to be
certain at what point the 'I' of Solomon gives place to the 'I' of
Qoheleth himself".[74] Nevertheless, there are strong reasons for
seeing the royal fiction as extending as far as 2:26, not least
because of the self-evident and recognizable unity of 1:12-2:26.
Thematically, 1:12-2:26 bears the character of an introduction as
it contains Qoheleth's self-introduction as king, and the laying
out of the purpose of his pursuit.[75] As Whybray points out, "All
the principal themes of the book are treated here and are
specifically related to Qoheleth's main purpose."[76] Structurally,
the literary unit is marked by two poems of roughly equal
length, that is, the poem on cosmology (1:3-11) and another on
time (3:1-8). The limits to 1:12-2:26 is further supported by the
presence of an *inclusio*. At the beginning and end of the literary

---

72 E.g. Barton (1912, 76); Zimmerli (1962, 129); Barucq (1968, 62); Lauha (1978, 42-
    3); Rousseau (1981, 213); Crenshaw (1987, 171); Whybray (1989, 46); Fischer
    (1991, 72-83); Lohfink (2003, 44).

73 Although Gordis argues that the Solomonic guise is limited to 1:12-2:11, he does
    admit that there are occasional allusions to Israel's wisest king beyond this limit
    (e.g. 7:20; 1968, 278). Seow, although writing that "Beyond that fictional royal
    autobiography in 1:12-2:11, there is no hint that the text stems from the royal
    court" (1997, 98), nevertheless recognized the use of conventional royal
    language in later passages in the work. Murphy hesitates to define precisely
    the limit of the royal fiction, arguing that while the self-reference to kingship
    remains clearest within 1:12-2:11, royal themes may still be found beyond this
    passage of text (1992, 13-14). Fox, likewise, is open to both possibilities (1999,
    153). For the majority of commentators today, Qoheleth is seen to put on the
    royal guise in order to establish his credentials and authority at the start and
    once this is done he abandons his royal persona.

74 Whybray 1989, 46.

75 Thus the passage has been described as "Solomon's testimony" (Whybray),
    "the royal experiment" (Crenshaw), and "Solomon's confession" (Rousseau).
    Barton describes the unit as containing Qoheleth's experiments and conclusion
    as carried out "in the character of Solomon" (1908, 76). Similarly Perry (1993,
    65).

76 Whybray 1989, 47.

unit there is the mention of God: God is the one responsible for giving human beings the grievous task to be occupied with (1:13), yet He also gives them the possibility to enjoy it (2:24-26).[77] And set within the *inclusio* we find the basic details surrounding Qoheleth's purpose and experiment, namely, Qoheleth's intention to investigate "all that is done under heaven" (1:13), the reason for the investigation – which is to discover what is good (or best) for humans to do (2:3) – and, following a preliminary conclusion to his investigation, Qoheleth's recommendation for living (2:24a). Despite holding the view that the royal fiction is limited to 1:12-2:11, Loader also recognizes 1:12-2:26 as a coherent literary unit which contains the king's self-introduction, the announcement of his royal experiment, and their results.[78] He adds that 1:12-2:26 introduces "the collection of reflections between the prologue and epilogue".[79]

For the rest of this section of the chapter, I shall discuss the evidence for the royal voice in 1:12-2:26 according to the following five subsections which I have delineated for convenience of discussion. The divisions are logical and commonly accepted, with the exception of 1:12, which I shall treat separately in view of the amount of discussion to follow for this verse.

1:12	Qoheleth's self-introduction
1:13-18	The purpose and object of Qoheleth's experiment
2:1-11	Qoheleth's experiment with pleasure
2:12-23	Qoheleth's experiment with wisdom
2:24-26	The conclusion to Qoheleth's experiment and his practical advice for living

---

77   Whybray (ibid.); Fischer (1991, 83-6).
78   Loader (1979, 19, 35-39); (1986, 24-33). Similarly, Seow who, although arguing that the royal fiction is limited to 1:12-2:11, sees 1:12-2:26 as a coherent unit, comprising Qoheleth's introduction, his recitation of his accomplishments and wealth, his meditation on the subject of death and toil, and finally his conclusion (1997, 142-58). This double analysis of Loader and Seow is awkward in the light of the coherence of the voice until 2:26.
79   Loader 1986, 24.

A. Qoheleth's Self-Introduction (1:12)

Qoheleth's narration begins in 1:12 with what clearly is a well-recognised formulaic ancient Near Eastern royal self-introduction, intended no less to impress the royal setting of the work upon the listeners. Qoheleth's opening remark of

אֲנִי קֹהֶלֶת הָיִיתִי מֶלֶךְ עַל־יִשְׂרָאֵל בִּירוּשָׁלָם

in fact parallels very closely the language and style of the self-introductions found in West Semitic and Akkadian royal inscriptions. Loretz and others have pointed out that Qoheleth's self-introduction, which consists of the first, common singular, independent, personal pronoun followed by his name and his position as king, follows the literary formula commonly used to introduce the king in Semitic royal inscriptions.[80] Mesha's Inscription, the stele of Zakkur of Hamath, and the Yehaumilk Inscription provide clear examples of this. In Mesha's Inscription, for example, we read אנך משע ... מלך מאב "I am Mesha... king of Moab". Similarly, in Zakkur's Inscription, there is אנה זכר מלך חמת ולעש "I am Zakkur, king of Hamath and Lu'ath".[81] Qoheleth's use of this well-recognized royal self-introductory formula at the start of his narration creates the impression that the narrative to follow belongs to a king. More will be said of this in Chapter 3 where I shall discuss *Qoheleth* in the context of ancient Near Eastern literature.

Qoheleth's declaration of the place of his kingship, which is described as "over Israel" and "in Jerusalem", is the earliest and clearest of all Solomonic allusions in the work. The pair of descriptions, when read together, quite clearly refers to the kings of the united monarchy. As Seow points out, the phrase "king over Israel" is only used elsewhere in the Old Testament to refer to the kings of the Northern Kingdom (1 Kgs. 14:13-14; 15:25; 16:29; 22:52; 2 Kgs. 2:25) while the Judaean kings, who are said to rule "in Jerusalem", have never been identified by this phrase.[82] Both these phrases, when taken together with the reference in the

---

80 E.g. Loretz (1964, 62); von Rad (1970, 56-58); Fox (1989, 174); Seow (1995, 279-287).

81 See further discussion in Chapter 3, pp. 65-69.

82 Seow (1995, 277), (1997, 98).

superscription (1:1) to Qoheleth as "son of David", leave readers in no doubt that Solomon is being referred to here. Many commentators see a further allusion to Solomon in the author's use of the *nom de plume* קֹהֶלֶת Qoheleth (1:1, 2, 12; 7:27; 12:8, 9, 10), which in its verbal form means "to assemble", or "gather", as used of people. Traditionally the title is seen as an implicit reference to Solomon's assembling (יַקְהֵל שְׁלֹמֹה, 1 Kgs. 8:1, 2) of the people (קָהָל "assembly", 1 Kgs. 8:55) to hear his speech at the dedication of the Temple as recorded in 1 Kgs. 8. Seow argues that the title may further hint at Solomon's role as the "gatherer" of wisdom since gnomic sayings were collected under Solomon's name (Prov. 1:1; 10:1; 25:1, cf. Hezekiah in Prov. 25:1). Furthermore, Solomon might also be seen as "the archetypal person who had *gathered* everything for himself but yet was subjected to the vicissitudes of life".[83]

B. A Solomonic Experiment (1:13-18)

This next literary unit might best be described as the blueprint of Qoheleth's narration in that here we have Qoheleth stating the purpose of his investigation and the object and means by which he will carry it out. The subsequent observations of Qoheleth are tied to this first declaration of his intent to embark upon a royal quest to test and examine wisdom. Interestingly, we find in 1:18 an early allusion to the mood of resignation in which Qoheleth eventually finds himself at the conclusion of his search. Qoheleth's acknowledgement and acceptance of God's role in humankind's labour similarly receives first mention in 1:13b.

The royal character of Qoheleth is reflected very clearly in his language, namely in his tendency to speak in universal terms. His research is comprehensive and covers הַכֹּל "everything", and embraces אֶת־כָּל־הַמַּעֲשִׂים שֶׁנַּעֲשׂוּ תַּחַת הַשָּׁמָיִם "all that has been done under heaven" (1:14).[84] The language of his ambitious

---

83 Seow 1997, 99. Italics his.

84 The scope of Qoheleth's search covers three areas: the world כָּל־אֲשֶׁר נַעֲשָׂה תַּחַת הַשֶּׁמֶשׁ "all that has been done under the sun" (1:14), חָכְמָה "wisdom" (1:17a), and שִׂמְחָה "pleasure" (1:17b) (Brown 2000, 29); cf. Fox who sees

intention is serious: he is keen to research and probe. Qoheleth's use two infinitives, לִדְרוֹשׁ "to seek" and וְלָתוּר "and to search out", following וְנָתַתִּי "and I set" (my heart), underlines the seriousness of his task. Only a person with a privileged background would dare to undertake such a project. As Crenshaw similarly points out, the enormity of the task that Qoheleth sets out to accomplish can only belong to the office of the king. Only the king has the necessary resource and ability not only to carry it out, but also to handle any unforeseen consequences.[85] Qoheleth's exaggerated claims of superior wisdom (1:16) and the boasting of the comprehensive-ness of his investigation (the depth and breath of his quest כָּל־אֲשֶׁר נַעֲשָׂה תַּחַת הַשָּׁמָיִם, 1:13) similarly exudes a royal aura.[86] Seow argues that the rhetorical language evidenced here shares a common ground with ancient Near Eastern royal literature. Seow points to Ashurbanipal II's boast of searching "heaven and earth, the wisdom of Shamash and Adad" as a very close parallel to Qoheleth's own investigation.[87] Seow also sees Qoheleth's description of וְנָתַתִּי אֶת־לִבִּי לִדְרוֹשׁ וְלָתוּר בַּחָכְמָה "I applied my heart to seek and to explore by wisdom" (1:13) as alluding to Solomon, paralleling in particular the texts of 1 Kgs. 3:12; 4:29-34; 10:23-24; and 2 Chron. 1:11-12; 9:3, 5-7, with their reference to Solomon's "wise heart".

Qoheleth's investigation, which constitutes the main subject of his narration, is a royal one. Qoheleth's purpose and his ensuing experiment to discover the meaning of one's toil are wrapped up in his status and position as king. According to Israel's own wisdom tradition, such an investigation belongs to the realm of royal pursuits. As Proverbs 25:2 declares, "It is the glory of God to conceal a matter; to search out a matter is the glory of kings."[88] The royal context is unmistakable as even wis-

---

"wisdom" as the means but not the object of Qoheleth's investigation (1989, 175).

85 Crenshaw 1987, 71.

86 Murphy sees this as possibly alluding to Solomon's wisdom, which was said to encompass a broad range of disciplines including judicial, experiential, and nature wisdom (cf. 1 Kgs. 3-10; 1992, 14).

87 Seow 1997, 121.

88 As Brown aptly puts it, "the world is the king's classroom, his laboratory" (2000, 29).

dom and its truths are included in the range of subjects under Qoheleth's investigation.[89] As Kamano remarks, "With his supreme wisdom, Qoheleth has decided to engage in the acqui-sition of knowledge of wisdom and folly, a task appro-priate only to Qoheleth, the wisest king."[90]

Qoheleth's boast of being the wisest in the land, and even wiser than his predecessors, again echoes the literary conven-tions of the Mesopotamian royal inscriptions where kings would record their deeds and accomplishments which were often described as exceeding those who had ruled before.[91] Some scholars have argued that such a claim would not fit Solomon since only one other Israelite king in Jerusalem, which is David, may be said to precede him. It is possible that the Canaanite kings who had ruled in Jerusalem before David are implied here[92], although it is more likely that the emphasis on Solomon's renowned wisdom is intended in hyperbolic fashion.[93] Quite clearly, a loose and rhetorical association rather than a more literal reference to Solomon is intended here. Another possible allusion to Solomon lies in the phrase וְהוֹסַפְתִּי חָכְמָה "and I increased in wisdom" (v.16) which, as some scholars argue, closely parallels the queen of Sheba's praise of Solomon's great wisdom הוֹסַפְתָּ חָכְמָה (1 Kgs. 10:7).[94]

C. A Test of Pleasure (2:1-11)

Following the revelation of his intent and the object of his quest in the preceding passage, Qoheleth embarks on what Murphy describes as the "Solomonic experiment"[95] of שִׂמְחָה "pleasure", a

---

89 It is important to note the distinction between wisdom as a subject of teaching (as in a corpus of doctrine) and wisdom as a method of investigation. Qoheleth's investigation (by way of wisdom, through seeking, seeing, etc.) brings him into conflict with wisdom teaching. See Murphy (1992, lxii-iii) for further discussion on the distinction.

90 Kamano 2002, 61.

91 See Chapter 3 for further discussion.

92 Cf. Josh. 10:1-11; Hertzberg (1963, 84); Isaksson (1987, 52 n.67).

93 So Hertzberg (1963, 84); Lauha (1981, 395); Murphy (1992, 14).

94 Seow 1995, 277.

95 Murphy 1992, 19.

topic which defines this next passage of text.[96] The abundance of frivolity and the indulgence[97], which Qoheleth led himself to enjoy for the purpose of his experiment, reflects a life of luxury (2:1-3).[98] An extravagant living is further suggested by Qoheleth's keen pursuit of his enquiry, which he is said to want to continue עַד אֲשֶׁר־אֶרְאֶה אֵי־זֶה טוֹב "until I could see what was good" (2:3). That throughout the length of his experiment Qoheleth did not hold back anything his eyes desired and, in addition, he was "generous"[99] in giving his heart enjoyment (2:10) further implies a life of great privilege. Laughter (v.2), drunkenness (v.3), and merry-making (v.1) were the main sources of pleasure for Qoheleth and yet eventually, and retrospectively, they were found to have no significant or lasting meaning for him (vv.1-2). From his experiment with sensual pleasure, Qoheleth turns to describe the enjoyment of his material achievements.

Qoheleth's list of accomplishments and wealth in 2:4-11 is clearly suited to a king. Gardens, parks, vineyards, and pools were common projects of pride for kings in ancient times,[100] often carried out for the sole purpose of self-aggrandizement. Qoheleth's manner of boasting in 2:4-11 bears a further similarity with the ancient Semitic royal language of boast. I shall examine these parallels further in Chapter 3. Scholars have pointed to the similarity between Qoheleth's list of building works and that in Mesha's Inscription, both of which bear the parallel mention of a reservoir, park, and cisterns.[101] Seow[102] has gone further in his attempt to match the building works and properties described in

---

96 שִׂמְחָה in 2:1 and 2:10 forms an inclusio to mark the passage as another pericope. Likewise, the הֶבֶל judgment in 2:1 and 2:11.

97 This may be inferred from the words מְהוֹלָל "madness", לִמְשׁוֹךְ "to draw, drag" (v.3), and the suggestive phrase וְלִבִּי נֹהֵג בַּחָכְמָה "and my mind (still) guiding (me) by wisdom" (v.3).

98 Similarly, Murphy writes, "One can judge from what follows that שִׂמְחָה is to be understood as the good life, not the mindless joy of Prov. 21:17 ('the one who loves pleasure…') or something superficial" (1992, 17-8).

99 Kamano 2002, 68.

100 Cf. other biblical references to royal projects such as the "King's garden" (e.g. Jer. 39:4; 52:7; 2 Kgs. 25:4; Neh. 3:15), the "King's Pool" (e.g. 2 Kgs. 18:17; 20:20; Isa. 36:2), and Solomon's vineyard in Baal Hamon (Song 8:11).

101 See KAI 181.

102 Seow (1995, 278).

2:4-11 to those in Jerusalem which may have a specific connection to Solomon, such as Solomon's vineyard in Baal-Hamon (Song 8:11), the "King's Garden" in the Kidron Valley (Jer. 39:4; 52:7; 2 Kgs. 25:4; Neh. 3:15), the "King's Pool" (Neh. 2:14), the Siloam Pool (Neh. 3:15), and another reservoir near Jerusalem which is traditionally ascribed to Solomon (as mentioned by Josephus[103]). Although the royal fiction in this passage undoubtedly plays on the renowned achievements of Solomon, most scholars today are well aware that the Solomonic association made here is carried out with considerable freedom.[104] The point of recounting Qoheleth's building projects in vv. 4-8 is to emphasize the use of royal prerogatives for his experiment. The list of Qoheleth's achievements and wealth speak of the power and riches of his kingship. As Crenshaw remarks, "Like a king, Qoheleth did things on a grand scale."[105]

Qoheleth's description of his wealth in verses 7-9 is similarly couched in the conventional language of ancient royalty in that the possession of slaves, livestock, precious metal, and provinces (2:7, 9) is typically featured in the royal accounts of the ancient Near East. Parallel expressions are found in abundance in the Assyrian kings' lists of treasures and acquisitions. More will be said of this in the next chapter. Loretz points out that the expression "male and female singers" is likely to be in reference to a royal harem, following the occurrence of a similar expression found in the El Amarna letters.[106] The items on Qoheleth's list further parallel some of Solomon's known possessions, such as slaves (1 Kgs. 9:20; 10:5), flocks of livestock (1 Kgs. 5:3 [ET 4:23]), gold and other precious metals (1 Kgs. 9:28; 10:2, 10-11, 14; 7:15, 27), and jurisdiction over provinces (1 Kgs. 4:7). Furthermore, Qoheleth's boast of having more than anyone before him, like his claim of superior wisdom in 1:16, also reflects

---

103 Josephus, BJ. v.4.2. as cited by Barton (ibid., 80).
104 Gordis (1968, 209); Hertzberg (1964, 87-8); Lauha (1981, 395); Crenshaw (1987, 78); Murphy (1992, 17). It is often said that the absence of reference to Solomon's Temple here is surprising. On closer analysis, this omission is actually logical since Qoheleth's recitation here is of his past and meaningless achievements. See also the discussion on p.80-81.
105 Crenshaw 1987, 78.
106 Loretz 1964, 155 n.94.

the stereotypical language commonly found in ancient Near Eastern royal texts.

The description of the care with which Qoheleth's experiment was conducted, that is, with wisdom – וְלִבִּי נֹהֵג בַּחָכְמָה "and my mind guiding (me) by wisdom" (2:3), אַף חָכְמָתִי עָמְדָה לִּי, "also my wisdom remained by me" (2:9) – echoes the legendary talent of Israel's wise king *par excellence*. The phrase, וְגָדַלְתִּי וְהוֹסַפְתִּי מִכֹּל שֶׁהָיָה לְפָנַי בִּירוּשָׁלָם "and I became great and surpassed all who were before me in Jerusalem", which bears a close similarity to the description of Solomon's renowned wisdom and wealth as told in the historical narratives of 1 Kgs. 5:9-14 [ET 4:29-34]; 10:23 and 2 Chr. 9:22, provides a further and clear link to Israel's famous wise king. Another possible allusion to the Solomonic legend lies in Qoheleth's use of the word שָׁאַל "desire" in 2:10 which echoes the account of Solomon's "desire" for wisdom in his dream in Gibeon (1 Kgs. 3:5, 10, 11, 13; 2 Chron. 1:7, 11).[107] Seow sees a further parallel between the description of Qoheleth's "toil" in 2:11 ("all my labour which I toiled") and the reference to the king's "toil" (Gilg. I i 8) and all his "troubles" (Gilg. I i 26) in the prologue to the Middle-Babylonian version of the Gilgamesh Epic.[108]

D. An Experiment With Wisdom and the Issue of Royal Legacy (2:12-23)

In contrast to the résumé style of boast in the preceding passage, the unit of 2:12-23 turns to a more reflective style of narration. This section marks the start of Qoheleth's meditative enquiry. Having established his royal credentials in the previous passage, Qoheleth now embarks on a preliminary investigation into the merits of wisdom and folly in the context of death.[109] The royal context is clearly reiterated in the opening verse (v.12) of the

---

107 Seow 1995, 277.

108 Seow 1997, 133.

109 More accurately, Qoheleth reconsiders "wisdom" here, having done so previously in 1:17.

section where readers are led to ponder, along with Qoheleth, on the matter of succession.[110]

Turning to consider wisdom and foolishness, Qoheleth laments at the thought that his successor might not be able to extend his accomplishments (vv.12, 17-21) thus resulting in his wise deeds being forgotten (vv.16, 17-19). This concern, over the lack of remembrance of one's deeds, is the predominant reason for the creation of "monumental inscriptions" in ancient times, where the name and deeds of kings and other heroes are often engraved on objects and building structures in order to commemorate the benefactors and be lasting memorials to their name.[111] This concern is also occasionally expressed in the "literary compositions". For example, in the Egyptian Royal Instructions for King Merikare, the son of the king is admonished with the words, "May I see a brave man who will copy it, who will add to what I have done; a wretched heir would disgrace me."[112] Qoheleth despairs at the possibility that for those who are to come after him, there is no remembrance of what he has accomplished. "There will not be any remembrance of them" (1:11), and "the memory of them is lost" (9:5).

Qoheleth's misery is compounded when he dwells on the related issues of inheritance and succession (vv.18, 19, 21), matters which are clearly relevant to a king. Qoheleth laments at the thought of having to leave his accomplishments, so laboriously gained through "toilsome labour" and "anxious striving" (vv.18-23), to a successor who may turn out to be a fool (vv.18-19). All the striving for power and the wealth that Qoheleth has achieved, of which he has just made a boast, are but a vanity in that his accomplishments will be inherited by someone who will not have worked for it (v.21). Qoheleth is vexed at the thought that he is unable to know to whom all his achievements and wealth will pass, and whether his legacy will

---

110 Both Michel (1989, 21-22) and Fischer (1997, 203) read הָאָדָם שֶׁיָּבוֹא אַחֲרֵי הַמֶּלֶךְ as a reference to those who come after the king in rank. Reference to the king's successor is what is probably meant here, which is made clearer in the rest of the passage.

111 Hallo and Simpson (1998, 154-57); Grayson (1981, 151).

112 *AEL1*, 103, as cited by Crenshaw (1987, 83-4).

be preserved and his name remembered. Hence this influences
Qoheleth's advice for living.

Despite the change in the style of narration, this passage
displays continuity with the preceding section. This is seen in
Qoheleth's reconsideration of the theme of wisdom which is first
mentioned in 1:17. In addition, Qoheleth's contemplation of the
inevitability of death brings out issues of inheritance, succession,
and legacy, matters which are indeed relevant to a king. This
finds a natural link to Qoheleth's earlier royal representations
and provides evidence for seeing his royal voice as continuing
beyond 2:11.

E. Qoheleth's Practical Advice for Living (2:24-26)

The description of Qoheleth's intention and the pursuit of his
investigation comes to a climax in these final three verses of his
introduction.[113] Following the preliminary conclusion of his
investigation that "all" (all gains, all achievements, all toil) is
ephemeral (2:22-23), Qoheleth's practical advice for human
beings is to enjoy life, as God wills and gives them the opportunity to do so. That God holds the key to an individual's fate
and destiny is clear: God, who נָתַן "gives" human beings a
grievous task to be occupied with (1:13), is in the end the same
God who "gives" them the possibility of enjoyment 2:24b, 26).[114]
Because it is God who determines the חֵלֶק "lot" of human beings
and is responsible for the moral workings of the world, there is
no better thing to do than to eat, drink, and experience the
pleasures that God "gives" (v.24).

---

113 Cf. Whybray views 2:11 as the "climax" to Qoheleth's experiment although he
   also contends that the "theological implication" of Qoheleth's preliminary
   conclusion in 2:11 comes later in 2:24-6 which is that "all satisfaction in life
   comes as God's gift" (1998, 261). As I shall argue further in Chapter 4, the
   answer to Qoheleth's main inquiry of "what is good for man to do under
   heaven" (2:3) is properly given in 2:22-3 which reiterates the main question
   with the words מֶה־הֹוֶה לָאָדָם בְּכָל־עֲמָלוֹ וּבְרַעְיוֹן לִבּוֹ שֶׁהוּא עָמֵל תַּחַת הַשָּׁמֶשׁ
   (cf. the preliminary and off-the-cuff conclusion in 2:11). This is appropriately
   followed by Qoheleth's practical advice in 2:24-6. Thus, I would argue that 2:22-
   23 is best seen as the proper or formal conclusion to Qoheleth's experiment and
   2:24-26 as a further point arising from this conclusion.
114 Cf. 3:10, 11; 5:17-18 [ET vv.18-19]; 8:15; 9:9.

In verse 25, the royal fiction is brought to bear, as Qoheleth throws his authority and position behind his recommendation with the words: "for who can eat and have enjoyment if not I?" As the wisest and wealthiest king over Jerusalem, Qoheleth as Solomon is not only the most capable to undertake the experiment, but he qualifies as humankind's best representative to do so. His unrivalled position honours him with the necessary authority and allows him to claim universal validity for his conclusions.[115] If Qoheleth, in all his royal prerogatives and unsurpassed wisdom, can find no lasting profit from his toil, then neither can anyone else who does not enjoy his position.[116] Nevertheless Qoheleth *has* had enjoyment in his toil (2:10b) and it is this that he positively recommends (2:24).

F. Summary

Qoheleth's language, which appears to parallel the literary conventions of ancient Near Eastern royal texts, highlights the extent to which the language and content of 1:12-2:26 are rooted in ancient Near Eastern royal ideology and literary practice. This section is also, as Murphy points out, "freely modeled on the Solomonic tradition".[117] As seen above, the formulaic self-introduction, the boast of Qoheleth's grand accomplishments and extraordinary wisdom and knowledge, the superiority of his achievements over his predecessors, and his great deeds echo the language of the royal compositions of the ancient Near East. In addition, several themes, which clearly belong to a royal context, are found in this beginning section of Qoheleth's narrative, such as the issue of royal legacy and succession (2:12-23). It is clear that Qoheleth's royal representations draw upon the themes of Solomon's legendary wealth and wisdom activities (1 Kgs. 5:9-

---

115 Whybray sees the "Solomonic episode" as characterizing a moral tale and the concluding moral as "what is true of the life of the world's most privileged person is bound *a priori* to be true of the lives of us all" (1998, 261).

116 Similarly Kamano 2002, 92.

117 Murphy (1992, 17). Similarly, Crenshaw comments, "Solomon's vast wealth supplies the imagined context for the royal experiment comprising these verses" (1987, 320).

14). As Loretz aptly points out, the Solomonic link is hinted at by the way in which Qoheleth emphasizes the sapiential character of his kingship (which is evidenced in his interest in wisdom, cf. 1:17), in the manner which he glorifies himself in his wisdom (which is said to surpass that of his predecessors, 1:16), and in the description of his wealth which is portrayed as a consequence of his wisdom (2:9).[118] Although the idea of Solomon as the author of *Qoheleth* is no longer held today, on the basis primarily of the dating of its language alongside other issues such as style and theology, the majority of scholars are still not averse to recognizing a Solomonic Qoheleth in the work even though why this link is not made any clearer by the author remains a puzzle.[119]

II. Does the Royal Voice Speak Beyond 2:26?

Even though the majority of scholars are of the view that Qoheleth's use of a Solomonic guise ends at 2:26, many still acknowledge that occasional allusions to the royal fiction may still be found after Chapter 2. Hertzberg,[120] despite arguing that the royal fiction is limited to 2:11, (in following Gemser) read the reference in 7:28 to the "thousand" women from whom Qoheleth could not even find one "upright woman" as recalling the character of Solomon with its allusion to Solomon's "thousand" women in 1 Kgs. 11:3 ("seven hundred wives of royal birth and three hundred concubines").[121] Gordis, who similarly suggests that the Solomonic fiction is restricted to 1:12-2:11, points out that the phrase in 7:20 – כִּי אָדָם אֵין ... אֲשֶׁר ... וְלֹא יֶחֱטָא – is almost a direct quotation of a part of Solomon's prayer at the dedication of the Temple in 1 Kgs. 8:46 כִּי אֵין אָדָם אֲשֶׁר לֹא יֶחֱטָא.[122] Beentjes has recently argued that the vocabulary of Eccl.

---

118 Loretz 1964, 149.
119 Thus Childs writes that one of the unresolved issues in the book is why "the author is identified with Koheleth, and yet immediately described in a way which is only approximate to Solomon" (1979, 384).
120 Hertzberg 1963, 158.
121 Barton similarly views 7:27-8 as alluding to Solomon (1908, 147).
122 Gordis 1968, 278.

8:2-5 echoes the text of 1 Kgs. 2:43-44 [ET vv.42-43] (cf. שָׁמַר,
מִצְוָה, שְׁבֻעַת יהוה, יָדַע, הָרָעָה), which is a narrative about
Solomon.[123] Seow further identifies the use of royal polemic
language in 10:16-17 and 20. The majority of scholars who hold
the view that Qoheleth abandons the royal guise after Chapter 2
argue that allusion to Solomon or kingship is considerably less in
the later chapters. This assumption, as we have just seen above
(and will also see in our next section), needs further clarification
and discussion.

Proponents of the prevailing view of Qoheleth's temporary
use of a royal guise have further argued that the notion of royal
authorship is contradicted by the epilogist who describes
Qoheleth as a חָכָם "wise man" and by the observation that the
royal fiction is not found at the start of the book as one would
expect for a royal text.[124] Both of these arguments are not as
strong as they appear in view of the possibility that the book of
Qoheleth may have been edited or reorganized and that portions
of it (viz. its epilogue) might not be part of the original work but
instead belong to the hand of a subsequent redactor or editor.[125]
By far the strongest argument for seeing the royal fiction as a
temporary guise is the charge that Qoheleth's perspective
supposedly changes from a royal personage to that of a subject
after Chapter 2. This supposition, which is based on the presence
of purportedly "anti-royal" passages, will be examined in the
final part of this chapter. As for my next discussion, I shall
examine closely the two arguments recently put forth for the
pervasive-ness of the royal voice which appear to strengthen my
own argument for a greater role for the royal voice in the work
as whole, but will be seen to have limitations in their approaches
and conclusions.

---

123 Beentjes 1998, 306 n.19.
124 E.g. Zimmerli (1962); Ellermeier (1967); Crenshaw (1988); cf. discussion in
    Chapter 1, pp. 21-23.
125 See earlier discussion in Chapter 1, pp. 21-23.

III. Arguments for the Pervasiveness of the Royal Voice

It was against the background of a new and rapidly growing interest in comparative research between Egyptian and Biblical wisdom writings in the 1930s[126] that Galling made the suggestion that *Qoheleth* was written in the form of a Royal Testament (*Königstestament*) by the author who on his death bed offered words of advice to his successor. Galling saw *Qoheleth* as following after the Egyptian Instructions, namely the royal didactic texts (*Königslehre*) such as the Instruction for Merikare and the Instruction of Amenemhet to His Son.[127] Von Rad took a similar view, claiming that the literary structure of the Hebrew work was an "offshoot" of the court-originated wisdom *Gattung* of Royal Testament which originated from ancient Egypt.[128] For both Galling and von Rad, the constancy of the royal voice was implied by the *Gattung* of Royal Testament which the Hebrew work was thought to have adopted from Egypt.[129] More will be said of this parallelism in Chapter 3.

In this section, I shall examine the recent arguments of Perdue and Christianson for the pervasiveness of the royal voice. It should be noted that there are others who have made cursory mention of the possibility of the royal voice being implicitly pervasive but, because of the lack of clear and comprehensive treatment on the specific issue in question, they are not made the

---

126 This is following Budge and Erman's theories of dependence between Proverbs (notably 22:17-24:22) and the Instruction of Amenemope in 1923 and 1924.

127 Galling (1932, 298f). So Eissfeldt (1934, 552, 557-8; ET 1965, 493, 499); Lauha (1978, 2, 12, 44f); Fox (1989, 1999). Fox, in his most recent work, still holds to his earlier view that *Qoheleth* reflects most closely the form of the Egyptian Instructions, although he does suggests two other possible categories of genre for *Qoheleth*, i.e. "royal autobiography" in the manner of the Egyptian Instructions, and the more general classification of "reflections" (1999, 152). Fox also follows the majority of scholars in seeing the work as a royal parody.

128 Von Rad 1970, 292 [ET 1972, 226].

129 Galling, in a later work, remarked how the royal fiction remained "totally overlooked" after chapter 2 (1964, 510-1). Others, such as Zimmerli (1962, 151) and Fohrer (1968, 336), although recognizing a parallel feature of the royal introductory voice with the Egyptian didactic texts, nevertheless did not think that it was applied for the entire length of the work.

main focus of the discussion here.[130] For example, Salyer,[131] who approaches the work with a reader-response perspective, sees the royal fiction as being maintained throughout the work through the author's creation of a suspension of belief for the readers, although whether this is successfully achieved is dependent upon the skill of the individual reader to capture correctly the intention of the author. Salyer, however, contends that Qoheleth does contradict his royal persona at various points in the work. Some of these contradictions are unintentional (and inevitable as in all private narrations), whilst others are due to Qoheleth's unstable mood and character as well as the nature of the work as a debate between Qoheleth's private knowledge and the epilogists', editors', and readers' response to it (which are also reflected in the work).

A. Perdue – the Royal Testament of Qoheleth

Galling's earlier argument that *Qoheleth* reflects the genre of Royal Testament has recently been revived by Perdue who contends that the Egyptian Royal Instructions provide the closest form-critical parallel to the Hebrew work in that they contain the key elements of first-person narration and didactic sayings. Perdue sees in *Qoheleth*, a voice from the distant past, the literary fiction of a dead Solomon who "speaking from the tomb undertakes to instruct the living in the wisdom of life".[132] He argues that the Hebrew work, which follows the form of a Royal Testament, belongs to the hand of a sage who assumes the character of Solomon and engages in the quest to find the good in human existence.[133] According to Perdue, the purpose of the work is didactic and the original audience probably students at a school in Jerusalem who are preparing for civil and religious scribal

---

130 E.g. Galling, von Rad, Eissfeldt, Zimmerli, Fohrer, Lauha, and Fox.

131 Salyer 2001.

132 Perdue 1994, 202. This suggestion, of the voice of Solomon speaking from the dead, follows Galling's and is based on the presence of the perfective verb in Qoheleth's self-representation of his kingship in 1:12 (...אֲנִי קֹהֶלֶת הָיִיתִי מֶלֶךְ). Hertzberg, Loretz, and more recently Seow, have both argued decisively against this view. See further discussion in Chapter 3, pp. 123-125.

133 Ibid., 238-9.

careers.[134] Perdue argues that the Solomonic fiction is employed throughout the book in order to fulfil the sage's purpose of examining the wisdom themes of cosmology and anthropology, since the king is generally perceived to be the one responsible for establishing and maintaining cosmic and social order and hence is the best and most qualified speaker on the subject.[135]

Perdue points out that there are indirect as well as direct allusions to Solomon throughout the work. For example, the instructions and admonitions concerning cultic activity in the Temple (4:17-5:6) find a natural connection to Solomon. Qoheleth's admonition to be careful when speaking to God (5:5 [ET v.6]) alludes to Solomon's speech about God's omnipresence in 1 Kgs. 8:27-30.[136] A more general connection is seen between the large collections of proverbial sayings in the work and Solomon's reputation as the patron of Israel's wisdom literature (1 Kgs. 5:9-14). In the parable of the foolish old king and the wise youth in 4:13-16, Perdue argues that the Solomonic persona may be hinted at in "the one who comes after" (i.e. the "second one" in v.15, cf. 1 Kgs. 1-2), as also David (the poor youth) and Saul (the king whom the youth later supplants) in the other characters of the story.[137]

As for the passages which scholars often suggest are incongruent with a royal voice, for example, 4:1-5:19 which is usually read as words spoken in criticism against the king, Perdue argues that this theme is commonly found in the Egyptian Royal Testaments where the admission of the king's failures and weaknesses is made by the king himself (e.g. the Instruction of Amenemhet and the Instruction for Merikare). Perdue argues that this is also evidenced elsewhere in the Old Testament, for example, in 1 Kgs. 3-11 (viz. chapter 11) where, he writes, "the criticism of the tyranny of Solomon's rule is found even in a largely pro-Solomonic narrative".[138] Although Perdue's observation of the presence of royal self-criticism in Egyptian

---

134 Ibid., 202.
135 Ibid.
136 Ibid., 222-3.
137 Ibid., 222.
138 Ibid., 220.

Royal Testaments is correct, explicit criticism of kingship as an institution is absent from these Egyptian texts. I shall argue in the final section of this chapter that, similarly, in *Qoheleth*, explicit criticism of the monarchy is lacking. A careful study of the Hebrew passages in question will help to clarify whether we have, in *Qoheleth*, explicit criticism of the monarchy or not. This will be undertaken in our examination of the allegedly "anti-royal" passages.

Perdue's use of the Deuteronomistic account of Solomon's reign as an analogy is also fallacious because the passage being referred to (i.e. 1 Kgs. 3-11) is not comparable with the Egyptian Royal Testament texts in a form-critical sense.[139] In relation to Eccl. 4:1, Perdue argues that Qoheleth acknowledges that the king is guilty of tyranny and oppressive rule in this verse, but contends that the author nevertheless lays the final blame on God. Perdue views Qoheleth's subsequent lament in 4:3 as a protest against God (cf. Job 3; Jer. 20:14-18), accusing Him as the one ultimately responsible for the existence of oppression in the world. Perdue sees the passage as a deliberate attempt by the author to highlight not only the "subversive" actions of the king, but also to emphasize God's apathy in not protecting the impoverished and the abused.[140] Similarly, in relation to Eccl. 5:7 [ET v.8], Perdue reads this verse, along with other similar texts which deal with the theme of social injustice, as affirming the radical sovereignty of God; God being the one who arbitrarily decides on the place and power of human rulers (10:5-7, 16-17, 20), who ignores the cries of injustice (4:1-3), and who rules in secluded obscurity.[141] Interestingly, Perdue does not see Qoheleth's protest of injustice in these passages as incompatible with the royal voice, arguing that God, and not the king, is the one ultimately responsible for the lack of justice in the world. Perdue's interpretation that Qoheleth is attacking God in 4:3 is unnecessary as this verse could merely be an expression of

---

139 Arguably a more comparable text would be 1 Kgs. 2:1-12 which contains the words of David's parting speech and instruction to Solomon at his death-bed. This text, however, does not hold any obvious similarity with *Qoheleth*.
140 Ibid., 221.
141 Ibid., 226-32, 238-42.

Qoheleth's frustration at the incomprehensibility of God, namely the mysterious operation of His justice in the world. In fact, Qoheleth does believe that God will judge – which he speaks of earlier in 3:17 and reiterates in 5:5 [ET v.6] and 11:9 – but that judgment comes only according to God's time (3:1-15).[142] Perdue appears to have also misinterpreted 4:1 in his argument that Qoheleth is engaging in self-criticism in this verse. I hold that what we have in this verse is more likely a general musing by Qoheleth on the ongoing occurrence of injustice in the world than a self-referential lament by Qoheleth of his own tyranny. I shall discuss the interpretation of this verse in more detail below. Perdue's argument, that *Qoheleth* is written in the form of a Royal Testament, is unpersuasive for the same reasons that Galling's suggestion of the same has not been taken up by scholars.[143] Moreover, it is difficult to imagine how a book which allegedly attacks God and accuses Him of moral irresponsibility, and which is further associated with Israel's legendary wise king, could be readily accepted and sanctioned by the orthodox sage of the epilogue and the canonical editors.

B. Christianson – Telling the Story of Qoheleth

Christianson has recently forwarded another argument for the pervasiveness of Qoheleth's royal voice which builds upon Fox's earlier theory that the whole book of *Qoheleth*, save its title (1:1), is by a "frame-narrator" who "is looking back and telling his son the story of the ancient wise-man Qohelet".[144] According to Fox, all the third-person references in the book (i.e. in the prologue, epilogue, and 7:27) belong to the frame-narrator who has

---

142 Fox (1989, 104); Murphy (1992, lxvi).

143 See discussion in Chapter 3, pp. 123-125.

144 Fox 1997, 91. Fox makes the suggestion that both the epilogue and the "main story" of Qoheleth is written by the same author who deliberately sets the attitude of the epilogist at a distance from Qoheleth and his teachings in order to enhance the credibility of Qoheleth's radical teaching and to prevent it from being "violently rejected" (pp. 100-3). This argument, whilst possible, is unconvincing.

deliberately put them in to remind readers of his presence.[145] For the rest of the work, the frame-narrator uses his created persona of Qoheleth to tell the "story" of his search for knowledge and understanding of the world in the form of a first-person account.

Following Fox and his "frame-narrative assumption", Christianson argues that the book of *Qoheleth* is about a frame-narrator telling the "story" (or "narrative"[146]) of Qoheleth and his journey of personal experience and discovery. Christianson explores the element of royal fiction in the work, arguing that the author or frame-narrator adopts a Solomonic guise as a means of giving himself the freedom to venture and articulate his very own intellectual inquiry, as well as to validate the conclusions of his own search. For Christianson, the Solomonic persona is a literary device adopted for the purposes of protecting the author from criticism, as well as for gaining authority for a message which is subversive in intent.

Christianson argues that the "Solomonic guise proper" is established in the first two chapters of the book. Nevertheless, for the rest of the work readers are reminded of the guise by the various literary "throwbacks" that the author uses, such as recurring motifs which are first introduced in the "guise proper" and subsequently repeated throughout the book (e.g. phrases such as "absurd and a pursuit of wind" and "what is crooked cannot be made straight", 1:15; cf. 7:13). Christianson points out that many of the first-person verb forms relate to Qoheleth's experiment (e.g. "I observed", "I applied myself", "I tested") and his conclusion (e.g. "I said in my heart", "I said to myself concerning..."), and their usage helps to enhance the unity of the

---

145 Fox writes, "Virtually all the 'story' he [the frame-narrator] tells is a quotation of the words of the wise-man he is telling about. This speaker, whom I will call the frame-narrator, keeps himself well in the background, but he does not make himself disappear" (ibid., 91).

146 Christianson uses the term "narrative" in the sense of a literary genre, that is, as a "story". Christianson understands this term in a post-critical way and in relation to its use in the field of modern literary criticism. Although I reject Christianson's definition of "narrative", I do not totally reject the use of the term in relation to *Qoheleth*, as it remains an appropriate literary description for the main body of text (1:12-11:6), which is composed in narration.

narrating voice while reminding readers of the Solomonic presence in the work.[147]

Although Christianson admits that the Solomonic guise is at times "elusive", "lurking", and "multifaceted", he nevertheless argues that it may be felt throughout the work as readers are sufficiently reminded of the royal persona through the hints that are given by the author at various points in the work.[148] Christianson contends that there are also several clear allusions to Solomon to be found beyond Eccl. 2. These include the author's use of the idiomatic phrase "eat, drink, and be happy" (2:24; 3:13; 5:17 [ET v.18] ; 8:15), which parallels the description of Solomon's abundant provisions for his people in 1 Kgs. 4:20[149], and Qoheleth's negative judgment on women in 7:25-29 which, Christianson suggests, echoes the tradition of Solomon's experience with women (1 Kgs. 11:1-8).[150] Christianson discerns another Solomonic reference in 3:10-11, in the phrase "he has placed eternity in their hearts", which, he argues, comes close to Solomon's own experience of receiving wisdom "which God had placed in his heart" (1 Kgs. 10:24; 2 Chron. 9:23).[151] Following Fox, Christianson also argues that the epilogist, who is the same sole author of the entire work, continues with the Solomonic fiction in the epilogue in his use of the traditional celebrated image of Solomon as sage *par excellence* (1 Kgs. 5:11-14) [ET 4:31-34].

For much of his work, Christianson focuses on proving the "narrative" quality of the text. Among other issues, he defines the narrative plot as a "character-oriented" one, which is described as Qoheleth's quest and journey of self-discovery. For Christianson, the "dynamic narrative motion" is reflected in the "character's development through what it says and/or does and

---

147 Christianson 1998, 147, n. 61.
148 Ibid., 159. Christianson's argument for Qoheleth's consistent use of the Solomonic guise, on closer examination, is confusing as he contends that the royal guise is sometimes worn, sometimes removed, and even sometimes exchanged for an independent Qoheleth (see ibid., 148, 156-9, 164).
149 Ibid., 133.
150 Ibid., 144-5. Christianson further admits that Qoheleth's criticism of women in 7:26 does become a challenge to the Solomonic guise (ibid., 145)
151 Ibid., 163.

not necessarily how it interacts and develops in relation to others". The progress and tensions of the "story" are found in the unfolding of the character of Qoheleth as told by the frame-narrator. It is clear that Christianson does not rely on the traditional definitions of narrative in reading *Qoheleth* as a narrative. Thus, his arguments for the classification of *Qoheleth* as a piece of sustained literary narrative seem awkward, if not forced at times. For example, one notices the conspicuous lack of actors in the "story", and a number of the "narrative events", which he claims are present in every chapter, are questionable. Furthermore, one is hard-pressed to detect any kind of "dynamic narrative motion" in the collections of didactic sayings which are located towards the end of the book (interestingly, Christianson acknowledges that the first-person narration extends only until Eccl. 10 and not to the end of the work).

Christianson argues that in the author's journey of self-discovery, he questions and challenges traditional wisdom as he observes realistic truths about life's absurdities. In the process, Qoheleth "deconstructs" his Solomonic persona since in his examination of life's absurdities he includes the issue of the king's failure in exacting justice.[152] The allegedly "anti-royal" passages reflect the author's subtle challenge of the authority and status of kingship and reveal his true subversive intent despite posing as a self-critical royal figure who, according to Christianson, is also speaking as a moralist. Christianson writes, "if anything, it is imperative to regard Qoheleth's voice as the king's here and in any text that even remotely hints at the limits of the king's power, precisely because by doing so Qoheleth is seen to question the potency of the king and continues... his strategy of deconstructing the socially unquestioned power and authority of the king".[153] Christianson's argument, in essence, is similar to the view espoused by the majority of commentators today that the royal guise is deliberately used by the author for the purpose of criticizing and correcting the concepts and traditions relating to the institution of the monarchy. While other scholars see a distancing of or even a change in the character of

---

152 Ibid., 136-7, 164.
153 Ibid., 136.

the narrator from the initial royal characterization in the introduction to the alleged passages of criticism, Christianson assumes instead that these are projected as a self-criticism even though he admits that the real intention is that of satirizing the king.[154]

C. Summary

Aside from being unconvinced of Christianson's proposed genre of "narrative" for *Qoheleth* (that is, according to his own definition of the term and his arguments for it), I do not agree with Christianson's theory of the "deconstruction" of the royal voice, which is similar to that of Perdue. In essence, both scholars view the work as satirical and argue that the Solomonic persona provides the author with the means to subvert the monarchy (and God, in the case of Perdue) and the values that it represents. I believe that the royal persona is given a more positive role by the author than is suggested in these two arguments. Although the adoption of the royal guise by the author is primarily to gain authority and persuasiveness for his message, nevertheless the author does also use the Solomonic persona to address issues to do with kingship in general, issues which would be of concern to rulers and those in positions of authority. In essence, there is very little difference between the views of Christianson and Perdue and the views of those who see the royal fiction as limited to the early chapters of the work, in that a number of such views have largely taken the work to be ultimately an attack on the king and the institution of the monarchy.[155] Christianson contends that it is necessary for the readers to see the Solomonic guise as being maintained throughout the work if the author's subversive purpose is to be realized.[156] I find

---

154 Michel (1989, 23-4), for example, argues that Qoheleth puts on the royal guise in 1:12-2:12 in order to establish his credentials at the start and, once this is done, he abandons the literary royal character to take on the supposedly different role of philosopher (which does not necessarily have to exclude Qoheleth's royal persona).

155 E.g. Crenshaw (1988); Seow (1997); Vinel (1998).

156 Christianson 1998, 136.

Christianson's idea here unconvincing for reasons which I will give in the following chapters. Instead, I suggest that it is more likely that a coherent and authoritative Solomonic persona was intended to be portrayed throughout *Qoheleth*, and that, in the course of his comprehensive quest for the meaning of life, Qoheleth discovers and acknowledges his own vulnerability in life as king, in that rulers too are exposed and affected by the absurd realities of reversed social conventions and political oppression. These thoughts are not direct criticisms of the king; they are merely the pessimistic musings of a royal personage who sees his position and authority as being subject to the same vicissitudes of life as his subjects, only on a grander scale. Hence there is added pessimism about the royal role on his part. I shall explore these ideas further in Chapter 4.

Despite these points of disagreement, I do agree with Christianson's identification of several key characteristics of the work, namely the prevalence of the "I", and the revelation of the character of Qoheleth as conveyed through the narration. Of significance also, is his argument for the coherence of the narrating voice and how the "I" references in the book link up with the fuller representations that are found in the introductory passage of 1:12-2:26. I shall discuss this matter further in Chapter 4, where I shall suggest a better way of defining these key features of the book.

The predominant reason for viewing the work as a royal satire and the royal voice a temporary literary artifice is the alleged presence of anti-royal passages in the book. Christianson has examined a few of these passages, which are often quoted by commentators as evidence for rejecting the use of the royal guise, but his analysis has not been different from the others in the way he has approached these passages with a view to proving their satirical nature. In an attempt to answer this common charge of the presence of anti-royal passages in the book, I shall now investigate these passages with the purpose of testing whether they might or might not be compatible with a royal voice.

IV. Examination of the Allegedly "Anti-Royal" Passages

In this section, I shall examine passages which have been considered by some commentators to suggest an "anti-royal" perspective, indicating that there could be other voices in the text in opposition to the royal voice which we have identified primarily, at present, in the first two chapters of the book. It is argued in particular that the voice changes from that of a ruler to that of a subject. We shall need to test this argument. The passages under consideration are, in textual order, Eccl. 3:16-17; 4:1; 4:13-16; 5:7-8 [ET vv.8-9]; 8:1-5; 10:5-7; 16-17 and 10:20. In what follows I shall consider, first, passages that contain general musings on injustice which have been said to be the voice of the powerless or the oppressed; and second, those that concern kingly rule.

A. The Problem of Injustice

1. 3:16-17

16 וְעוֹד רָאִיתִי תַּחַת הַשָּׁמֶשׁ מְקוֹם הַמִּשְׁפָּט שָׁמָּה הָרֶשַׁע וּמְקוֹם
הַצֶּדֶק שָׁמָּה הָרָשַׁע:

17 אָמַרְתִּי אֲנִי בְּלִבִּי אֶת־הַצַּדִּיק וְאֶת־הָרָשָׁע יִשְׁפֹּט הָאֱלֹהִים
כִּי־עֵת לְכָל־חֵפֶץ וְעַל כָּל־הַמַּעֲשֶׂה שָׁם:

16 Moreover, I have seen under the sun, in the place of justice there was wickedness and in the place of righteousness there was wickedness.

17 I said in my heart, "God will judge the righteous and the wicked for there is a time for every matter and concerning every work there".[157]

---

[157] שָׁם at the end of the verse is unusual. It is unlikely to be a reference to the world to come where God will finally dispense absolute justice (e.g. Qoh. Rab., Tg) since this would then contradict Qoheleth's own interpretation in 9:10 that there is no work or thought or knowledge or wisdom in the place of the afterlife, Sheol. Although many commentators have suggested emending the particle to a finite verb, the position of a verb at the end of the clause and at a distance from its object (עֵת) makes this option unlikely (McNeile 1904, 63). Moreover, the proposed syntax does not fit well with the rest of Qoheleth's

This passage poses two problems: v.16 bewails the prevalence of wickedness instead of justice and righteousness and the question is raised: Is this then a specific criticism of a particular king's malpractice in terms of a system of justice? Furthermore, would a king make such a complaint or could this be the voice of an outsider to the court who lacks the power to correct the human oppression expressed? Second, verse 17 suggests that God will judge the wicked; thus the king as dispenser of justice might here be said to be out of a job!

It is important to note that in relation to verse 16, Qoheleth is not referring to a specific place, such as the law court, where justice should be dispensed. Rather, he is more likely to be referring to all "places" where justice and righteousness should be practised.[158] Thus, this verse need not be seen as a specific criticism of a specific justice system under an Israelite or other king, but it is likely to be a broader reference that could even have been voiced by a king who felt the helplessness of the human condition in general, and in particular, in relation to the ideals of justice and righteousness (cf. 7:15). This verse should also be interpreted in the light of the section that follows in vv.18-22 in which the general theme of injustice is continued in reference to death as the great leveler of humans and animals alike. Man and beast share the same fate in that they both die (v.19). Because they also share רוּחַ there is no distinction between man and beast in regard to life and death. As Grant writes, this is the greatest injustice which "extends beyond human causation and lies at the heart of human existence itself", a thought which one who has enjoyed a privileged royal life

---

style of writing. It is perhaps best to see it as a reference to שָׁמָּה in 3:16, and hence read as "there" (so Crenshaw (1987, 102); Murphy (1992, 30)). Murphy adds that שָׁם "there" could also refer to God's judgment in verse 17 itself (ibid., 30, 36).

158 Most commentators see the expression (מְקוֹם הַמִּשְׁפָּט ... וּמְקוֹם הַצֶּדֶק) as a general reference to all areas where justice should be realized rather than to any specific and official place, such as the law courts and tribunals, e.g. Delitzsch (1891, 265); Lauha (1978, 74); Ogden (1987, 59); Whybray (1989b, 77); cf. Barton (1908, 108), who believes that the passage describes the corrupt administration of Qoheleth's time. Fox's suggestion that both phrases may be read as part of a hendiadys, i.e., "the place of righteous judgment" is possible (1989, 197).

might have more to feel uncertain and even fearful about than most.[159]

When we turn to verse 17, we find the premise, in true wisdom style, that God will judge the righteous and the wicked and we find an echo of the poem on time (3:1-8). The idea that God is ultimate judge, rather than the king who is simply a temporal ruler, is being expressed here and it is not in tension with the king's dispensation of justice. This may be a quotation of a traditional wisdom sentiment,[160] which is then relativized in what follows in verses 18-22 with the thought that there is no substantive difference between human beings and animals, with the inference perhaps that since animals do not have expectations of reward, this too is an illusion. When taken in isolation then, such a musing on the nature of God's dispensation of justice as found in verse 17 would not be out of place in the thought of a king who might well muse on God's justice being greater than that of any human, even that of a king. The two verses taken together indicate that human systems of justice are inevitably flawed and that only God can resolve such apparent injustices once and for all. That the king might muse on such an issue is possible and so this passage should not be seen as "anti-royal" or out of keeping with the sentiments of a royal persona.

2. 4:1

וְשַׁבְתִּי אֲנִי וָאֶרְאֶה אֶת־כָּל־הָעֲשֻׁקִים אֲשֶׁר נַעֲשִׂים תַּחַת הַשָּׁמֶשׁ
וְהִנֵּה דִּמְעַת הָעֲשֻׁקִים וְאֵין לָהֶם מְנַחֵם וּמִיַּד עֹשְׁקֵיהֶם כֹּחַ
לָהֶם מְנַחֵם:

1 Again I saw all the oppressions that were committed under the sun and behold, tears of the oppressed; they had no comforter. And from the hand of their oppressors came power; but they had no comforter.

In verse 1, we find an observation of oppression with no one to comfort. Many see the presence of this verse as being

---

159 Grant 2000, 183.
160 So McNeile (1904, 99); Barton, (1908, 111); Crenshaw (1987, 102); Whybray (1989, 76-7). See Chapter 4, pp. 164-168 for the discussion of the theory of quotations.

incongruous with the position of a king who might reasonably be expected to correct injustice in his land.[161] However, we can again argue that the reference made here is quite general and that a king might well be frustrated by injustice, and the lack of comforters, which is part of what he sees as inevitable to the human condition.[162] Oppression is a universal phenomenon from which rulers are neither excluded nor protected. Wars and military conquests are ongoing realities, both for king and subject. Thus, it could be that verse 1 is less an admission by Qoheleth of his own powerlessness than an acknowledgement that it is a reality of life that power sometimes lies on the side of the oppressor (who could indeed be the king's enemy as indicated by עֹשְׁקֵיהֶם "their oppressors") and is used to cause others to suffer.[163] It may also be that as king, Qoheleth feels a greater frustration on his part, at being unable to influence the miscarriages of justice that he sees as ongoing under his rule on a more local level.[164] Perhaps we are to read the verse in the wider context of verses 2 and 3 in which being dead is thought to be better than being alive, and not even having existed even better than both these options. Here, we have Qoheleth at his most pessimistic! The idea here is not that death is preferable to life, but that, given the situation of the weight of oppression in the land, it would have been better not to have lived to see it. Perdue's argument that Qoheleth's lament over the observed injustice implies the

---

161 Cf. 2 Sam. 8:15; 1 Chr. 18:14.

162 Crenshaw sees the idiomatic phrase וְשַׁבְתִּי אֲנִי , which may be translated adverbially here ("again I"), as indicating that oppression and injustice are recurring phenomena (1988, 106). He further suggests that rather than a recounting of a historical situation, an "abstract notion of oppression" may be referred to here (ibid., 105).

163 This is repeated again in 8:9b.

164 Fox notes that although Qoheleth bemoans the misery of the oppressed he does not see himself as a possible help in the suffering of others, nor does he encourage others to do so (1989, 200-1). Although Fox's observation is not incorrect, he has nevertheless misconstrued the sentiments expressed in this passage. Qoheleth's sympathy and grief is not so much over the individual cases of observation, but over the ongoing phenomenon of injustice in the world. Furthermore, as is commonly noted (e.g. Galling, Lauha, Murphy, Seow), Qoheleth does not call for a social transformation, but rather resigns to the fact that the observed injustice is just another ongoing vanity in life. Qoheleth calls on his listeners to accept this as a part of life since human beings are powerless to control, much less prevent, their occurrence.

total absence of divine judgment[165] is unconvincing as it fails to take into consideration those passages where Qoheleth clearly affirms life (e.g. 9:4-5) and where he calls upon individuals to enjoy the pleasures that it may bring (e.g. 2:24; 3:13; 5:18; 8:15; viz. 9:9). As Murphy similarly notes, for Qoheleth, death is preferable in specific situations of great suffering but "outside of these extenuating circumstances death is totally unwelcome".[166]

3. 5:7, 8 [ET vv.8, 9]

7 אִם־עֹשֶׁק רָשׁ וְגֵזֶל מִשְׁפָּט וָצֶדֶק תִּרְאֶה בַמְּדִינָה אַל־תִּתְמַהּ
   עַל־הַחֵפֶץ כִּי גָבֹהַּ מֵעַל גָּבֹהַּ שֹׁמֵר וּגְבֹהִים עֲלֵיהֶם:
8 וְיִתְרוֹן אֶרֶץ בַּכֹּל הִיא מֶלֶךְ לְשָׂדֶה נֶעֱבָד:

7 [8]   If you see the oppression of the poor and the robbing of
          justice and righteousness in the province, do not be astonished
          at the matter; for a high official is watching over (another) high
          official and (there are even) higher ones over them.
8 [9][167] The advantage of land is paramount; (even) a king is subject to
          the land.

---

165 Similarly Crenshaw 1987, 102.
166 Murphy 1993, lxvii.
167 The text of 5:8 [ET v.9], which Gordis describes as an "insuperable crux" (1968, 250), is notorious for its obscure nature and its meaning remains largely uncertain. There are three major difficulties in this verse: first, the presence of the demonstrative pronoun הִיא and the question of its supposed function (the Qere הוּא is supported by many Hebrew MSS, LXX, and Syr). Second, the meaning of בַּכֹּל is unclear in this verse. Third, should נֶעֱבָד be construed with לְשָׂדֶה or with מֶלֶךְ ? To answer the first question, a Qere reading, which seeks to match the predicate and subject in terms of gender, is unnecessary since הִיא may also function as a neuter ("the advantage of a land is *this*" i.e. what follows; Delitzsch (1891, 294); Murphy (1992, 46)). As for the second question, בַּכֹּל may be interpreted as "in all respects" or "on the whole", e.g. Gen. 24:1, so McNeile (1904, 70); Murphy (1992, 46); or "in all things" e.g. Ezra 10:17 or "to all" e.g. 1 Chr. 7:5, so Delitzsch (1891, 294). In relation to the third question, opinions vary with LXX, Syr, Theod, and Jerome deciding on the former, while Vg and Tg take on a freer translation in their adoption of the latter. Translations have largely varied according to the different perceptions of the context and meaning of the verse. The following are the better-argued translations: (1) Delitzsch argues that whether נֶעֱבָד is to refer to לְשָׂדֶה or מֶלֶךְ is immaterial since the meaning of the verse is that the king is subject ("has become a servus") to the cultivated land, that is, the nation is praised for its agriculture-king "who is addicted not to wars, lawsuits, and sovereign stubbornness in his opinions, but who delights in peaceful advancement of the prosperity of his country and who takes an interest in husbandry and the cultivation of the land". Delitzsch gives the translation of "but the advantage of a country

Although there is reference to a king in verse 8, a verse which remains largely uncertain in meaning (see discussion in footnote 167), I have included these verses in this section because the main theme is oppression and we find again the two keywords of "justice" and "righteousness". Verse 7 is often understood as pointing to the existence of bureaucratic hierarchy with each official jealously guarding his own interests, although they may also be supporting each other in corruption.[168] This could be the

---

consists always in a king given to the arable land" (1891, 294-5). (2) Barton (1908, 127, 131), in following Haupt (1905, 19, 40), sees the verse as speaking of the advantage of having a monarchy, especially for a land that is well established in terms of its agriculture and population. Despite all the drawbacks of a monarchy, there are to be found some advantages, as even Herod was said to have carried out some good works, e.g. preventing plundering raids (cf. Josephus Ant. xvi, 9.1; xvii, 2.1, as cited by both Barton and Haupt). Haupt translates the verse as "After all a country will profit – a civilized land – by a king". Barton reads "But an advantage to a country on the whole is a king – (i.e.) an agriculture land" (1908, 126). (3) Both Michel (1989, 144) and Murphy (1992, 51) take the king to be a corrective to the situation of corrupt officials in v.7 to translate "an advantage of the country for all would be this: a king for the cultivated country". Michel also views verse 8 as a political slogan, which Qoheleth is quoting to make his point, which would help explain its awkward syntax and relation to its surrounding context. (4) Gordis sides with Rabbinic literature in its emphasis on agriculture to read, "the advantage of land is paramount; even a king is subject to the soil". (1968, 166, 250). (5) Whitley adopts a Mishnaic Niphal reading of נֶעֱבָד ("is served", "benefits") which is linked to the king, hence "a king benefits from a field" (1979, 51). (6) Lauha identifies the use of quotations in vv.7b and 8 based on its "poetic feature" (*poetischen Merkmale*). He adds that verse 8 is likely to be an interpolation since it forms no logical link to the preceding verse and that it is used by the redactor as a counterpoint to the corruption in government described in verse 7, and that the existence of a monarchy provides a recourse to the unwelcome state of government. Lauha translates verse 8 as, "however, it is advantageous for all of a country that the cultivated country has a king" (1978, 103-5). It is difficult to make sense of this very problematic verse. I have followed Gordis's translation for verse 8 as it gives the sense of Qoheleth being in sympathy with his people. Such a reading would parallel the concern found in his opening remark to "not be surprised" at the corruption observed in the administration. It would further tie in with Qoheleth's mood of resignation. In verse 8 then, we have Qoheleth empathizing with the general populace that even he, as king, is indirectly subject to the maladministration of his own land.

168 Some commentators take verse 7b to refer to the situation of each official looking out for his own interests, e.g. Barton (1908, 127), with a possible further inference that corroboration exists between officials in that they are looking out for each other, so McNeile (1904, 69). Others see a competitive spirit being inferred here, e.g. Crenshaw (1987, 118). Both meanings are possible and both can support the general point of the verse about the existence of corruption in the official and governmental system. Fox takes the verse too far in reading it

recognition by a king of the moral treachery that is happening in his own administration, which he is helpless to influence, hence his warning to his corrupt officials in the following verses (9-14 [ET vv.10-15]) that the love of money does not bring satisfaction. It could also be a more general musing on the corruption of administration in general.[169] However, even this might reflect indirectly upon the king and add to his general frustration and pessimism. In verse 8, mention of the king is an interesting feature, although it is unclear whether the king is in some sense subject to the land or whether he is benefiting from it. In context with the previous verse, it may be that the king, in sympathy with his people, is expressing the limitations of being king despite his ownership of land.[170]

4. 10:5-7

‏5 יֵשׁ רָעָה רָאִיתִי תַּחַת הַשָּׁמֶשׁ כִּשְׁגָגָה שֶׁיֹּצָא מִלִּפְנֵי הַשַּׁלִּיט
‏6 נִתַּן הַסֶּכֶל בַּמְּרוֹמִים רַבִּים וַעֲשִׁירִים בַּשֵּׁפֶל יֵשֵׁבוּ׃
‏7 רָאִיתִי עֲבָדִים עַל־סוּסִים וְשָׂרִים הֹלְכִים כַּעֲבָדִים
עַל־הָאָרֶץ׃

---

as a reference to the difficulty of rooting out corruption in the bureaucracy because of the presence of officials watching out for one another (1989, 212-3).

169 Similarly Lauha 1978, 104.

170 Perdue argues that in this passage the institution of the monarchy is portrayed as being part of the hierarchy of tyrannical rule that eventually reaches "the throne of the God" (1990, 474-5). His argument is based on the reading of גְּבֹהִים in v.7 [ET v.8] as a plural of majesty in reference to God. This is in contrast to Siegfried and others (e.g. GKC §124h, BDB 147 citing earlier commentators e.g. Ewald et al.) who similarly see a reference to the divine in this verse though contending that the verse is a gloss added by a pious interpolator to convey the point that God, who is at the top of the hierarchy, is ultimately the one who is able to correct the injustice narrated in the preceding verse. Although the suggestion of a divine context is possible, the reference to earthly rulers is most likely meant here, so LXX ὑψηλὸς ἐπάνω ὑψηλοῦ φυλάξαι καὶ ὑψηλοὶ ἐπ' αὐτούς; Vg; Syr; Ginsburg (1861, 345-6); Plumptre (1885, 150); Delitzsch (1891, 294); McNeile (1904, 69); Barton (1908, 130); Galling (1969, 69); Lauha (1978, 104); Murphy (1992, 51). This would go well with the reference to וְגֵזֶל מִשְׁפָּט "wresting of justice" in v.7 [ET v.8]. Furthermore, the progression of thought would find a fitting climax in my suggested description of the king in verse 8 [ET v.9].

5   There is an evil that I have observed under the sun. The kind[171] of (foolish) error[172] that proceeds from the ruler.[173]
6   Foolishness is set in high places while the rich remain in a low estate.
7   I have seen slaves on horses and princes walking like slaves on foot.

This passage is seen by some commentators as words spoken in criticism of a king or ruler. However, it need not be so as it may simply be explained in terms of one royal personage criticizing another, in that this could be a comment on the foolish rulers with whom the king might have to deal. It may also, more subtly, refer to the fact that errors are made from the top down (v.5) and that sometimes the status quo of the wise ruling is not in fact the case. Instead, the foolish are given positions of power (vv.6a, 7a) and the world sometimes looks topsy-turvy. The issue that is raised here is of the observed chaos in the usual structure of society, where fools and slaves rule over the rich and the powerful. This passage is yet another observation that the reality of life goes against usual expectation, in this case, of the structure

---

171 Taking כ in כְּשְׁגָגָה to have a comparative function indicating a similarity, "the kind of..." ; so the ancient versions, LXX ὡς; Vg quasi; Murphy (1992, 96). It is also possible to read it as an asseverative particle ("indeed", so Gordis 1968, 319). The more important issue is the relationship between the error, the ruler, and the described social chaos in the following two verses. See the following footnote.

172 This is a reference to the thoughtless errors (BDB 993), which would be commonly associated with fools, cf. 5:5 [ET v.6]. Some commentators argue that the meaning of v.5b is not so much about putting the blame of the problem of vv.6-7 on those in authority, but that such rulers – who undeservedly occupy positions of authority because of the reversal of social conventions described in the following vv.6-7 – are found to make inadvertent mistakes, e.g. Ogden (1987, 167); Seow (1997, 324). Murphy instead sees הַשַּׁלִּיט as committing the error which is the social chaos that is described in the next two verses (1992, 101). It would provide for greater consistency and emphasis if the ruler who commits foolish errors is also seen as a representative of this chaotic social structure (vv.6-7) which Qoheleth describes as רָעָה and שְׁגָגָה . In any case, both views are not mutually exclusive in that the ruler, whose position might be a part of the described social chaos, may himself be responsible for promoting similar errors.

173 הַשַּׁלִּיט is more likely a reference to a person who wields power than to a specific political position or status. Lohfink, in his attempt to match the different political titles found in Qoheleth (i.e. שַׁלִּיט , מוֹשֵׁל , מֶלֶךְ) to possible administrative office and officials in the third century B.C. temple state of Judaea, concludes that both מוֹשֵׁל and שַׁלִּיט are broadly defined terms which essentially refer to a person having power over others (1982, 542-3).

of society. Whether this is in reference to an Israelite context or to a foreign one in historical terms is a matter of debate amongst scholars, but it appears that it is more likely to be a general reference to the way societies, and not just individuals, can go against the normal pattern that the wise might expect.[174] That Qoheleth describes this observation as רָעָה[175] reflects his concern for the hierarchical status quo. Such a concern would belong better to a royal personage who would be most keen to protect his unrivalled status and position in society. Thus this passage, far from being incongruent with a royal voice, strongly supports it.

To conclude, our analyses above have shown that the above passages that contain general musings on injustice are not inherently contradictory to a royal voice. Instead, they clearly are in keeping with and do support a royal voice.

B. The Nature of Kingship

The following four passages of texts contain some reference to the king and his rule. Two of the passages are exhortatory and are found in the didactic portions of the work, while the other two consist of a parable and an illustrative saying.

---

174 Many scholars note that the theme of a hierarchical change in society as expressed here is a typical wisdom topos and appears to be one commonly found in the wisdom literature of the ancient Near East. Examples include Prov. 19:10 and 30:21-30, the Instructions of Ipuwer, and the Admonitions of a Prophet. Seow points out that similar examples may be found in Assyrian and Babylonian letters (1997, 314). On the basis of his study of comparative ancient literature, van Leeuwen argues that, despite their conventional form, these observations of social chaos are likely to be genuine expressions of concern for the stability of society rather than humorous works of social satire (contra McKane 1979). Van Leeuwen points to Prov. 30:21-3 as an example of the depiction of a similar topos of "the world upside down" used for the purpose of legitimizing the hierarchical status quo from a royal perspective (1986, 609-10).

175 Grant notes that in the other passages of observed social chaos in *Qoheleth*, "the reversal of social conventions was matched by a corresponding reversal in moral values, usually seen in the form of a rejection of wisdom, but in the case of 10:5-7, the violation of morality is itself the reversal of social norms" (2000, 217-8).

1. 4:13-16

13 טוֹב יֶלֶד מִסְכֵּן וְחָכָם מִמֶּלֶךְ זָקֵן וּכְסִיל אֲשֶׁר לֹא־יָדַע לְהִזָּהֵר עוֹד:

14 כִּי־מִבֵּית הָסוּרִים יָצָא לִמְלֹךְ כִּי גַּם בְּמַלְכוּתוֹ נוֹלַד רָשׁ:

15 רָאִיתִי אֶת־כָּל־הַחַיִּים הַמְהַלְּכִים תַּחַת הַשָּׁמֶשׁ עִם הַיֶּלֶד הַשֵּׁנִי אֲשֶׁר יַעֲמֹד תַּחְתָּיו:

16 אֵין־קֵץ לְכָל־הָעָם לְכֹל אֲשֶׁר־הָיָה לִפְנֵיהֶם גַּם הָאַחֲרוֹנִים לֹא יִשְׂמְחוּ־בוֹ כִּי־גַם־זֶה הֶבֶל וְרַעְיוֹן רוּחַ:

13   Better a poor but wise youth than an old but foolish king who no longer knows how to take admonition.

14[176] For from prison[177] he had gone forth to rule, even though he was born poor in his kingdom.

---

176 There are many syntactical ambiguities in this passage (4:13-16), with uncertainties surrounding the pronouns and verbal suffixes as well as the number of persons being spoken of or described. In relation to verse 14, the subject of the two verbs is unclear. Do both verbs refer to the poor and wise youth in verse 13 who had been born poor and now gone on to be king, or do they refer separately to the youth and the foolish king? Further, there is the issue of the two כִּי conjunctions. Seow applies each כִּי in verse 14 separately to the young man and the old king to give the following translation – "for (one) went forth from the prison to reign, while (another), though born into his kingship, is impoverished" (1997, 184). This interpretation views the two כִּי conjunctions as referring separately to the destiny of the youth and the fate of the foolish king, and the particle גַם is read concessively. A simpler approach would be to see "the poor and wise youth" in verse 13 as the subject of the two verbs. McNeile, who takes this path, explains that the two adjectives which are applied to the young man in the preceding verse are consequently explained by the two separate facts which are introduced by the כִּי conjunctions, i.e. "he was wise – *for* he managed to escape from prison to be king; he was poor – *for* even in his kingdom he was born poor" (1904, 66-7). Whybray also takes the youth in verse 13 to be the subject of the two verbs in verse 14, although reading both כִּי conjunctions as coordinating conjunctions which qualify טוֹב in verse 13 (1989, 89). Murphy similarly views the wise youth in verse 13 as the subject of the two verbs, but reads the second כִּי conjunction as functioning concessively to the first ("even though"). In essence, all the last three interpretations see the wise youth in verse 13 as the subject of the two verbs in verse 14, although they differ in their interpretation of the function of the second כִּי conjunction. The second uncertainty, in verse 14, is of the suffix in בְּמַלְכוּתוֹ , that is, whether it is referring to the old king (Delitzsch 1981, 280), or to the youth who is presently king (McNeile 1904, 67); Murphy (1992, 41-3). There are no further means to clarify this ambiguity, and again either reading will not materially affect the main point of the story which comes at the end of the passage in verse 16.

177 All the ancient versions and most scholars today see the root as אָסַר , observing an elided aleph in this case (GKC §35d; for a similar phenomenon see 2 Kgs. 8:28; 2 Chr. 22:5).

15[178] I saw all the living, those who walked under the sun with the
second youth, who was to succeed him[179].

16[180] Yet there is no end to all the people, all who lived before them,
nor will those after them be happy with him, this also is vanity
and a chasing of wind.

In this passage, we have what is commonly read as a parable or
fictitious story.[181] The טוֹב saying in v.13 introduces this new unit
and proceeds to describe what Qoheleth sees as the "better"
situation of the two described, that is, the poor but wise youth
who rises to kingship, in comparison to the foolish king who
does not heed advice. Qoheleth then turns "to look" at a second
youth who could have risen through a similar difficult circumstance as the first youth (vv.15-6).[182] It is possible, as has been
suggested, that the old king, who has been deposed, was
perhaps once a poor and wise youth himself who took the throne
like the "first" youth, but this is not made clear.[183] The parable
however has a paradoxical twist at the end, which is that even
the second youth who succeeded the first, who had it "better"

---

178 In this verse, we have the problem of the "second youth", that is, whether he is
the same person as the first youth in verses 13 and 14, or another youth who
now becomes his successor (תַּחְתָּיו "in his place" cf. Dan. 8:22-3). Gordis (1968,
245) and Lauha (1978, 94) argue that הַיֶּלֶד הַשֵּׁנִי ought to be read in opposition
to each other to mean "successor". This argument, however, is based on a
rather doubtful analogy with Hos. 2:9, as both Crenshaw (1988, 113) and Fox
(1989, 207) have pointed out. Galling (1969, 100); Fox (1989, 208); and Seow
(1997, 185) read הַשֵּׁנִי as meaning "the next", after the first wise youth. McNeile
(1904, 67) and Barton (1908, 119-20) similarly read the phrase as meaning the
second youth ("another") who succeeds the first, and not that the first youth is
now the second king after the foolish one. I have chosen the simpler reading,
which sees the "second youth" as being in opposition to the first in verse 13.

179 Cf. Dan. 8:22-3.

180 It is unclear as to whether the subject of הָיָה is "the people" or "the rulers".
Murphy views the text as too ambiguous and contends that either one would
do (1992, 42). However, Gordis raises the pertinent point that the king is
usually "before" his people (e.g. 1 Sam. 18:16; Ps. 68:8; 2 Chr. 1:10) and not his
people "before" him (1968, 245-6; followed by Crenshaw (1988, 114). Following
Gordis then, the phrase אֲשֶׁר־הָיָה לִפְנֵיהֶם "who lived before them" (i.e. the old
king and his young successor) is held in opposition to הָאַחֲרוֹנִים to refer to the
earlier and later generations (cf. 1:10-1), and consequently, the plural suffix in
לִפְנֵיהֶם would then refer to the rulers in the previous verses.

181 It is commonly described as a Standesmärchen in German scholarship, e.g.
Galling (1940, 67); Zimmerli (1962, 185); Lauha (1972, 91).

182 Cf. discussion in previous footnote 178.

183 Fox 1989, 207-8.

with his rise to kingship, did not end up in a better position than any of his predecessors. In the end, the multitude of people who lived before the rulers, as well as the succeeding generations who came after, were not happy with their ruler.

Aside from the issue of the historicity of the event[184] and the ambiguities surrounding the personalities involved, the point of the story – which comes at the end of the passage – is that a king's power and position lie in a vulnerable state before the ever-changing sentiment of the populace. As Lohfink points out, "The rapidity of this description of a sequence of three leaders and the gently ironic presentation of the approval 'of all the living who walked about under the sun,' underline stylistically what this is about: the fickleness of popular favor and the insecurity at the top of the political ladder."[185] That a king might contemplate the issue of the precarious nature of kingship (which is consistent to Qoheleth's other musing on the threat of social order) is possible. The rise and fall of a monarch, and the power of the populace to affect the fate of rulers, are unwelcome realities of life for a king. The adulation of the public is unreliable, and in the light of the ephemeral quality of popularity (v.16c), striving for power is an illusion and a vanity.[186] The

---

184 On the question of the reality of such a situation, Fox argues, in the minority, that the elliptical character of the narration gives the impression that the event described in vv.13-14 is known to his audience. He contends that the fact that certain details of the story, such as the youth coming forth from prison (v.14b), are not typical features of the event and do not do much for the message, but nevertheless are recounted, indicates that the author was recalling an authentic historical event.   Schunck goes further in his attempt to relate the story to a specific historical situation during the rule of the Seleucids in Judaea (1959). Both Fox and Schunck's views are at best speculative since historical references in the passage are almost non-existent and the identities of the characters are obscure.   Furthermore, as many scholars acknowledge, the story has the appearance of a sapiential work, with its use of conventional wisdom forms and the distinctive wisdom theme of the old king and rising young ruler, which suggest that it is but a "fictional example story".   Similar kinds of stories are found in ancient Near Eastern texts, such as the Instructions for Merikare and the Aramaic Sayings of Ahiqar, where they are also generally viewed as fictitious.

185 Lohfink (2003, 73). Similarly, Crenshaw describes the story as illustrating "the speed with which people forget rulers, regardless of their achievements" (1988, 112).

186 Fox draws out several other possible meanings from the story, e.g. that political power, like wealth, will be passed on to those who may not even have the

concern expressed in the narrating of this story would favour rather than preclude a royal voice.[187]

2. 8:1-5

מִי כְּהֶחָכָם[188] וּמִי יוֹדֵעַ פֵּשֶׁר דָּבָר חָכְמַת אָדָם תָּאִיר פָּנָיו 1
וְעֹז פָּנָיו יְשֻׁנֶּא:

אֲנִי פִּי־מֶלֶךְ שְׁמוֹר וְעַל דִּבְרַת שְׁבוּעַת אֱלֹהִים: 2

אַל־תִּבָּהֵל מִפָּנָיו תֵּלֵךְ אַל־תַּעֲמֹד בְּדָבָר רָע כִּי כָּל־אֲשֶׁר 3
יַחְפֹּץ יַעֲשֶׂה:

בַּאֲשֶׁר דְּבַר־מֶלֶךְ שִׁלְטוֹן וּמִי יֹאמַר־לוֹ מַה־תַּעֲשֶׂה: 4

שׁוֹמֵר מִצְוָה לֹא יֵדַע דָּבָר רָע וְעֵת וּמִשְׁפָּט יֵדַע לֵב חָכָם: 5

1[189] Who is like the wise man? Who knows the meaning of a thing? A man's wisdom makes his face shine and the boldness[190] of his countenance is transformed[191].

"appropriate" background to claim it, that is, the youth who was born poor and who came from prison to reign, although he did gain the throne by wisdom. Another is that political power, even though gained by wisdom, is not lasting as is seen in the second youth taking over from the first (1989, 206). These should be taken as secondary issues of the text. Clearly the main point of the parable lies at the end of the story (v.16) with its focus on the successive generations' displeasure with their ruler.

187 This story also links up with Qoheleth's earlier lament in 2:18-26 over the unpredictability of the character of his successor and the consequences to his legacy.

188 The unassimilated definite article, though unusual, is attested elsewhere in the Bible (GKC §35n; Jöuon §35e). LXX's Τίς οἶδεν σοφούς "who knows (like) the wise" is likely to be a corruption with οἶδεν being mistaken for ὧδε, so Euringer (1890, 93-4) as cited by Seow (1997, 277); and followed by Gordis (1968, 286); Murphy (1992, 80). The Greek traditions apparently read כה חכם for כהחכם but there is no need for this. The MT is supported by the Syr, Vg, and Tg.

189 There is some debate about whether 8:1 or 8:2 marks the start of the section to follow. Some commentators, e.g. Galling (1969, 76); Loader (1979, 50-54); Whybray (1989, 128); Lauha (1978, 139-147) see verse 1 (viz. 1a and b) as the conclusion to the preceding passage of 7:23-29 where Qoheleth speaks of his failure in his quest for wisdom. Verse 1a and b are thus read as rhetorical questions (i.e. "Who is so wise? And who knows the solution of anything?" No one!). However, the whole of verse 1 could be viewed as the opening verse to the subsequent sayings on the positive value of wisdom in a court context. This latter option is more likely in view that firstly, 8:1 anticipates the didactic sayings which follow on proper conduct in the royal court (vv.2-5); secondly, there is a notable change in Qoheleth's style of narration at 8:1, i.e. from first-person discourse to second-person address. Thirdly, verse 1 (especially v.1c) finds a natural connection with vv.2-5 with its affirmation of the value of wisdom, i.e. it gives the wise the ability to discern the particular situation that

2   < >[192] Keep the king's command according to the manner of a
     sacred oath.[193]

---

they are in and consequently the opportunity to adapt their behaviour and
demeanour accordingly (vv.1c, 3, 4, 5) thereby avoiding unnecessary harm.
Fourth, as Seow points out, verse 1 contains several catchwords (such as דָּבָר
and יוֹדֵעַ) which are repeated in the verses after (i.e. vv.3, 4, 5, 7). Fifth, the
question of 8:1 "who is like the wise man... who knows...?" finds a matching
though ironic answer at the end of the chapter in 8:17b, that "no one can
comprehend what goes on under the sun... even if a wise man claims he
knows, he cannot really comprehend it". As I will argue later, in Chapter 4, this
change in the narrating posture may be viewed as a change in Qoheleth's role
from king to wise teacher.

190 All versions read the adjective עַז for עֹז following עֵז פָּנִים in Deut. 28:50; Dan.
8:23, so McNeile (1904, 76); BDB 738; Lauha (1978, 144); Murphy (1992, 80).
However, the phrasing of the purportedly parallel idiom is not exact, so Gordis
(1968, 286-7); Seow (1997, 278-9). The suggested emmendation is also
unnecessary since עֹז could also be read as a noun in the construct state.

191 The root is more likely to be שׁנה "change" in this context, following the
analogy of ל"א verbs (GKC §75rr; and the majority of commentators) than
ישׂנא "hate" (LXX μισηθήσεται and Syr). A similar expression is found in Ben
Sira 13:24 which supports this reading: לטוב אם לרע לב אנוש ישׁנא פניו אם
(Gordis 1968, 287) "the heart changes the countenance, either for good or for
evil" (NRSV).

192 The presence of אֲנִי at the start is peculiar. Among the many suggested
emendations are, (1) a modification of the pronoun to אָמַרְתִּי (cf. 2:1, 3:17, 18),
so Ginsburg (1861, 391); Delitzsch (1891, 338-9); Hertzberg (1963, 164); (2)
converting it to the sign of the direct object אֵת (Barton 1908, 152); or (3) to בְּנִי
after the "father-son" wisdom terminology (cf. 12:12, so Wildeboer 1898, 149),
and (4) treating it as the object suffix of the preceding verb, with "a partial
dittography of the aleph and the graphic confusion of waw and yod" (Seow
1997, 279). Crenshaw reads אֲנַפֵּי ("in the presence of") following a supposedly
similar passage in the Aramaic Sayings of Ahiqar (1988, 150). Whitley, who
likewise notes the similarity with Ahiqar, suggests a rearrangement of the MT
phrase to parallel the Aramaic text to read אֲנַפֵּי מֶלֶךְ "in the presence of the
king" (1979, 71-2). As none of the proposed solutions are decidedly persuasive,
and because the omission of the pronoun does not materially affect the
meaning of the verse, I have chosen to leave it out (similarly LXX; Syr; McNeile
(1904, 76); Lauha (1978, 146)).

193 There is uncertainty over the meaning of וְעַל דִּבְרַת שְׁבוּעַת אֱלֹהִים , in
particular, the function of עַל דִּבְרַת and whether שְׁבוּעַת אֱלֹהִים should be read
as an objective or subjective genitive. The different translations are a result of
the different interpretations of these two issues (i.e. the oath of God or to God,
and whether עַל דִּבְרַת is read as a causal or modal clause). These include, (1)
keeping a king's command because of the oath one has sworn to the king before
God, so Barton (1908, 149); Gordis (1968, 288), (2) because God has sworn an
oath to the king, so Hertzberg (1963, 161-2, 163-4); Lauha (1978, 148), (3) in the
manner that one keeps an oath sworn to God (Seow 1997, 279). McNeile (1904,
106) and Fox (1989, 246) read the waw as intrusive, and thus divide the verse
into separate clauses which leads to a reorganization of the subsequent verse
divisions (similarly LXX, Symm, and Syr which take it with the subsequent

3   Do not hurry to leave[194] from his presence. Do not persist in an
     unpleasant matter, for whatever he pleases he does.
4   Because a king's word is supreme, who may say to him "what are
     you doing?".
5   Whoever obeys a commandment[195] will not experience harm. The
     heart of a wise man will know the time and judgment.

It has been argued that this passage must reflect the voice of a
subject to the exclusion of a king because of the didactic form
that the text takes and because the king is mentioned in it.[196]
Such an argument is flawed because the reasons suggested for
the "anti-royal" perspective could equally apply in support of a
royal voice, in that the shift in the style of narration (from first-
person discourse to second-person address) might indicate a
shift in the role of Qoheleth from king to wise teacher as he dispenses *his* wisdom on the subject on which he is most qualified
to speak. In this passage, Qoheleth calls on the individual to be
sensitive to the prevailing mood in the court (8:5-6; 10:4), and to
be conscious of proper timing and appropriate behaviour before

---

clause אַל־תִּבָּהֵל) – "Observe the commands of a king, but on account of [thine]
oath to God, be not frightened. Out of his presence shalt thou go", McNeile
(ibid.). This emendation, however, is unnecessary since good meaning may still
be derived from the MT verse structure. It is important to note that, despite
their difference, the basic point of the verse is retained in all the above
interpretations, in their emphasis on the seriousness of keeping the king's
decree. Nevertheless, Seow's suggested interpretation is preferable in view of
our ignorance about Israel's practice of taking oaths of loyalty to the king before
God.

194 The advice here to be wise in one's behaviour in court is similar to the one in
10:4 (cf. 7:9). תֵּלֵךְ would coordinate to complement תִּבָּהֵל (GKC§120c), so
Gordis (1968, 288); Murphy (1992, 80). LXX; Syr; McNeile (1904, 106); Seow
(1997, 279-80) read אַל־תִּבָּהֵל with the preceding verse 2 to interpret the
remaining verse 3 as advice to depart quickly and not linger in stupor in the
king's presence. This latter reading is less likely as it would then be
inconsistent with its clear meaning of "applying calm" in 5:1 [ET v.2] and 7:9.

195 This may also be read as a royal command in view of the court context of the
passage (cf. 1 Kgs. 2:43; 2 Kgs. 18:36; 2 Chr. 8:15; Isa. 29:13; Jer. 35:18). The
phrase שׁוֹמֵר מִצְוָה is also found in Prov. 19:16 where מִצְוָה quite clearly refers
to the saying of the teacher (Murphy 1992, 83). This phrase, in Eccl. 8:5, is likely
to be a *double entendre* referring to both the word of God and the orders of the
king. As Crenshaw comments, "the attitude of wisdom literature toward
royalty is ambiguous, but there is never any refusal to recognize the awesome
power resting in a ruler's hands" (1988, 150).

196 Gordis argues that there is a real sense of fear of royal authority in this passage
(1968, 41). He further suggests that Qoheleth is here speaking as a sage to warn
against the potential incidence of harm (v.5).

the king (vv.1c, 3, 4, 5) so as to avoid any harmful consequence. Far from being incongruous with the king as speaker, this passage might represent the didactic function of the king as wise man who knows many more truths than most about appropriate behaviour in the king's presence.[197]

In the following verses (vv.6-9), the merits of wisdom are relativized in the wider context of life, against the mysterious ways of God.[198] Whereas in court the wise man is able to "know" how to interpret the demeanour of the king and act appropriately, thereby ensuring his own safety, in the wider context of life he remains helpless and unable to discover his own fate (8:8).[199] Although there is a "proper time" for everything, man is unable to grasp this completely.[200] Qoheleth's argument, which begins with a specific and determinable context (i.e. a royal court, where a wise man is able "to know" and be in control of his situation) proceeds to a wider and more complex setting (i.e. the larger context of life, where man is unable to predict future events – no matter how wise he claims to be (cf. 8:1, 17) – especially the hour of his death (8:8)). Read in the wider context of vv.6-9, the point of the admonitions in 8:1-5 is that

---

197 Some commentators have argued that this passage implicitly draws a parallel between the king and God in terms of their undisputed authority and their use of power. Grant, for example, suggests that this passage speaks of the capriciousness of God and the king in their use of power (2000, 154). This suggestion is unconvincing. To be sure, absolute power of the king is indeed emphasized here, hence Qoheleth's call for "wise" conduct when one is before the monarch. However, supreme power does not necessarily imply caprice. In this context, it is clear that loyal obedience to the king's decrees will have its reward otherwise such advice would be superfluous. Thus, the admonition to avoid dealing with an unpleasant matter in 8:3 emphasizes the benefit of applying wisdom when in the presence of a king so as not to incur his wrath (Prov. 16:14; 19:12; 20:2; Eccl. 10:4). Murphy likewise points out that verse 15 "certainly promises the traditional sapiential value; the wise person will succeed... the knowledge of the wise... is commended in positive fashion" (1992, 83).

198 The opening יכִּ in 8:6 serves as an asseverative particle, as in 3:1, to mark Qoheleth's return to private meditation from his didactic role. We may also note the change in tone, from one that is assertive and positive to one that is pessimistic and resigned.

199 This echoes Qoheleth's earlier thought on the powerlessness of man to control future events, their timing and occurrence, which God alone knows and sets (3:1-15).

200 Thus Qoheleth too found his own search for wisdom to be futile (e.g. 7:23-4; 8:17).

whilst human beings should accept the limits of their wisdom they should also take advantage of those situations where wisdom can bring them benefit (and vice versa). That the court-specific advice of 8:1-5 might come from a king who is assuming his didactic role is thus possible.[201]

3. 10:16-17

16 אִי־לָךְ אֶרֶץ שֶׁמַּלְכֵּךְ נָעַר וְשָׂרַיִךְ בַּבֹּקֶר יֹאכֵלוּ׃

17 אַשְׁרֵיךְ אֶרֶץ שֶׁמַּלְכֵּךְ בֶּן־חוֹרִים וְשָׂרַיִךְ בָּעֵת יֹאכֵלוּ
בִּגְבוּרָה וְלֹא בַשְּׁתִי׃

16   Woe[202] to you, O land, where your king is an immature[203] and your princes feast in the morning.

17   Fortunate are you, O land, where your king is a son of nobles[204] and your princes feast at the proper time, in strength and not in drunkenness.

---

201 Noticeably, the theme of power saturates the final verses of the wider passage (vv.8-9), but is developed in a convoluted manner – man is powerless against the events of life (v.8), but when and where he does have power he uses it to the detriment of others (v.9). A similar irony appears in 4:1. This passage in fact raises the question why such specific instructions for proper conduct before a king might be included if the work was indeed meant as a royal travesty or parody, as many commentators posit, or if the royal fiction was supposed to have ended in Eccl. 2. Furthermore, Qoheleth's exhortation to obey the king is not only found in this passage, but also elsewhere, e.g. 10:4, 20, and the association between פִּי־מֶלֶךְ " the king's decree" and שְׁבוּעַת אֱלֹהִים " the oath of God" in 8:2 helps to further emphasize the power and authority of the king.

202 This is likely to be a late form of אוֹי , so Murphy (1992, 40); Schoors (1992, 149); Seow (1997, 182), which, in this context, may be translated as "woe" (cf. 4:10; Isa. 6:5).

203 McDonald has argued that a נַעַר is always of high birth (1949, 149), but this is unlikely to be correct since there is evidence to suggest that it carries a reference to the role and status of a servant. The word has a varied etymology and it carries a wide range of possible meanings not exclusively relating to the age of the person but possibly including his position in a royal administration (Avishur 2000, 107-8). נַעַר in the above passage is likely to allude to the characteristics commonly associated with a person's youthfulness which in this particular context are likely negative, i.e. the "instability", "irresponsibility", and "rashness" (Lauha 1978, 194). The reading of "servant" in order to balance the comparison with בֶּן־חוֹרִים , e.g. Zimmerli (1962, 237); Fox (1989, 271) is unlikely since the contrast is really on the בֶּן־חוֹרִים feasting with proper self-control. Similarly, the idea of the king being a former "servant" is just as unlikely since the verse is making a contrast between wisdom and foolishness rather than referring to the difference in social standing, so Lauha (ibid., 195).

204 1 Kgs. 21:8-11; Neh. 2:16, 5:7.

It has been argued that this passage contains criticism of kings and thus must be words spoken by a subject. However, a closer examination of the text suggests that it could also reflect an admonition by a king who is advising other rulers about appropriate royal behaviour and responsibility. In this passage we find that the contrast is made between the immature and foolish rulers who lack proper restraint, and those who exert self-control, with the point being that good kingship depends on the cultivation of self-discipline and growing in maturity.[205] The literary style of the passage suggests that its main purpose is didactic and that the issue of whether it is referring to a real or contemporary setting is secondary.[206] The didactic aim of the passage is further underlined by Qoheleth's use of the formulaic phrase אִי־לָךְ (which echoes the prophetic admonitions, e.g. Isa 5:8f) to express his disapproval of the slothful behaviour of the foolish rulers. As with the other didactic passage of 8:1-5, Qoheleth might, in this text, be taking up his didactic role of wise-king again. Criticism is expressed against rulers who are described as "immature" and "self-indulgent" in their attitude and behaviour, while encouragement is given to kings to guard their conduct and not neglect their responsibilities.[207] Far from having an "anti-royal" perspective, this passage in fact suggests a royal context in which such wisdom about kings might not only be spoken by monarchs, but also would be of interest and concern to them as well.[208]

---

205 Not only is advice given on how to behave (which is a common biblical wisdom topic) but the commended behaviour is also to be seen as evidence of wisdom. There is also a faint echo of the poem on time (3:1-15) in the admonition on the appropriateness of time.

206 The stylized nature of the passage, with the presence of antithetical parallelism (marked by the "woe"/אַשְׁרֵי forms), and the repetition of keywords מֶלֶךְ and שַׂר in both verses, suggests that a fictional context is being described here, so Lauha (1978, 193); Ogden (1987, 175-6); Murphy (1992, 105) cf. Whybray who believes that the author's own situation is depicted in the verses (1989, 156).

207 Cf. the two earlier passages that deal with the issue of the precarious and insecure nature of kingship. In 2:12, 18-24 Qoheleth laments over the possibility that his successor might be a fool, thereby laying his legacy of achievements and good deeds to waste. In 4:13-16 Qoheleth despairs over the absurd reality that the fate of a king's rule depends upon the unreliable support of his subjects.

208 Seow detects the use of political polemical language in this passage. He argues that the word "youth" is sometimes used as a derogatory term by kings in the

4. 10:20

גַּם בְּמַדָּעֲךָ מֶלֶךְ אַל־תְּקַלֵּל וּבְחַדְרֵי מִשְׁכָּבְךָ אַל־תְּקַלֵּל 20
עָשִׁיר כִּי עוֹף הַשָּׁמַיִם יוֹלִיךְ אֶת־הַקּוֹל וּבַעַל כְּנָפַיִם יַגֵּיד
דָּבָר:

    20   Even in your thought[209] do not curse the king and in your bedroom
        do not curse the rich; for a bird in the sky will carry the news, or a
        winged creature will report what is said.

In what is the last reference in *Qoheleth* to the king, we have
another exhortation to obey and be loyal to the monarch (cf. 8:2-
5). This verse warns its listeners against criticizing the king and
those in power, with a further advice to refrain from "even" (the
opening גַּם is emphatic) harbouring any negative thoughts about
the ruler or speaking ill of wealthy and important people, lest
they may be persecuted for their lack of loyalty. This verse
clearly supports the status of the king, as well as the wealthy,
which is exempt from any criticism.[210] Listeners are warned of
the ubiquitous presence of spies and informers. This text is
clearly seeking to discourage criticism and potential rebellion
against those in power – themes which support the authority of

---

    ancient Near East to refer to their rival rulers in criticism of their lack of
    wisdom and political naiveté. Seow points to the example of the Hittite king,
    Mursilis II, whom his enemy calls "a youth" who is unable to defend his land,
    and Nabonidus's criticism of the son of a rival ruler who is described as "a
    minor who had not yet learned how to behave" (1997, 339-40). Seow's
    argument would support a royal context to the passage.
209 Most commentators read it as "thoughts" as derived by extension from the
    Aramaized מַדַּע "knowledge" (2 Chr. 1:10-12; Dan. 1:4, 17; so BDB 396; McNeile
    (1904, 83); Barton (1908, 179); Gordis (1968, 149); Hertzberg (1963, 197-8). Levy
    argues persuasively that the thought-sequence of the first two clauses would
    support this reading: "A *king* is not to be cursed even in *thought*; while a *rich
    man* whose power is less (and whose spies are less ubiquitous) not in the
    privacy of one's *bed-chamber*", as cited by Gordis (1968, 329). Others have
    suggested an emendation to בְּמַצָּעֲךָ "on my bed" in order to achieve a
    parallelism of a noun indicating place with "bedroom" (Perles who first
    suggested this, is followed by *HALOT* 497b; Lauha (1978, 196)). LXX, and some
    versions (e.g. Vg, Syr, Tg) reflect the MT consonantal text. Thomas (1949, 177)
    suggested a revocalization to מֹדְעֲךָ to read "your rest" following the Arabic
    mawdû (so NEB "in your ease"). This is also unnecessary. As Murphy points
    out, rigidity in parallelism should not be expected (1992, 105).
210 As Crüsemann observes, "the king and the wealthy, whose incorporation into
    the apparatus of the state is shown here more clearly than anywhere else"
    (1984, 71).

the king – hence would more naturally belong to a royal voice than a person who is against the monarchy. In fact, this verse poses an obstacle to the "anti-royal" view in that its warning against speaking ill of the king and the wealthy would be ironic in the light of the purported presence of "anti-royal" passages in the book.[211]

C. Summary

In the first set of passages, we saw that these might be read to reflect the general musings of a king on the issue of social injustice, which is an ongoing reality in life and against which even he and his government are not immune. Because this reflects indirectly on Qoheleth, it adds to his general frustration and pessimism. We have also seen that there is nothing inherently incompatible with a king using examples involving other rulers for the purpose of illustrating a point.

As for the passages to do with the nature of kingship, we noted that these consist of didactic sayings and a parable. Their didactic form and the mention of the king in them have prompted some commentators to suggest that an outsider of the court is the author of these texts. However, as we have seen, it is still possible to render these passages of didactic sayings as being addressed by a royal personage. The passage of 8:1-6[212], for example, would, as I have argued above, more likely belong to a royal voice than to the voice of a subject, the latter being commonly argued by commentators today. We have also seen how the passages of 4:13-16 and 10:16-17 might carry the didactic purpose of inculcating proper behaviour and discipline among rulers, a matter which would be of concern for kings, especially in the light of the precarious nature of their power and reign (4:13-16; 10:5-7).

Therefore, it is unnecessary to view the above passages as reflecting Qoheleth's subversion of royal wealth and power (of

---

211 Fox admits that "Verse 20 seems to be an ironic warning directed against Qohelet's own words in the opening verse of this passage" (1989, 270-1).

212 10:4 carries a similar admonition.

which, to remind ourselves, he makes a boast in the opening chapters of the book). Rather, Qoheleth's narrative is dialectic in nature. He uses his observations and experience (which often begin with a royal context) to validate conventional wisdom where applicable, or where it is not, to challenge his listeners to rethink. In arguing for the possibility of reading a royal voice in these passages, we have seen how the message and themes display coherence and consistency. In fact, we often find, in the above passages of texts, a repetition of themes spoken of earlier in the book which are sometimes echoed again in later chapters. Furthermore, the dialectic shifts in Qoheleth's argument appear to reflect his unique style of thought, which very often is nuanced. We have briefly seen, for example, in the passages of 4:13-15 and 8:6-9 how Qoheleth often makes a statement only to subsequently pose a counter-argument or modification to the initial assertion. This unique style of argument, which Hertzberg described as a *zwar-aber Tatsache* or *Aussage*, has often been interpreted as reflecting different voices in the text or as part of a deliberate rhetorical strategy of satirizing the king.[213] However, my argument is that the royal position of Qoheleth *is* consistent with the words spoken in these texts, especially if his advice is appreciated in the light of his intent to examine carefully and comprehensively the subject of wisdom which includes also matters involving the king. In his testing, Qoheleth shows that whilst he does not deny the truth of conventional wisdom he is neither averse to showing its inapplicability in certain contexts.

V. Concluding Remarks

We have seen from the above investigations that there is stronger evidence for than against the idea of a royal voice in *Qoheleth*. In fact, all of the allegedly "anti-royal" passages appear to assume a court context wherein topics of the problems of injustice and the nature of kingship would have found an appropriate audience. For my next step, I shall turn to test further my argument for the

---

213 See Chapter 4, pp. 178-184 for further discussion of Qoheleth's *zwar-aber* style of argument.

pervasiveness of the royal voice by considering *Qoheleth* in the context of comparative ancient Near Eastern literature. I shall investigate comparative ancient literature to see whether the argument for the royal characterization of the work finds support in the literary traditions of the ancient world from which Qoheleth could have adopted or imitated. If significant parallels can be found it will strengthen my argument for a cohesive royal voice in the work as a whole.

Chapter 3

Qoheleth in the Context of
Ancient Near Eastern Literature

In this chapter I shall examine ancient Near Eastern texts and
compositions to strengthen further my argument for the coherence and pervasiveness of the royal voice in *Qoheleth*. The
analysis to be carried out in this chapter seeks to deepen the
conclusions reached in Chapter 2, thereby paving the way for a
more detailed analysis of the royal voice in *Qoheleth* in Chapter 4.
The following study will focus on textual materials and compositions with a royal theme (where the king is featured as either
the protagonist, author, or main narrator of the work) and will
highlight the parallels between *Qoheleth* and these ancient works
which will further support my argument for the unity and
pervasiveness of Qoheleth's royal voice in the work. The analysis
will be synchronic in its approach in view of the diverse origins
and fragmentary condition of a few of these texts and also
because there is no clear genre category with which *Qoheleth* is
analogous. Our investigations in this chapter will be divided into
two sections, the first of which will focus on the similarity of
language between *Qoheleth* and ancient Semitic royal inscriptions. In the second, I shall examine previous arguments on the
comparability of literary forms and structures between ancient
texts and *Qoheleth*.

Section 1: The Royal Language of *Qoheleth*: *Qoheleth* and Ancient Semitic Royal Inscriptions

As Baumgartner once pointed out, on the basis of the Hebrew
language alone, Mesopotamia's influence upon Israel is

undeniable.[214] Loretz has added further that not just from the fact
of the relatedness of the Semitic languages but "auch aus seiner
ganzen Art und Weise der Darstellung und seiner Probleme"
that Israel's wisdom literature can be seen to share in the rich
and ancient literary traditions of Mesopotamia.[215] This is perhaps
to be expected given the geographical proximity of the nations
and their common ancestral heritage. In this first section, I shall
examine Qoheleth's language, namely his use of formulaic expressions in his introduction, which is said to parallel the ancient
Semitic royal inscriptions.[216] The texts to be analysed in this first
section are from the genre of "monumental inscriptions" and
comprise royal inscriptions from the West Semitic region and
Assyria.

I. West Semitic Royal Inscriptions

The corpus of West Semitic royal texts which will come under
our analysis comprise the inscriptions of Azatiwada, Bar-Rakib
(i), Panammu I's votive inscription to Hadad ("Hadad"),
Kilamuwa, Mesha, Bar-Rakib's dedicatory inscription to his
father Panammu II ("Panammu"), Zakkur, Yehaumilk, Tabnit,
and Eshmunazar. These eleven texts are all well known.
Although they do not all belong to the same genre category, they
are generally known as "monumental inscriptions" set up by
kings for public display and as enduring records.[217] These texts
are considerably varied in their historical origins. The majority of
the inscriptions belong to the once small states of Syria-Palestine,
with two others from the small Neo-Hittite and Aramaean state
of Sam'al (modern Zinjirli in south-central Turkey). These texts
date from the ninth century B.C. (Kilamuwa, Azatiwada, Zakkur,
Hadad, Panammu) to the fifth century B.C. (Yehaumilk). The
different genres that are reflected in this collection of texts
include building inscriptions (Azatiwada, Kilamuwa, Bar-Rakib),

---

214 Baumgartner 1959, 229.
215 Loretz 1964, 90.
216 Loretz (ibid., 62); von Rad (1970, 56-58); Fox (1989, 174); Seow (1995, 279-287).
217 Millard (1972, 99); Hallo (1998, 155).

cultic inscriptions (Hadad, Kilamuwa, Zakkur, Yehaumilk), inscriptions commemorating victories in battle (Mesha), votive inscriptions (Panammu), and sepulchral inscriptions (Tabnit, Eshmunazar).[218] Although there are some observable variations in style and form, a commonality of language is nevertheless identifiable in their formulaic expressions and the stereotypical hyperbole and rhetoric used, all of which hint at a common underlying royal ideology. I shall begin with the examination of the stereotypical "royal" expressions found in the West Semitic corpus which *Qoheleth* appears to also share.

A. The Formulaic Self-Introduction

Qoheleth's opening remarks of אֲנִי קֹהֶלֶת הָיִיתִי מֶלֶךְ עַל־יִשְׂרָאֵל בִּירוּשָׁלָם in 1:12, as I have mentioned earlier in Chapter 2, is commonly acknowledged as paralleling the formulaic self-introductions of West Semitic royal inscriptions.[219] The similarity lies in the syntactical structure of the phrase concerned, which carries the formula "I... RN, am king over..." (i.e. the first-person, common, singular, independent personal pronoun followed by the royal name and the extent of his kingship). Although the royal introductions in the West Semitic texts often vary in length and detail, they nevertheless typically consist of the identification of the king by his name (I am...) and his office (king of...). Quite often, there is also the patronymic element (son of...).

One of the earliest extant examples of the use of the "I... RN" self-identification formula is found in Kilamuwa's Inscription from Zinjirli, written in Old Phoenician and dated to the ninth century B.C.

אנך כלמו בר חיא 1
אנך כלמו בר חיא ישבת על כסא אבי... 9

---

218 These genre categories are not meant to be definitive as some clearly reflect a mixture of forms, e.g. Panammu, Zakkur, Yehaumilk have elements of the memorial and dedicatory genres; see Miller (1974, 12); Parker (1997, 85, 108); Younger (*COS* 2.37).

219 So Loretz (1964, 62); von Rad (1970, 56-8); Loader (1979, 20 n.71); Isaksson (1987, 50 n.55); Fox (1989, 174); Seow (1995, 279-87).

1   I am Kilamuwa, the son of Ḥayya
9   I am Kilamuwa, the son of Ḥayya, I sat upon my father's throne...
(*KAI* 24.1, 9)

In the inscriptions of Mesha, Zakkur, Panammu I, and Yehaumilk, the self-introductions include a further reference to the king's territory.

אנך משע בן כמש[ית] מלך מאב... 1
...' אבי מלך על מאב שלשן שת ואנך מלך 2
תי אחר אבי... 3

1   I am Mesha, the son of Kemosh[-yat], king of Moab...
2   ... My father was king over Moab for thirty years, and I was king
3   after my father...
(*KAI* 181.1-3)

[א]נה זכר מלך חמת ולעש... 2

2   I am Zakkur, the king of Hamath and Lu'ath...
(*KAI* 202.2)

אנך פנמו בר קרל מלך יאדי... 1

1   I am Panammu, the son of QRL, king of Y'DY...
(*KAI* 214.1)

אנך יחומלך מלך גבל בן יחרבעל בן בן ארמלך מלך 1
גבל... ממלכת על גבל... 2

1   I am Yehaumilk, king of Byblos, son of YḤRB'L, grandson of
     Urimilk, king of
2   Byblos, ... made king over Byblos...
(*KAI* 10.1-2)

Further examples of this literary formula may be seen in two fifth-century B.C. Phoenician inscriptions on the sarcophagi of the Sidonian kings Tabnit and his son Eshmunazar II. In Eshmunazar, we find the unusual inclusion of his mother's name in the recitation of his genealogy.

אנך תבנת... מלך צדנם בן 1
אשמנעזר... מלך צדנם... 2

1   I am Tabnit... king of the Sidonians, son of
2   Eshmunazar... king of the Sidonians...
(*KAI* 13.1-2)

13 ... אנך אשמנעזר מלך צדנם בן
14 מלך תבנת מלך צדנם בן בן מלך אשמנעזר מלך
צדנם ואמי אמעשתרת

13 ... I am Eshmunazar, king of the Sidonians, son of
14 King Tabnit, king of the Sidonians, grandson of King Eshmunazar,
     king of the Sidonians, and my mother Amotashtart[220]
(*KAI* 14.13-14)

Interestingly, the shorter form of the 1cs independent personal pronoun אני , which Qoheleth uses to the exclusion of the longer form אנכי , and which some scholars have taken as evidence for suggesting a late date to the book[221], is found in the Arad Inscription, Ostracon No. 88. This inscription, which is dated to the seventh century B.C., is thought to be a copy of a part of a letter from a king proclaiming his enthronement.[222] A further interesting detail to note in this fragmentary inscription is the author's use of a perfective verb to describe the king's claim to the throne, a phenomenon, which is also observed in Qoheleth's opening remark of הָיִיתִי מֶלֶךְ in 1:12.

1 אני מלכתי בכ[ל]...

1 I have become king in [all] ...[223]

The issue of Qoheleth's use of the perfective verb to describe his kingship has attracted considerable discussion both in the past as well as the present and will be looked at next.

Qoheleth's Rule: Past or Present?

In addition to the formulaic style of his royal self-introduction, another similarity which Qoheleth shares with the West Semitic royal inscriptions is the use of the perfective verb to describe the author's kingship. In the Kilamuwa, Panammu, and Mesha

---

220 *SSI* 3, 112 n.13-14, cf. McCarter (*COS* 2.57, n.9).
221 E.g. Whitley (1979, 14); Schoors (1992, 47); see also Seow (1996, 661).
222 Aharoni 1981, 103-4. The specific historical origin of the inscription remains unclear although it is widely held to be a copy of a royal proclamation (see e.g. Pardee (*COS* 3.43M n.36); Malamat 1988).
223 Smelik (1991, 104-5); Pardee (ibid., n.37); Aharoni: "I have come to reign in all..."(ibid.) which is the same.

Inscriptions, a perfective verb is also used to clearly refer to the king's existing reign. The same holds true for the Arad Inscription.

אנך כלמו בר חיא ישבת על כסא אבי 9

9   I am Kilamuwa, the son of Ḥayya, I sat upon my father's throne
(*KAI* 24.9)

גם ישבת על כסא אבי 8

8   Moreover, I sat on my father's throne
(*KAI* 214.8)

ואנך מלכתי אחר אבי 3

3   and I have reigned after my father
(*KAI* 181.3)

It is clear that the above idiomatic expressions, which are used in the West Semitic royal inscriptions to depict the enthronement and rule of kings (e.g. "I sat on my father's throne", "I have reigned after my father"), are no different to Qoheleth's own – הָיִיתִי מֶלֶךְ – in that they all imply that the king is still reigning.[224] That a present state of affairs is meant in these ancient writings is clear from the observation that these idiomatic phrases are often used to represent the king's attempt at legitimizing his claim to the throne, an intent which clearly speaks of the king's existing reign. The translation of הָיִיתִי to "was" in English regrettably causes confusion as it has been consequently interpreted by many as expressing a past tense which suggests Qoheleth's dethronement.[225] On the contrary, Qoheleth appears to present his kingship as an existing and present state rather than as a past fact, as further affirmed by the didactic role which he assumes in his composition.[226]

---

224 Seow 1995, 280.
225 Thus the vivid Talmudic legends that arose from reading the perfective verb as referring to a past fact, which saw Qoheleth as Solomon writing as a dethroned monarch (y. Sanh. 20c; b. Git. 68a-b); also the versions e.g. LXX (ἐγενόμην), Vg (*fui*), and scholars such as Galling and Perdue who subsequently took it as the basis for arguing that the text was written in the form of a Royal Testament. Others, such as Rankin saw the phrase as "carelessly expressed" (1956, 31).
226 Kings in ancient Israel usually ascend to the throne following the death of their predecessor. The few exceptions include cases of co-regency, rebellious coup

Read against the background of West Semitic royal inscriptions, the verb הָיִיתִי in Qoheleth's opening self-introduction should be understood to indicate a present state which has its beginning in the past (especially as it is also a stative verb).[227] The option of reading הָיִיתִי in the sense of an English past tense to imply "no longer" (i.e. a once but no longer king) is further precluded by the author himself in 2:18 – where Qoheleth laments over not knowing who his successor will turn out to be, whether a wise man or a fool – as well as indirectly, by the writer of the superscription of 1:1.[228] Quite clearly, the problem lies with the English translation rather than the Hebrew, as English verbs, unlike Hebrew, always possess tense and cannot express aspect and mood without it.[229] Hence, all English translations of Hebrew verbs will inherently reflect tense, as understood by the translator.

The above investigation shows that the style of Qoheleth's opening words in 1:12 follows after the self-introductory formulae of kings in West Semitic royal inscriptions. The comparison between *Qoheleth* with these ancient Semitic texts has enlighten us on the often-discussed issue of Qoheleth's use of the perfective verb הָיִיתִי to describe his kingship.

B. The Royal Boasting of Deeds

Another prominent literary feature of the West Semitic royal inscriptions and one which is often composed rhetorically is the king's boastful recitation of his deeds and achievements. This literary motif forms an essential part of the royal propaganda, heralding the king's great accomplishments to the public as well

---

(Jeroboam), or where they were deposed or imprisoned by foreign powers (e.g. Manasseh) or God (Saul). It is unlikely that Qoheleth adopted the persona of any of these kings in the work.

227 Similarly Hertzberg (1963, 81); Seow (1997, 119). Isaksson similarly does not see the use of הָיִיתִי in 1:12 as a serious interpretative issue, arguing that its presence need not be read as a "significant deviation" from the common formula of royal self-introductions used in the West Semitic royal inscriptions (1997, 50).

228 Ibid., 46, 48; also Loretz (1964., 64); and Seow (1997, 119).

229 Gibson (1994, 60).

as to posterity. As mentioned earlier in Chapter 2, Qoheleth appears to have adopted this literary convention although there is a notable difference in content between the extravagant description of his accomplishments in 2:4-9 and those found in the West Semitic royal texts.

The boasting of the West Semitic kings in their inscriptions often comprise deeds done on behalf of their people. Economic prosperity and peace in the land are often spoken of and "filled granaries" and the abundant harvest of crops such as maize, barley, wheat, and garlic with the occasional mention of livestock appear to be the clichés of the day. Thus we read, in Azatiwada, of the abundant supply of grain and filled granaries, fine food, and new wine (*KAI* 26 A I.6; A II.7-8; A III.7-9), and in Hadad, there is mention of the richly cultivated land of barley, wheat, and garlic, as well as the abundant provision of food and drink for the people (*KAI* 214.5-7, 9). There is also the mention of a vineyard כרם (*KAI* 214.7; cf. Eccl. 2:4). In Kilamuwa, we read of the king's boast of securing livestock, gold and silver, and linen for his people (*KAI* 24.11-13). Similarly, in Bar-Rakib's dedicatory inscription to his father ("Panammu"), there is the boasting of the economic and social well-being of the citizens during the days of his father's rule, where prisons were done away with and the captives set free (*KAI* 215.8), and wheat, barley, corn, and millet were plentiful and inflation was kept at a minimum (זלת מוכרו "cheapness of price"[230] *KAI* 215.9-10)! "Everyone had plenty to eat and drink" (*KAI* 215.8-9). In clear contrast, Qoheleth's boasting is centred on his self-indulgent merry-making activities.

The recitation of a king's building projects is a major feature of West Semitic royal inscriptions and is found in all of our inscriptions, with the exception of Bar-Rakib i and Panammu, which may be explained by their original function as apologetic pieces of work aimed at reaffirming the vassal king's loyalty to his Assyrian suzerain. The list of building works carried out includes the erecting of memorial statues, temples, the king's palace, defence and civil works, and the rebuilding of cities.

---

230 On the motif of "ideal prices" in the West Semitic inscriptions and the OT, see Hawkins (1986, 93-102); Younger (1986, 96-8); Greenfield (1991, 122).

Mesha's list of construction projects is particularly interesting as it matches quite closely Qoheleth's list. In Mesha, there is mention of the repairing of what appears to be parkland walls and the building of a reservoir with a supplementary irrigation system, items which are also found in *Qoheleth*, although in Mesha, these projects are mentioned as part of Moab's recovery efforts after their supposed break from Israelite lordship rather than as projects which reflect a nation with well established powers.

9   ... ואבן את בעלמען ואעש בה דאשוח...
21   אנך ... בנתי קרחה חמת היערן וחמת...
22   העפל ואנך בנתי שעריה ואנך בנתי מגדלתה וא
23   נך בנתי בת מלך ואנך עשתי כלאי האשו[ח במע]ין
     [ב]קר[
24   הקר...

9   ... I rebuilt Baal-meon, and I made a reservoir in it...
21   ... I have rebuilt Qarḥōh[231], the parkland walls and the walls...
22   of the acropolis, and I rebuilt its gates and repaired its towers, and
23   I repaired the king's residence, and I made retaining walls for the
     reser[voir at the spr]ing inside
24   the town...
(*KAI* 181.9, 21-24)

cf. Eccl. 2:4-6

4   הִגְדַּלְתִּי מַעֲשָׂי בָּנִיתִי לִי בָתִּים נָטַעְתִּי לִי כְּרָמִים׃
5   עָשִׂיתִי לִי גַּנּוֹת וּפַרְדֵּסִים וְנָטַעְתִּי בָהֶם עֵץ כָּל־פֶּרִי׃
6   עָשִׂיתִי לִי בְּרֵכוֹת מָיִם לְהַשְׁקוֹת מֵהֶם יַעַר צוֹמֵחַ עֵצִים׃

4   I did great works: I built houses for myself, I planted for myself
     vineyards.
5   I created for myself gardens and parks, and planted fruit trees of
     every kind in them.
6   I made for myself reservoirs of water, using them to irrigate the
     grove of flourishing trees.

Whilst temple projects are an important feature in a king's boast of building constructions, we find no mention of this in *Qoheleth*. However, there is no need to make much of this absence in

---

231 Possibly meaning "citadel", see Lipiński (1977, 95); also Emerton (2005, 294-5).

Qoheleth's list since it is improbable that any Israelite king would have thought it necessary to sup-plement Solomon's temple, which is clearly implied in the background. From the text, we are told that Qoheleth, who apparently lived in Jerusalem, was an eyewitness to the regular events that took place at the "holy place" (8:10 cf. 4:17 [ET 5:1]; 5:5 [ET v.6]).[232] Furthermore, the mention of Solomon's temple would not have been appropriate to the rhetorical purpose of the passage since the listed achievements were eventually viewed as a "vanity".

Finally, there is considerable freedom of expression in the boasting of the king's private wealth, which typically includes a description of his silver and gold. The accumulation of precious metals was in fact understood in ancient times as a symbol of one's power.[233] This is in contrast to Qoheleth's preoccupation with his self-centred achievements and projects. In his boasting Qoheleth declares that the palaces that he built were לִי just as the vineyards which he planted were לִי. The gardens and parks were created לִי, as were the canals of water לִי. הָיָה לִי male and female slaves, sons of the house, abundant cattle, and flocks of livestock. Qoheleth gathered לִי silver and gold, the treasure of kings and the province, male and female singers, and a harem. In all, לִי is emphatically used eight times in the five lines of boasting in 2:4-9. Thus, while Azatiwada, Hadad, Kilamuwa, Mesha, and Panammu were all keen to speak of the good that they had done for their people in terms of securing peace and prosperity for the land, Qoheleth's focus lay solely on making known the extent of his private wealth and past lifestyle of indulgent merrymaking.

In addition to the formulaic self-introduction of 1:12, Qoheleth's boasting of his achievements reflects another well known literary convention found in almost all the West Semitic royal inscriptions although, as we have noted, there is a difference in content between the works.

---

232 McNeile 1904, 9.

233 In Bar-Rakib i, there is the equating of a ruler's power with his accumulation of silver and gold by the asyndectic phrase מלכן רברבן בעלי כסף ובעלי זהב "powerful kings, possessors of silver and possessors of gold" (KAI 216.10-11).

C. Comparison With Predecessors and Contemporaries

The boast of unparalleled accomplishments is another literary feature commonly found in West Semitic royal inscriptions, which Qoheleth appears also to have adopted for his work (e.g. 1:16a; 2:7b; 2:9a; 2:12). In Kilamuwa's inscription, we find the boasting of the king's accomplishments against those of his father and other relatives, who are described as having "achieved nothing"! Following the "I... RN" formula, we read, from the second line onwards in Kilamuwa, the following:[234]

2 מלך גבר על יאדי ובל פ[על]
3 כן במה ובל פעל וכן אב חיא ובל פעל וכן אח
4 שאל ובל פעל ואן[ך] כלמו בר תמ-מאש פעלת
5 בל פעל הלפני[ה]ם...

2 Gabbar was king over Y'DY, but [accomplished] nothing.
3 There was BMH, but he accomplished nothing. Then there was my father, Ḥayya, but he accomplished nothing. And then there was my brother
4 Š'L, but he accomplished nothing. But I, Kilamuwa, the son of TM-, what I accomplished
5 those who were before me did not accomplished...
(*KAI* 24.2-5)

In Panammu's Inscription, Bar-Rakib, in praising his father Panammu II, speaks of his father's glorious achievements as follows:

9 ... בית אבה והיטבה מן קדמתה...

9 ...his father's house, and he made it better than it was before...
(*KAI* 215.9)

In Bar-Rakib's own inscription (i), there is the boasting of his own greatness which, he claims, surpasses even that of his father and the other kings:[235]

---

234 *SSI* 3, 33-4
235 The boast continues with the following lines,

16 בי טב לישה לאבהי מ
17 לכי שמאל הא בית כלמ
18 ו להם פהא בית שתוא ל
19 הם והא בית כיצא ו
20 אנה בנית ביתא זנה

16 There was no good house for my fathers, the kings

11   ... ואחזת
12   בית אבי והיטבתה
13   מן בית חד מלכן רברב
14   ן והתנאבו אחי מלכי
15   א לכל מה טבת ביתי...

11   ... I have taken over
12   my father's house, and have made it better
13   than the house of any powerful king.
14   And my brother kings were envious
15   of all the good (fortune) of my house...
(*KAI* 216.11-15)

In Azatiwada, we read of the humbling of his enemies which Azatiwada claims none before him had ever achieved. The boasting sometimes consists of the king's criticism of his predecessors.

18   ... ועך אנך ארצת עזת במבא
19   שמש אש בל ען כל המלכם אש כן לפני וא
20   נך אזתוד ענתנם ירדם אנך...

18   ... And I subdued strong lands in
19   the West, which none of the kings who were before me had been able to subdue; but
20   I, Azatiwada, subdued them. I brought them down...
(*KAI* 26 A I.18-20)

Qoheleth's claim of being the greatest and wisest of all in Jerusalem in his opening introduction (viz. 1:16a; 2:7b, 9a, 12b) clearly parallels this well-recognized motif of boasting. The comparisons made with his predecessors and contemporaries are

---

17   of Sam'al. They had the house of Kilamuwa,
18   and it was their winter house,
19   and it was (also) a summer house.
20   But I built this house (!).

as idiomatic and rhetorical as those found in the West Semitic
royal texts.

16a ...אֲנִי הִנֵּה הִגְדַּלְתִּי וְהוֹסַפְתִּי חָכְמָה עַל כָּל־אֲשֶׁר־הָיָה לְפָנַי
עַל־יְרוּשָׁלָ͏ִם236

16a ...Behold, I have grown and increased in wisdom surpassing all
   who were before me over Jerusalem

7b הָיָה לִי גַּם מִקְנֶה בָקָר וָצֹאן הַרְבֵּה הָיָה לִי מִכֹּל שֶׁהָיוּ לְפָנַי
בִּירוּשָׁלָ͏ִם

7b I also owned large herds and flocks, more than anyone who had
   been before me in Jerusalem

9a וְגָדַלְתִּי וְהוֹסַפְתִּי מִכֹּל שֶׁהָיָה לְפָנַי בִּירוּשָׁלָ͏ִם

9a Thus I became great and surpassed all who were before me in
   Jerusalem

12b כִּי מֶה הָאָדָם (יַעֲשֶׂה) שֶׁיָּבוֹא אַחֲרֵי הַמֶּלֶךְ אֵת אֲשֶׁר־כְּבָר
עָשׂוּהוּ

12b For what can the man who comes after the king (do, i.e. add) to
   what has already been done?[237]

---

237 Many manuscripts and the ancient versions have בִּירוּשָׁלָ͏ִם instead of
עַל־יְרוּשָׁלָ͏ִם. The more difficult MT reading would imply a reference to past
kings who ruled before Qoheleth. Many commentators argue that the plural
nature of the referent (i.e. many kings) would be historically incongruent to a
Solomonic Qoheleth. Delitzsch, Wildboer, McNeile, and Barton believe that the
phrase is anachronistic here and that it is unlikely that the author had in mind
the Jebusite kings, Melchizedek (Gen. 14:18), Adonizedek (Josh. 10:3 cf 2 Sam.
5:7), or Ethan, Heman, Calcol, and Darda (1 Kgs. 4:31) (which Hengstenberg,
Nowack, and Plumptre suggest). I would say that there is no need for a literal
interpretation, as the language used here quite clearly reflects typical royal
rhetoric and propaganda and therefore need not be seen as erroneously
anachronistic. See Barton for further discussion on the problem (1908, 79).

237 Verse 12 is a notoriously difficult text and suggestions for emendation include
swapping vv.12a and 12b around (e.g. Siegfried, Galling, Gordis, RSV) or
moving it further ahead (e.g. NEB and REB to v.18) to provide for a supposedly
more logical flow of thought. The second half of v.12 poses a greater problem
as the text is obscure. A number of different readings based on various textual
traditions have been suggested. The interpretation of the final verb in the
sentence is especially problematic. Despite the textual difficulties in the verse,
the main idea of it is still clear (Gordis 1955, 211). Qoheleth in v.12b is making
the point that it is unnecessary for anyone coming after him to attempt his
experiment; they ought instead to learn from his experience and conclusion.

The rhetorical language used in these self-laudatory royal accounts has been described as "often spilling into bombast".[238] A similar hyperbolic language is witnessed in Mesha's claim that he was successful in battle against "all" his enemies, prevailing over "all" of them (l.4), and that Israel had "utterly perished forever" (l.7). The use of heavy rhetoric is likewise witnessed in Kilamuwa's boast of benevolence, that to those who had never seen the face of a sheep or an ox, he made them the owner of a flock and a herd (ll. 11-12). The same may be said of Qoheleth who clearly employs the rhetorical techniques of exaggeration both in his introductory boasting and elsewhere in his narrative (e.g. 5:5; 6:6; 7:19; 8:12). It is commonly acknowledged that the royal writings of the ancient Near East, in line with their royal propaganda, often contain the language of rhetoric.[239] Qoheleth's boasting of his accomplishments and his exaggerated claims clearly also reflect the rhetoric commonly found in the ancient royal inscriptions. Furthermore, Qoheleth repeats his boast (four times), as do most of the royal inscriptions. Read in the light of the ancient royal inscriptions, Qoheleth's kingship claims of being "ruler over Israel in Jerusalem" (1:12, 2:9) and having done better than "all" his predecessors clearly reflect the same hyperbolic language of the ancient royal inscriptions.

Conversely, if Qoheleth, as king, has already conducted his experiment, then it is best for others to follow his example and instruction. V.12b may be read as a rhetorical question with a reference to his successor, whom Qoheleth does not expect to be able to improve upon his accomplishments. Thus, in line with this interpretation, one may either read the last plural verb as having an impersonal force, i.e. "what has been done" (e.g. Ibn. Ezra; Fox (1989, 183); Seow (1997, 134)) or adopt the variant reading עָשָׂהוּ which is attested in several mss. (68 according to Driver in BHK, also V, Pesh), i.e., "he (i.e. the king) has done" (so Gordis 1955, 211). In keeping with the suggested interpretation and for the purpose of emphasis, I have followed Tyler and Plumptre's argument to replace a possible elliptical omission, i.e. adding יַעֲשֶׂה after הָאָדָם ; similarly RSV; Crenshaw (1988, 83).

238 *SSI* 3, 33.
239 See, for example, Younger (1990) on the evidence of rhetorical language in the Solomonic narrative of 1 Kgs. 1-11.

D. Royal Wisdom

Seow argues that Qoheleth's wisdom quest – to explore all things under heaven through wisdom – is more a reflection of the royal ideology of the ancient Near East than a mere echoing of Solomon's fame in the field of wisdom.[240] Although the kings of the ancient Near East were viewed as wise rulers by their subjects, a closer look at the West Semitic royal inscriptions reveals that wisdom is rarely mentioned as an attribute of the king. However, where it is found, it is often described alongside the virtue of "righteousness".

In the Panammu Inscription, Bar-Rakib, in praising his father, attributes the latter's deliverance by the gods and his possession of precious metal to his wisdom and righteousness.

1   דק[צ]ב [.] [ו]נמ[פ בא]א ... 1
2   אבה פלטוה אלה יאדי מן שחתה... 2

1   … my father Panammu, because of his father's righteousness
2   the gods of Y'DY delivered him from destruction…
(*KAI* 215.1-2)

10   ... [א]
11   בי לו בעל כסף הא ולו בעל זהב בחכמתה
ובצדקה...

11   … my father, though[241] he possessed silver and though he
possessed gold, because of his wisdom and his righteousness…
(*KAI* 215.11)

In Azatiwada, we have the following:

11   וישב אנך על כסא אבי ושת אנך שלם את
12   כל מלך ואף באבת פעלן כל מלך בצדקי ו ...
13   בחכמתי ובנעם לבי...

11   And I set him on his father's throne and I established peace with
12   every king, and indeed every king treated me as a father because
of my righteousness, and
13   because of my wisdom, and because of the goodness of my heart…
(*KAI* 26 A I.11-13)

---

240 Seow 1995, 281.
241 *SSI* 2, 81; cf. Younger (*COS* 2.37).

Although righteousness as a virtue is more frequently extolled in the ancient royal texts, wisdom might be said to be implied in the king's successful administration of the land. In the case of Azatiwada, wisdom is explicitly mentioned: other kings looked up to him because of his wisdom and righteousness, and it was because of his wisdom that his people have been able to enjoy peace and prosperity.[242] In the West Semitic corpus, royal wisdom is more often implied in the outstanding deeds of the king for his people.[243] In contrast, the theme of wisdom pervades the entire narrative of Qoheleth.

E. A Political and Military Background

Descriptions of intense political upheavals, coups, and strife among leaders and rulers of the ancient Near East are commonly found in the royal inscriptions. This is perhaps to be expected since warfare, as Parker notes, was a relatively common experience for the inhabitants of the Syro-Palestinian states especially during the Iron Age and thereafter.[244] Thus it is no surprise that the threat of enemies and foreign invasions and the king's reciprocal conquest and reconquest of land are topics frequently found in the royal texts. Quite often there is mention of the quashing of rebel groups, and the subduing of "strong lands" resulting in the extension of borders and peace in the land. Zakkur, in his memorial stele, boasts of his victory over the coalition of sixteen Syrian rulers led by the king of Aram whose incursion is vividly described in thirteen lines of writing (ll.4-17).

---

242 Kalugila interestingly points out that Azatiwada's prayer to his gods for long life and wisdom closely parallels Solomon's prayer for the same and suggests that the Danunian king could have emulated Israel's wisest king in his inscription (1980, 65-7). For this reading, Kalugila interprets רשאת as a metaphor for "wisdom" (KAI 26 A III.6, following Caquot) rather than "old age" (SSI 3, 62 n.6).

243 Solomon's wisdom is similarly associated with the exercise of justice (as seen, for example, in his famous judgment described in 1 Kgs. 3:16-28), the political administration of the kingdom (1 Kgs. 4:1-5:8 [ET 4:1-28]), and the strengthening of diplomatic and commercial ties with the surrounding nations (e.g. 1 Kgs. 5:15-21 [ET 5:1-7]; 9:10-14, 26-8; 10:11-12, 22).

244 Parker 1997, 43. Parker reckons that most adult males, during this period, would probably have been involved in at least one battle during their lifetime.

In the opening lines of Panammu, we read of the crushing of a coup upon the death of a king (ll. 2-3). The regular mention of political conspiracy and assassinations and the usurping of thrones reflect the constant political upheavals and unstable situation of the times, all of which were freely expressed in the inscriptions. Bar-Rakib, in his memorial inscription to his father Panammu II, describes how his great-grandfather (Panammu I) along with a group of royal family members were murdered, with the rest put in prison in a conspiracy (ll. 2-5). Through the help of the Assyrian king (Tiglath-pileser III) Panammu I was eventually able to claim back his throne (ll. 11-12), and following his death, Bar-Rakib was allowed by the Assyrians to succeed him (l. 19). The question of Azatiwada's kingship has in fact been a topic of much discussion amongst scholars, as he is not known to have been a king in other literary sources. Gibson points out that Azatiwada does not even accord himself the title "king" in his opening speech.[245] Suggestions as to his actual role and identity include a usurper, a regent to the son of Awarku (who was a king of the Danunians),[246] a local prince,[247] and "a kind of palace prefect".[248] A similar query arises over the background of Zakkur who uniquely does not mention his lineage, leading one to suspect that he too might have been a usurper.[249] The survival of kings and rulers in the ancient Syro-Palestinian states constantly hung on a delicate balance as political survival often depended upon establishing alliances (e.g. Zakkur's enemies who formed a coalition against him), eliminating rivals (e.g. Panammu against his conspiring relatives), waging and winning wars (e.g. Azatiwada, Hadad, Mesha, Panammu, Zakkur) and most securely, through becoming a vassal to the Assyrian overlord (e.g. Kilamuwa, Panammu, Bar-Rakib).

Although there is no mention of Qoheleth's involvement in military battles, the theme of rulers and military campaigns features quite prominently in the work. Qoheleth's observations

---

245 *SSI* 3, 43.
246 *SSI* 3, 43; Hawkins (1995, 1304).
247 Röllig 1992, 98.
248 Bron 1997, 268.
249 *SSI* 2, 6.

of oppression and social chaos (e.g. 4:13-16; 9:13-14; 10:5-7) appear to suggest a background of constant warfare and short-lived dynasties. It might also be argued that Qoheleth's exhortation to take heed and obey the king (8:2-6) could be words of advice offered to young or present rulers (of adjoining nations perhaps) who might one day be subject to the authority of another ruler.[250] Qoheleth could be warning his royal audience ahead of the possibility of a devastating reality. In contrast to the West Semitic royal inscriptions, Qoheleth does not speak of acting to correct any injustice or of defeating the enemy or oppressor, nor is there any mention of his involvement in any military exploits. Qoheleth's observation of young men being in positions of authority (4:13-15) parallels a similar situation described in Azatiwada (A.I.10-11), which recounts the king's successful effort in helping to contain an internal strife that was threatening a legitimate and known heir, who presumably was a minor.[251] As we shall soon see, in our examination of the Assyrian royal inscriptions, the Assyrian kings were notorious for installing young rulers upon the thrones of their defeated enemies.

F. Summary

From my investigations above, I maintain that *Qoheleth* shows a very close affinity with the West Semitic royal inscriptions in terms of the style and language of its formulaic self-introduction, rhetorical royal boasting, and comparison of achievements with predecessors and contemporaries. The close paralleling of the introductory self-identifications, which is syntactically almost absolute, suggests that Qoheleth was probably following the stereotypical royal language of the West Semitic royal inscriptions in his own opening introduction of 1:12. Qoheleth's many observations of oppression and political upheavals give a further

---

250 Interestingly, Qoheleth uses a "war" example in his subsequent instruction in 8:8.
251 *SSI* 3, 57-8.

realistic impression of a kingdom which is open to the threat of foreign invasions and internal coups.

Finally, and interestingly, the phrase שמש תחת "under (the) sun" (without the definite article) appears in two fifth-century B.C. Sidonian inscriptions of Tabnit and Eshmunazar. "Tabnit" was found on the base of a sarcophagus and "Eshmunazar" on the lid of a coffin, both serving to discourage potential tomb desecrators with their imprecations and threatening curses. This evidence goes against the argument (e.g. by Plumptre) that the use of the same phrase in *Qoheleth* is due exclusively to Greek influence:[252]

6 ... ואם פת
7 ח תפתח עלתי ורגז הרגזן אל י<כ>ן ל<ך> זרע
בחים תחת שמ
8 ש...

6   ... And if
7   you do open up my cover and disturb me, may you have no seed among the living under (the) sun...
(*KAI* 13.6-8)

11 ... המת אל יכן לם שרש למט ו
12 פר למעל ותאר בחים תחת שמש...

11   ... May they have no root below or
12   fruit above, or form[253] among the living under (the) sun ...
(*KAI* 14.11-12)

II. The Assyrian (Sargonid) Royal Inscriptions

The Assyrian royal inscriptions span a good two millennia and are notoriously copious, with many of the inscriptions having multiple exemplars. For our purpose, the following analysis will be limited to the inscriptions from the Sargonid period and to

---

252 Ibid, 103, 106-7. Similarly argued by McNeile (1904, 40 n.1); Loretz (1964, 46f.); Zimmerli (1962, 147); cf. Braun who prefers to attribute Qoheleth's use of the phrase to Greek cultural influence than to the author's knowledge of Phoenician tomb curses (1973, 49-50).

253 Or "visible presence", *SSI* 3, 111 n.12; McCarter (*COS* 2.57).

four literary features which are found in both the ancient inscriptions and *Qoheleth*.[254] From here on, "ARI" will refer to the Sargonid inscriptions unless indicated otherwise.

A. The Formulaic Self-Introduction

Qoheleth's opening words in 1:12 not only parallel closely the formulaic self-introductions of West Semitic royal inscriptions but also those of the ARI, although in the Assyrian inscriptions the 1cs independent personal pronoun (the "anaku") is usually placed at the end of the customary string of royal epithets. The Akkadian royal self-introduction typically begins with the king's name which is then followed by a lengthy "heroic" titulary (e.g. "king of the universe", "the great king", "the mighty king", "king of the four quarters", "king of the world", "king of Assyria"). The personal pronoun often comes at the end of the titulary. For example:[255]

> Sin-aḫê-eriba šarru rabû šarru dan-nu šar kiš-ša-ti šar Aššur... a-na-ku
> Sennacherib, the great king, the mighty king, king of the world, king of Assyria... am I.

The "anaku" pronoun is also sometimes found at the beginning of the royal self-introduction, although not as often as at the end. Examples of this may be seen in the building inscriptions of Esarhaddon and Assurbanipal, and occasionally in Sennacherib's annalistic and "sogenannte Prunkinschriften"[256].

> ana-ku ᵐᵈSin-aḫêᵖˡ-eriba šar ᴵAššur...
> I am Sennacherib, king of Assyria...[257]

> a-na-ku ᴵAš-šur-áhu-ídina šárru dan-nu šar kiššati šar mât A-š-šur [š]akkana[k] Bâb[il]Iᵏⁱ šar mât Šumer u Akkadîᵏⁱ...

---

254 It also happens that the best examples (in terms of having the closest similarity) of these four literary characteristics to be compared with *Qoheleth* are found in the inscriptions of the Sargonid kings who are Sargon II, Sennacherib, Esarhaddon, and Assurbanipal, who together ruled from c. 721-627 B.C.

255 *Annals* 147 (I 8), ll. 1, 9

256 Weber (1907, 229); *Streck* I, XL; also sometimes called "decoration inscriptions" (Olmstead 1916).

257 *Annals* 150 (I 22), ll. 1-2.

I am Esarhaddon, the mighty king, king of the world, king of Assyria, viceroy of Babylon, king of Sumer and Akkad...[258]

a-na-ku [ilu] aššur-bân-aplu [šarru] rabû šarru dan-nu šar kiššati šar[mâtu.ilu] aššur[ki] ...
I am Assurbanipal, the great king, the mighty king, king of the world, king of Assyria...[259]

These examples suggest a continuity between the literary traditions of the West Semitic royal inscriptions and the ARI, namely in the style of their introductory self-identification. They further suggest that Qoheleth's opening speech in 1:12 is likely to have imitated the well-recognized formulaic royal self-introductions typically used by ancient Semitic kings in their public inscriptions.

B. The Royal Boasting

One of the major subjects of boast in the ARI is the collection of tribute, which Luckenbill describes as being the "chief occupation" of the Assyrian kings from almost the beginning of Assyrian history until the very last of her kings.[260] However, it was only from the reign of Tiglath-pileser I (c. 1100 B.C.) onward that the Assyrian rulers started to carry out planned campaigns, setting their sights on world dominion.[261] Historians note that from then on, reports of the king's battle success were a standard feature in the inscriptions and descriptions of their military exploits were often repeated.[262] The military accounts, especially the annalistic inscriptions, are stereotypical in language and content, typically comprising the chronological listing of the deeds of the ruler, with the events of the years stated, followed by a record of places captured and booty taken and the tributes

---

258 Borger 1964, 8 §6: Ass. E. See also p. 9, § 7: Ass. F; p. 70, §35: Nin. O; p. 72, §44: Trb. B; p. 73 §45: Trb. C; and *ANET* 317 for examples in Neo-Babylonian royal historical texts, e.g. of Antiochus Soter.
259 *Streck* II 92, Cylinder B. Col. I, ll.1-2. Also 240, Stele S² l.1.
260 *Annals* 5.
261 *Annals* 6; *RIMA* 2, 6.
262 Weber 1907, 227.

received along the way, all drawn together by set formulae.[263] Even the non-annalistic "display" (*Prunkinschriften*) or "summary" inscriptions (*Übersichtsinschriften*, i.e. inscriptions on bricks, slabs, clay prisms, and cylinders) which were intended as architectural adornment – placed to face the palace walls or deposited as the corner stone of gates and building walls – would contain descriptions of the military campaigns which, according to Weber, included those fought up to the day of the placing of the material.[264]

By the time of the Sargonid era, two topics appear to dominate the Assyrian royal boast, which are, the king's building activities and his heroic war campaigns. Interestingly, it is these two themes which Qoheleth's own boasting closely parallels. In particular, some of Qoheleth's building achievements may be seen to parallel those found in the ARI. Qoheleth's list of possessions in 2:8 is also strikingly similar to the items commonly mentioned in the Assyrian standard booty list. We will begin with an examination of the boasting of building activities, for which the Assyrian rulers, namely the Sargonid kings, were particularly well known. Interestingly, we find that the closest parallels are from the inscriptions of Sennacherib which, when compared to the texts belonging to other Sargonid kings, is also the most pensive of all. The absence of any mention of temples in the descriptions of Sennacherib's large-scale building project at Nineveh (which experts find unusual),[265] parallels a similar omission in Qoheleth's own account.[266]

---

263 Olmstead 1916, 3-4. Olmstead argues that the annalistic genre emerged from the period of Arik-den-ilu's reign c. 1400 B.C. (ibid.). Weber similarly notes that there is a homogeneous pattern to the reports of the military campaigns observable from the start of the empire through to the Sargonid period (1907, 228).

264 Weber (1907, 227); Olmstead (ibid., 4-5).

265 Reade 1981, 164.

266 See my earlier point on the absence of reference to temple building in *Qoheleth* in p. 80-81.

1. Palaces, Canals, Gardens and Parks

Aside from the military accounts and the occasional gory description of the punishment meted on their rebellious enemies, the ARI regularly contain the boasting of the creation of royal gardens and orchards which reflect the peculiar interest of the Assyrian kings in importing plants and trees from foreign lands and defeated nations. The building of palaces and temples and city wall constructions are also regularly mentioned in the descriptions of their royal wealth and personal achievements. Many of these items are similarly found in Qoheleth's list of accomplishments such as the building of parkland walls, an irrigation system, and the more aesthetic works of creating parks and gardens with groves of fruit trees in them (cf. Eccl. 2:4-6).

In the inscription which is known as the "Broken Obelisk", there is a description of the repair and renovation works carried out by the king, thought to be Ashur-bēl-kala (1073-1056 B.C.), which included redigging a city moat which had fallen in, and surrounding a created garden with a system of irrigation: [267]

> I built the palace of cedar, box-wood, terebinth, (and) tamarisk in my city Ashur... The canal which Ashur-dan (I), king of Assyria excavated – the source of that canal had fallen in and for thirty years water had not flowed therein. I again excavated the source of that canal, directed water therein (and) planted gardens.

Ashurnasirpal II (883-859 B.C.), one of Assyria's great builder-kings, was known to have carried out an extensive building project at Calah. Among his building achievements there was the construction of a huge palace and several temples. Defence walls and a canal were also put in place and gardens with exotic trees were created in it. The boasting of his achievements over his predecessor is heard in the following inscription:[268]

> The ancient city Calah, which Shalmaneser, king of Assyria, a prince who preceded me, had built – this city had become dilapidated; it lay dormant (and) had turned into ruin hills. I rebuilt this city. I took people which I had conquered from the lands over which I had gained

---

267 *Annals* 56. The underlining of the parallel words and themes between the ARI and *Qoheleth* are mine.

268 *RIMA* 2, A.0.101.1 iii 11.32b-136. A similar account is found in *RIMA* 2, A.0.101.2, ll.52-62.

dominion, from the land… I settled (them) therein. I dug out a <u>canal</u> from the Upper Zab (and) called it Patti-ḫegalli. I planted <u>orchards</u> in its environs… I… dug down to water level; I sank (the foundation pit) down to a depth of 120 layers of bricks. I built its wall. I built (and) completed it from top to bottom.

In his dedicatory inscription of the Ninurta temple at Calah, we find a phrase very similar to Eccl. 2:5: [269]

I planted <u>orchards</u> with <u>all (kinds of) fruit trees</u> in its environs.

cf. Eccl. 2:5

5 עָשִׂיתִי לִי גַּנּוֹת וּפַרְדֵּסִים וְנָטַעְתִּי בָהֶם עֵץ כָּל־פֶּרִי

5 I created for myself gardens and parks and planted fruit trees of every kind in them.

In Sennacherib's annals, we find elaborate descriptions of extravagant building works which usually comprise greatly enlarged city walls and grand parks laid out throughout the city for all Ninevites to walk in and enjoy the flora, fauna, and menagerie collected from conquered nations. There is often also the setting up of an irrigation system for the city's inhabitants. In the inscription entitled "the Palace without a Rival", the building projects carried out under Sennacherib in Nineveh are spoken of twice. The following is from the second account:[270]

The area of Nineveh, my royal city, I enlarged.
I widened its squares, and made it shine like the day.
The outer-wall I built and made it mountain high.
Above the city and below the city I laid out <u>parks</u>.
The wealth of mountain and all lands,
All the herbs of the land of Hatti (Syria), myrrh-plants, among which fruitfulness was greater than in their (natural) habitat,
all kinds of mountain-vines, all the fruits of (all) lands (settlements),
herbs and <u>fruit-bearing trees</u> I set out for my subjects.

A glance through the annals of Sennacherib reveals the king's penchant for creating parks and gardens and planting exotic plants and trees in them. In another inscription written after his

269 *Annals* 154.
270 Ibid., 113-4, ll. 13-21.

eighth campaign, Sennacherib describes at length his irrigation project in Nineveh:[271]

> ... <u>waters</u> from the <u>canals</u> which I had caused to be dug [supplied] Nineveh, together with its neighbourhood. <u>Gardens</u>, <u>vineyards</u>, <u>all kinds of</u> ... products of all the mountains, the <u>fruits</u> of all lands, ... <u>I planted</u> (?), setting free the <u>waters</u> where they did not reach the thirsty (field), [and reviving] its vegetation, damaged (by drought) ... of all the <u>orchards</u>...

Similar descriptions of the building of canals and the creation of parklands and gardens are repeatedly found in many of Sennacherib's inscriptions. This more aesthetic aspect of the king's building activity is unique among the Assyrian accounts and parallels Qoheleth's boasting of the same.

2. The Treasures of Kings

Qoheleth's boast of acquiring the treasure of kings in Eccl. 2:8 bears striking resemblance to the ARI's booty list which typically comprises gold and silver, jewellery, officials, royal members of the family, a harem, slaves, court artisans, and singers. The similarity between Qoheleth's list of "acquired" goods and the Assyrian standard booty list, suggests that Qoheleth may have had the Assyrian accounts in mind when he penned the verse. The description of Qoheleth's accumulated wealth, as described in 2:8, echoes the lists of spoils typically found in the Sargonid inscriptions.

8 כָּנַסְתִּי לִי גַּם־כֶּסֶף וְזָהָב וּסְגֻלַּת מְלָכִים וְהַמְּדִינוֹת עָשִׂיתִי
לִי שָׁרִים וְשָׁרוֹת וְתַעֲנוּגֹת בְּנֵי הָאָדָם שִׁדָּה וְשִׁדּוֹת:

> 8 I also amassed for myself silver and gold, and the treasure of kings and the provinces. I got for myself men and women singers, and a harem.[272]

---

271 Ibid., 80, ll. 19-22.

272 "Harem" best captures the collective images of the two phrases וְתַעֲנוּגֹת בְּנֵי הָאָדָם "the delights of man" and שִׁדָּה וְשִׁדּוֹת . The meaning of the latter, a *hap. leg.*, is problematic although the context appears to suggest an interpretation closely related to the former (so the majority of modern translators; Whitley writes that it is probably an "amplification of the immediately preceding phrase 'the amorous pleasures of man'". 1979, 22), cf. most versions which carry non-

In a building inscription belonging to Adad-Nirari I, the king's spoils of war are described as follows:[273]

> I took and brought to my city, Ashur, the possessions of those cities, the accumulated (wealth) of his (Uasashatta's) fathers, (and) <u>the treasure of his palace</u>.... I took out from the city Irridu his "wife of the palace", his sons, his daughters, and his people.

In the inscriptions of Ashurnasirpal II, we find many similar booty lists. In one inscription, which describes the subduing of the rebellious city of Sūru, Ashurnasirpal recounts the ransacking of the city and the valuable spoils collected:[274]

> I carried off his <u>silver, gold, possessions,</u> property, bronze, iron, tin... <u>his palace women, his daughters,</u> captives of the guilty soldiers together with their property, precious stone of the mountain, his harnessed chariot, his teams of horses... linen garments, fine oil, cedar, fine aromatic plants...

During Sennacherib's reign, a new expression of boasting is coined: the sacking of the defeated enemy's treasure house. The list of items making up Qoheleth's boast in 2:8 comes closest to Sennacherib's standard list of spoils, which comprises precious silver, gold, jewellery, the defeated ruler's properties and assets (horses, chariots, etc.), stock of slaves, officials, singers, and his harem. In Sennacherib's successful campaign against the

---

sexual interpretations, e.g. LXX, Syr "male cupbearer and female cupbearers", Vg "cups and waterpots", Tg "baths and bath-houses"; Seow (1997, 131), who is followed by Kamano (2002, 63-4 note 150), reads "many chests". The singular-plural construct may be read as a hendiadys expressing multiplicity, e.g. דּוֹר דּוֹרִים Ps. 72:5, so Fox (1989, 181); also Kroeber "sehr viele Frauen" (1963, 81); Hertzberg "Mädchen und Mädchen" (1963, 75); Zimmerli "Frauen in Menge" (1962, 56). Zimmerli suggests "harem", following his observation of the mention of Hezekiah's concubines in Sennacherib's list of spoils (ibid., 158). Ellermeier has "Solomon's harem" (1967, 6). Lauha, following Zimmerli's argument similarly mentions the possibility of reading "a harem", suggesting that a translation with reference to women would fit with the topos of a "königlichen Schlemmens" (cf. 2 Sam 15:16; 16:21f.) (1978, 51). I am persuaded in my translation of "harem" by the striking similarity between the items of boast in Eccl. 2:8 and the ARI standard booty list. See the above main discussion.

273 *ARI* I, §393.

274 *RIMA* 2, p.199, A.0.101.1.i 83-88. These accounts are typically repeated in the same inscription, e.g. A.0.101.1 iii 20-25.

Babylonian ruler Merodach-baladan, the treasures collected thereafter are described, in an inscription, as follows:[275]

> I opened his treasure-house. <u>Gold</u>, <u>silver</u>, vessels of gold and silver, precious stones, beds, couches, palanquins… all kinds of property and goods, and without number, - an enormous treasure, his wife, his <u>harem</u>, his slave-girls (?), his chamberlains, his officials, his courtiers, <u>the male and female musicians</u>, the palace slaves, who gladdens his princely mind, all of the artisans, as many as there were, his palace menials (?), (these) I brought forth and counted as spoil.

The descriptions of the spoils collected after Sennacherib's first and last campaigns are largely uniform in style and content which suggests that these were following set formulae. Quite often, the same description is repeated for another account of a different military campaign which is also placed in the same inscription. Although the descriptions of the spoils are often elaborate, there are also the more succinct reports, which appear to parallel Eccl. 2:8 more closely: [276]

> I opened his treasure-house:- <u>gold</u>, <u>silver</u>, vessels of gold and silver, precious stones of every kind (name) goods and property without limit (number), heavy tribute, his <u>harem</u>, (his) courtiers and officials, <u>singers, male and female</u>, all of his artisans, as many as there were, the servants of his palace, I brought out, I counted as spoil.

Interestingly, we find a similar list of items in a description of Hezekiah's tribute to Sennacherib: gold, silver, precious stones, his daughters, a harem, and male and female musicians.[277]

The recitation of the king's wealth and accomplishments is clearly a common literary feature in the monumental inscriptions of the ancient Semitic kings, and Qoheleth's items of boast matches more closely those that are in the ARI than the West Semitic royal texts. These items are the building of palaces, gardens and parks with exotic trees planted in them, and the digging of canals and reservoirs of water, as well as other items of wealth such as gold and silver, male and female slaves and singers, the royal household, and a harem. This peculiar similarity, between Qoheleth's list of wealth and the Assyrian

---

275 *Annals* 52, ll. 31-33.
276 *ARAB* II, §234, §260, §270; *Annals*, 24, ll. 29-35; 52 ll. 31-2; 56, ll. 8-9.
277 *ARAB* II, §240, §312; *Annals* 34, ll. 42, 46-7; 70, ll. 31-2.

booty list which describes the riches acquired from defeated kings, most likely reflects the Hebrew writer's attempt at emphasizing his royal status through the description of his wealth in terms which are typical of rulers and not that he had conducted military campaigns himself.[278] This parallelism suggests an awareness on Qoheleth's part of these ancient texts and the likely "borrowing" of this particular literary feature of the ARI for his own composition.

C. Comparison With Predecessors

The motif of the surpassing achievement of the king over his predecessors is also found in the ARI, often alongside the list of the king's grand accomplishments. A few examples to demonstrate this point will suffice seeing as our earlier discussion has already made the case for a similar use of expression in *Qoheleth*.

This stereotypical style of boasting in the ARI is seen as early as in the reign of Shamshi-Adad I (1813-1781 B.C.), who, in boasting about his temple building skills, described his own talent in the following manner:[279]

> I, [Shamshi]-Adad, [king of] the universe, … and a ziqqurat, a great …, whose workmanship was greater and more skilful than before, I built. I erected the doorframes of that temple, the equal of which for perfection no king had ever built for the goddess Ishtar in Nineveh.

By the time of Sennacherib, the style of boasting is more descriptive and there is the additional use of exaggerated idioms to further praise the king's skills and abilities.[280]

> Sennacherib, the great king, the mighty king, king of Assyria, king without a rival… the god Assur, the great mountain, has intrusted to me an unrivalled kingship and above all those who dwell in palaces has made powerful my weapons.

---

278 Cf. Qoheleth's reference to his possessions which (he) קָנִיתִי "bought" (2:7), כָּנַסְתִּי "amassed" (2:8), and עָשִׂיתִי "acquired" (2:8).
279 *ARI* I, §141.
280 *RIMA* I, A.0.39.2 ii 1-20; *ARAB* II, §412.

> ... I greatly enlarged the site of Nineveh. Its wall, and the outer wall thereof, which had not existed before, I built anew, and raised it mountain high...

> In times past, when the kings, my fathers, fashioned a bronze image in the likeness of their members, to set up in their temples, the labor on them exhausted every workman; in their ignorance and lack of knowledge, they drank oil, and wore sheepskins to carry on the work they wanted to do in the midst of their mountains. But I, Sennacherib, first among the princes, wise in all craftsmanship, great pillars of bronze, colossal lions, open at the knees, which no king before my time had fashioned, - through the clever understanding which the noble Nin-igi-kug had given me, (and) in my own wisdom, I pondered deeply the matter of carrying out that task, following the advice of my head (will) and the prompting of my heart I fashioned the work of bronze and cunningly wrought it.

Experts point out that this stereotypical style of boasting by the king of his unsurpassed achievements carries a different meaning in the ARI as compared, for example, to the West Semitic royal corpus. With the ARI, they are intended to reflect what Assyriologists term a "heroic priority". In their inscriptions, the Assyrian kings are often portrayed as the very first to execute a particular action or, in the case of restoration work, to have undertaken works far superior to previous ones, all of which are in line with the Assyrian ideology of seeing the royal personage as the creator king.[281] Hence the purpose of such idiomatic expressions of boasting is more to show the continuation of the work of creation by the king in providing the creation dynamics into the cycle of the world than to merely declare his superiority over his predecessors. Whilst the motivation may be different, the motif of outperforming one's predecessor is, nevertheless, a common feature in ancient Semitic royal inscriptions. As we have observed earlier, there is a similar language of boasting in *Qoheleth* (1:16a; 2:7b, 9a, 12) which clearly resembles the ancient Semitic royal literary tradition of speaking of one's unsurpassed deeds and achievements.

---

281 Liverani 1979, 308-9.

D. Royal Wisdom

In the ARI, the king's wisdom is not mentioned as much or as explicitly as his military prowess, although again we see that the original function of the inscriptions may provide an explanation for this. With the Assyrian kings, the nature of the ruler's wisdom is often associated with the individual king's project of interest. [282] Thus, in the case of Assurbanipal, who is known for establishing a library and having copies of literary works made, his wisdom was related to the subject of learning and writing and the interpretation of dreams.[283] The image that he was keen to portray was that of a wise scribe. Wisdom is also at times tied to the gift of architectural design. Examples of this may be seen in the building inscriptions commemorating the king's achievements in construction, e.g. Assurnasipal's building of the temple of Ishtar (*ARAB* I, §528), Sargon II's extensive building projects in Dûr-Sharrukîn (i.e. Khorsabad) which included shrines and palaces (*ARAB* II, §105), and Sennacherib's building of the Temple of the New Year's Feast (*ARAB* II, §436) and palace in Nineveh (*ARAB* II, §391, 431).[284] With Adad-Nirâri, his wisdom lay in his military prowess (e.g. *ARAB* I §366).

There is a considerable number of Assyrian royal epithets with the theme of wisdom.[285] They include the following which, it should be added, are mostly found in the inscriptions belonging to the Sargonid kings: "wise" (*eršu*), "holder of wisdom" (*āḫiz nēmeqi*), "wise prince" (*rubū emqu*), "wise prince who considers/understands everything" (*rubū emqu ḫāsis mimma šumšu*), "the wise, competent prince, who understands everything" (*rubū emqu itpēšu ḫāsis kāl šipri*), "the expert (or competent) king" (*malku itpēšu*), "the competent shepherd" (*rē'ūm itpēšu*), "intelligent" (*ḫassu*), "ominiscient, knowing"

---

282 Loretz writes that it is rare that the Mesopotamian kings glorified themselves in the knowledge of wisdom or claimed fame for possessing great wisdom, a charge which upon closer inspection is incorrect (1964, 150).

283 E.g. *ARAB* II, §767, 986.

284 Kaligula 1980, 52-3.

285 According to Seux's analysis of Assyrian titulary, the theme of wisdom is not as prominent as those which describe the king's lineage, his piety and his benevolence, and his unrivalled status in the world (1967, 18-27).

(*mūdû*), "one who considers/ solicitous" (muštālam), "the cautious or prudent" (*pitqudu*), "the wise one" (*igigallu*).[286] The king's wisdom is also at times implied in the justice which he exercises and hence in epithets such as "the just, straight king" (*šarru kīnu; šar kīnāti*), "one who assures" (*kânu*), "speaks with integrity and justice" (*dabābu*), and "bearer of a just sceptre" (*ešēru*).[287]

We read in one of the Khorsabad texts, Sargon II's boast of his wisdom, which is said to surpass those of his predecessors:[288]

> In my all-embracing wisdom and the fertile planning of my brain, which thinking Ea and Bêlit-ilâni had made to surpass that of the kings, my fathers, (and) following the prompting of my heart, I built a city at the foot of Mount Musri, in the plain of Nineveh, and named it Dûr-Sharrukîn. Substantial shrines for Ea, Sin, Shamash, Adad and Urta, I constructed therein with (artistic) skill and built palaces of ivory… for my royal dwelling…

In a letter to Assur, Sargon's self-introduction is saturated with self-praise of his own wisdom:[289]

> I, Sargon, king of the four regions (of the world), … quick of wit… most wise prince of the regions (of the earth), who was created in wisdom and understanding…

In a cylinder inscription commemorating the founding of the new capital of Dûr-Sharrukîn, Sargon is seen once again to speak proudly of his wisdom, this time equating his brilliance to that of Adapa:[290]

> The sagacious king, full of kindness (words of grace), who gave his thought to the restoration of (towns) that had fallen to ruins, to bringing fields under cultivation, to the planting of orchards, who set his mind on raising crops on steep (high) slopes whereon no vegetation had flourished since the days of old; whose heart moved him to set out plants in waste areas where a plow was unknown in (all the days) of former kings… to cause the springs of the plain to gush forth, to open ditches, to cause the waters of abundance to rise high, north and south, like the waves of the sea… The king endowed with clear

---

286 Engnell (1967, 189-91); Seux (1967, 22).

287 Thus Seux's combining of the two themes under the single category of "wisdom and justice".

288 *ARAB* II, §105.

289 Ibid., §153.

290 Ibid., §119; similarly §407.

understanding, sharp of eye, in all matters the equal of the Master (Adapa), who waxed great wisdom and insight and grew old in understanding...

Wisdom, as a virtue, would have been seen to belong naturally to the Assyrian rulers. Nevertheless, kings were also keen to project themselves as wise leaders as part of the political propaganda to support their unquestionable status as the most powerful ruler in the known universe. In comparison, it may be said that Qoheleth's preoccupation with wisdom and his quest for the meaning of life not only finds a connection with Israel's wisest king Solomon, but is also very much in keeping with the royal ideology promulgated in the ancient Semitic world (of which Prov. 25:2 also speaks). Thus in the context of ancient Semitic royal literary and ideological traditions my suggestion for reading Qoheleth as a royal persona from start to end is clearly valid and possible.

E. A Warring Background

The predominant feature of the ARI is the vivid descriptions of their large-scale military campaigns and ongoing imperial conquests. Qoheleth's observation that the character of the rulers and the political and social structure of his world are not always desirable arguably matches the ups and downs of the battles frequently fought and described in the ARI. Luckenbill notes, for example, that the political situation in eighth-century B.C. Babylon was one where events moved rapidly. The ever-changing political scene is captured in an account in Sennacherib's annals:[291]

> In Babylon, one Marduk-zâkir-shumu, labeled 'son of a slave' in the King List, was proclaimed ruler (703). He had enjoyed royal dignity but a month when Merodach-baladan appeared on the scene and regained the throne from which he had been ousted by Sargon back in 709.

It is commonly known that Assyrian rulers would often place young men on the thrones of their defeated enemies. We read of

---

291 *Annals* 10.

Sennacherib, who after his successful campaign against Merodach-baladan, set Bêl-ibni (who is described as the "son of a master-builder" and "a scion of Babylon" and who "like a young hound" had grown up in the Assyrian palace) in his place as "king over Sumer and Akkad".[292] The description of these riotous events in the ARI parallels Qoheleth's observations of similar phenomena, such as those described in Eccl. 4:13-16 and 10:5-7, of ever-changing political scenes and a topsy-turvy state of governance where young men are found in positions of power and authority. Qoheleth's sighting of slaves on horseback and princes going on foot (10:7) is a typical wartime scene which is most akin to the Assyrian political practice of installing young common citizens of the defeated land in positions of governance and administration, thereby reversing the social norms and creating an upside-down state of political affairs.

F. Summary

As with the West Semitic royal inscriptions, our above investigation into the ARI establishes more solidly the evidence that the language used by Qoheleth in his introduction is clearly royal. The use of strikingly similar expressions in his opening introduction and in his language of boasting suggests that the ancient Semitic royal inscriptions were likely to have been a compositional source for the Hebrew author.

III. Concluding Remarks

From the sample of texts that were cited and discussed above, it is clear that *Qoheleth* does not belong to the same genre of composition as the West Semitic and Assyrian royal inscriptions, which are more correctly known, in their specialized field, as "historical narratives".[293] These official texts were engraved on monuments to commemorate the great deeds of the kings

---

292 *Annals* 54, 1.54.
293 See discussion on p.112f.

featured in the inscriptions. Despite the difference in genre, we are still able to observe a parallel use of the royal self-introductory formulae and stereotypical language of boasting in Qoheleth.[294] That Qoheleth may have followed the literary traditions of the ancient royal inscriptions when writing his own work (in order to enhance the literary portrayal of his royal persona) is possible, as such practices were prevalent in ancient times, where earlier inscriptions were either copied out of convenience (e.g. Shamshi-Adad who assumed a titulary belonging to an earlier king who had built the temple in Nineveh which he now possessed), or in order to exaggerate one's success through the imitation of the language and style of greater kings.[295] Having identified the main literary parallels and the possible source of Qoheleth's "royal language", I shall turn to examine other literary features which Qoheleth appears to also share with other ancient works.

I should add that, interestingly, in several of Sennacherib's inscriptions we find the use of a reflective type of discourse.[296] In one such inscription we see the Assyrian king giving thought and consideration, in his heart and mind, to the building of a great palace at Nineveh, which are described in words that echo Qoheleth's introspection and contemplative mood. In this parti-cular inscription we observe Sennacherib's musing over his work which has interesting overtones of Qoheleth's contemplative mood: [297]

> ...not one among them had given his thoughtful attention to, nor had his heart considered, the palace therein, the place of the royal abode, whose site had become too small; (nor) had he turned his thought, nor brought his mind to lay out the streets of the city, to widen the squares,

---

294 The literary features discussed above (e.g. the self-introductory formula, comparison with predecessors) are also evidenced in a few of the Hittite royal inscriptions.

295 In some cases, evidence of imitation is obvious especially where the style copied is clearly inappropriate and ill fitting, e.g. the imitation of Naram-Sin's style of boasting by a minor king of Kish which Liverani describes as sounding pathetic (1995, 2363).

296 Weber observes that by the Sargonic era, the royal inscriptions began to develop beyond the confines of the literary traditions with their formulaic themes and expressions to reflect more of the king's individual personality (1907, 228).

297 Ibid., §363 & 364.

to dig a canal, to set out trees (plantations) (363). But I, Sennacherib, king of Assyria, gave my thought and brought my mind to accomplish this work according to the command (will) of the gods...

These contemplative modes of expression demonstrate that some measure of freedom was exercised in the composition of the royal inscriptions which went beyond the confines of traditional literary conventions and that the public inscriptions were gradually showing a development in their literary style with their more personalized way of writing.

Section 2: *Qoheleth* and the Fictional Royal Texts of Akkad and Ancient Egypt

IV. Longman's "Fictional Akkadian Autobiographies"

Longman has recently argued that *Qoheleth* bears a close structural similarity to a group of fifteen Akkadian texts which he called "the fictional Akkadian autobiographies". The texts are dated between c.2000 B.C. to 150 B.C. According to Longman, these fifteen texts share four common literary characteristics[298], which are, (1) they are "fictional", (2) they are written in Akkadian, (3) they are autobiographical (which he defines as a first-person account of a past life), and (4) they are written in prose. Longman further argues that these texts all reflect a threefold structure, like the "official" Akkadian royal inscriptions, which comprise a first-person introduction or self-identification, a first-person narration, and an "ending". Longman argues that the main difference between the "fictional" inscriptions and the "royal inscriptions" is the "fictionality" of the former. For Longman, a "fictional text" describes non-contemporary events and imports many non-historical and folkloristic motifs while also possibly containing many statements that are historically true

---

298 Longman 1991, 199. Originally, in his dissertation, Longman included a fifth characteristic trait, which is "royal fiction". This is omitted in his subsequent works (as noted by Westenholz 1997).

although, he adds, it would be difficult to discern the time lapse between the writing of the texts and the events themselves.[299] Longman further views the fifteen fictional autobiographical texts as "imitations" of the "historical (non fictional) royal narratives".

Longman divides his collection of fifteen texts into four groups according to the distinctive "endings" that they have. The four "endings" are: the blessing and/or curse ending, the donation ending, the didactic ending, and the prophetic ending. Longman contends that, of the four categories of texts, *Qoheleth* parallels most closely the group with a didactic ending. This group of texts, to which Longman argues *Qoheleth* is comparable, consists of three compositions: the Adad-guppi autobiography, the Cuthaean Legend of Naram-Sin, and a Sennacherib autobiography.

A. Fictional Akkadian Autobiographies with A Didactic Ending

Longman argues that the similarities between *Qoheleth* and the Akkadian compositions with a didactic ending are to do with structure (tripartite) and form (self-discourse), with the Cuthaean Legend reflecting the closest parallel since, besides having these two features, it carries a further characteristic of "royal fiction". In terms of structure, Longman argues that it is not the entire book of *Qoheleth* but only "Qohelet's speech" in 1:12-12:7 which shares this three-part structure:[300]

Eccl. 1:12	first-person introduction
1:13-6:9	first-person narrative
6:10-12:7	first-person instruction

Two Assyriologists in their reference to and review of Longman's study have raised questions about his newly created genre. Westenholz argues that Longman's method of selecting

---

299 Ibid., 69-70.
300 Longman (1998, 19-20). This is his latest position on the general outline of "Qoheleth's speech" as given in his commentary which is slightly different to his earlier book (1991, 120-1).

the texts is "arbitrary" in that most of the four characteristics, which Longman uses to define the new genre, are debatable and even controversial, such as the ascribed elements of "fictionality" and "prose".[301] Westenholz further describes Longman's definition of the corpus as imprecise and contends that some of the suggested criteria would require either further justification (e.g. their prose character), or that they are irrelevant for the purpose of genre definition (e.g. that they are written in Akkadian language).

As for Longman's work with the original texts, Farber points out that a few of Longman's own translations, where they are provided, are wrongly divided or have missing lines.[302] Farber's criticism of Longman's treatment of the Akkadian texts does not directly affect our analysis as our focus is on three translated texts which, as it turns out, have not drawn any direct criticism from him. For the general description and translation of these texts (the Adad-guppi autobiography, the Cuthaean Legend of Naram-Sin, and a Sennacherib autobiography), Longman relies on the works of Gadd, Gurney, and Tadmor, which are well-accepted and, for our purpose, sufficiently reliable to allow us to proceed with our following discussion.[303]

There is, however, one particular criticism of Westenholz and Farber which is of direct relevance and importance to us. This is to do with the tripartite structure which, Longman argues, is discernible in all fifteen of his collection of texts. In his criticism of Longman's argument, Farber explains that the "ending" which purportedly makes up the third and final section of the

---

301 Westernholz 1997, 19.
302 Farber 1997, 229 n.5 and 6.   Farber also criticizes Longman for using the translations of others without exercising due caution, and for his neglect to incorporate more recent work.   He further complains that Longman's own translation of the Akkadian texts are "often incomplete, overinterpretive, misleading, or simply wrong" (ibid.; see n. 6–9).   According to Farber, Longman's "uncritical" method of study has led him "occasionally to a different classification of individual texts" (ibid.).
303 Longman can be seen to paraphrase the translation work of others in his book and at several places he gives a reading different to his source without further explanation. Where possible I have used the original translation works instead of Longman's paraphrases.   In the case of the Sennacherib autobiography, I have relied on Longman's work, as Winckler and Tadmor's translations were unavailable to me.

composition, and which is used by Longman to separate the fifteen texts into four further categories, "normally state the main purpose of the texts and occasionally make up more than 80 percent of the inscriptions".[304] Farber adds that the part which Longman describes as "autobiographical" "often looks like an introduction and may occasionally comprise as few as three lines".[305] A closer look at the Adad-guppi text, which is relevant to our discussion, appears to support Farber's criticism of Longman's unpersuasive identification of an alleged tripartite structure in the texts. In the Adad-guppi autobiography, the final section which Longman describes as its "didactic ending" is nothing more than a short epilogue containing an admonition to its readers to continue to be loyal to their gods. Longman clearly has exaggerated the extent and nature of this ending as it can hardly be described as "lessons from the life of Adad-guppi", particularly when viewed against its main narrative. Longman further describes this end part as containing "a series of commands to revere and worship the celestial deities" and argues that this "didactic section" helps qualify the composition as "wisdom literature"![306]   The following are the lines in question:[307]

44. Do thou, whether a king or prince…
(The remainder is too fragmentary for translation until,)
51. Fear (the gods), in heaven and earth
52. pray to them, [neglect] not [the utterance]
53. of the mouth of Sin and the goddess
54. …
55. - - - … make safe the … of thy seed
56. [ever(?)] and for [ever(?)].

Although Longman has clearly exaggerated the presence of a didactic end section in the work, it may still be said that the text does carry a didactic purpose, not in the way that Longman has argued, but on the basis of its main narrative content which has to do with the personal experiences of the narrator, which are

---

304 Ibid., 228 n.1.
305 Ibid., 229 n.1.
306 Ibid., 102.
307 Gadd 1958, 53.

described in order to remind readers of their religious obligations.

In the Cuthaean Legend of Naram-Sin, the argument for a didactic end section is better supported in that at the end of the text (i.e. in the Neo-Assyrian version which is the most complete) we find, e.g. in lines 147 to 151, a collection of aphorisms comprising mixed topics of political advice on domestic governmental policies and general advice on court etiquette. The text, using Gurney's translation, is as follows:[308]

    154. Be not bewildered, be not confused
    155. be not afraid, do not tremble,
    156. stablish thyself firmly,
    157. enjoy thyself in the bosom of thy wife,
    158. strengthen thy walls,
    159. fill thy trenches with water,
    160. thy chests, thy corn, thy money, thy goods and thy possessions
    161. bring into thy stronghold,
    162. tie up thy weapons and put them away in corners,
    163. spare the warriors and take heed for thy person.
    164. Though he wander through thy land, go not out to him,
    165. though he *slay* thy cattle, go not nigh him,
    166. though he eat the flesh of thy ...
    167. though he ...
    168. be meek, be hum[ble],
    169. answer them (!) "Here am I, my lord",
    170. respond to their wickedness with kindness,
    171. to kindness with gifts and *exchanges*,
    172. but do not go forth before them.

The didactic section is further marked by these preceding words:[309]

    152. Read this document and
    153. listen to the words thereof.

As to the third text called "A Sennacherib Autobiography", which is also known as "The Sin of Sargon", there is very little at the end of the text to suggest that there is an end "didactic section". What we have from line 18 onwards is an exhortation to the reader to take note of what has been described in the main body of text, which has to do with the narrator's (i.e.

---

308 Gurney (1955, 106-9), (1956, 164); cf. Hoffner (1970, 18-22).
309 Gurney 1955, 106-7 ll. 152-3.

Sennacherib) investigation, by way of divination, into the reason why his father was not buried in his tomb (whether this was due to a sin committed), in order that they may learn the lesson and avoid a similar ill fate. The final advice warns readers to learn the way by which the king had carried out the divination for his investigation. Line 18 is repeated as follows:[310]

> 18'. [Do] with your own hands these things about which I have informed you [ ] with your gods. Make peace with Aššur the king of the gods. Go about in a lordly fashion. The gods of heaven [ ] your shepherd [ ] reins of Šamaš and [Adad] handiwork of the gods [ ] on all of them [   ] I have informed you [   ].

These end admonitions are better described as general parting words of advice than as formal didactic instructions. Quite clearly, the primary didactic element of the work lies in the main narrative, which describes those particular events in Sennacherib's life which are meant to instruct its readers.

Farber and Westenholz have both raised a number of critical questions about Longman's interpretation and analysis of the Akkadian texts, which are mainly to do with his definitions and method of delineating the fifteen fictional autobiographies into four further subgroups. It is beyond the scope of this study to undertake a careful and thorough investigation of these criticisms. However, in line with my purpose, I shall now investigate Longman's claims of similarity between *Qoheleth* and the three fictional autobiographies with a didactic ending.

B. Longman's Analysis of *Qoheleth*

Longman's analysis of *Qoheleth* is problematic and appears to be misguided by his attempt at forcing the argument that the tripartite structure, which he argues is observable in his collection of Akkadian texts, is also evidenced in the Hebrew composition. This misplaced effort leads to several inaccurate analyses and comments, especially in relation to the structure of *Qoheleth*, such as the delineating and describing of the single verse of Eccl. 1:12 as the "first-person introduction", and 1:13-6:9

---

310 Longman 1991, 232, ll. 18f.

as "an extended first-person narrative".[311] Longman further claims that the "second half" of the Hebrew text, that is, 6:10-12:7, contains "a large block of exclusively instructional material".[312] This is clearly a misleading statement. Although a greater proportion of the didactic material in *Qoheleth* is found towards the end of the book, as is commonly noted, *Qoheleth*'s reflective discourse may still be seen, in significant portions, in Chapters 7 and 8, and to a lesser extent in Chapter 9, before finally ending in 10:7. Conversely, wisdom sayings and admonitions are also found in the "first half" of the book, a fact to which Longman admits but surprisingly does not address.

C. Summary

In summary, Longman's argument of a parallel between *Qoheleth* and the three fictional Akkadian autobiographies, in terms of a perceived similarity of a tripartite structure, is doubtful in the light of his inaccurate analysis and description of Qoheleth's narrative.

V. Pseudo-Autobiographies of the Kings of Akkad

Despite his unpersuasive argument, Longman has helped us by pointing us in the direction of the Akkadian *narû* texts, and in particular to one of its subgenres called "pseudo-auto-biography", to which the text of Naram-Sin also belongs. This latter corpus, on closer study, appears to share significant thematic parallels with *Qoheleth*. We will now investigate this further.

---

311 Longman 1998, 19.
312 Longman 1991, 121. In his commentary, Longman gives a different tripartite structure to "Qoheleth's speech" i.e. 1:12; 1:13-6:9; 6:10-12:7 (1998, 19-20) which is divided further to take into account his argument that the royal fiction is limited to 2:26 (ibid., 22):
   I.   Autobiographical Introduction (1:12)
   II. "Solomon's" Quest for the Meaning of Life (1:13-2:26)
   III. The Quest Continues (3:1-6:9)
   IV. Qohelet's Wise Advice (6:10-12:7)

This collection of Akkadian texts, which Grayson delineated and called "pseudo-autobiography", belongs to a wider corpus of texts called *narû* literature.[313] The "pseudo-autobiographies" are inscriptions which describe the legendary heroic deeds of the kings of the dynasty of Akkad in the third millennium B.C., to which some Assyriologists further include works relating to Akkadian deities (e.g. Marduk and Šulgi). Like *narû* literature, they are also known as "historical-literary" texts (in contrast to the "historical narrative" texts) and are fictional literary compositions about famous past kings of Akkad. They are written in the style of a first-person narrative purportedly by a king who is describing his deeds and experience as ruler of Akkad. Grayson defines the collection of "pseudo-auto-biographies" as simply "first person narrations by kings of their experiences".[314] According to Grayson, "the phenomena described are historical, legendary, and occasionally super-natural."[315] The Cuthaean Legend of Naram-Sin and the Sin of Sargon were the first two major texts assigned by Grayson to this genre, although other new fragmentary texts have since been included. A distinguishing feature of this collection of texts is the often negative portrayal of the narrator-king whose weaknesses are often openly described in the composition. The royal narrator is also sometimes singled out as the reason for the misfortune that is described in the text. Güterbock explains that the "good" and "bad" events in the texts are often the literary portrayals of the historical rise and fall of the king and his reign. He elucidates that these texts belong to the literary traditions which wrote about the *Heils- und Unheilsherrschers*[316], and were created primarily to provide lessons for future rulers, such as, to warn them to be loyal to their gods lest great calamities befall the land and its people. Naram-Sin appears to be a popular character in

---

313 Grayson (1975). These have been previously described, albeit more generally, as "historical inscriptions" (*historische Inschriften*). As these texts often reflected the form of a royal inscription and were purportedly engraved onto a stone monument (*narû*), Güterbock described them as "narû-literature" (1934). For discussions on the corpus and the history of attempts at classification, see Longman (1991, 43-8), Westenholz (1997, 16-24) and also Lewis (1980, 87-93).

314 Grayson 1975, 7.

315 Ibid., 8.

316 Güterbock 1934, 20.

this genre and is often portrayed as an *Unheilsherrscher*[317] as his character is often cast in the role of the archetypal ruler whose religious laxity brings condemnation, disaster, and misfortune to the nation.[318] Experts note that the characterization of a particular king may change with time and tradition. They further observe that the tradition tended to select and "affix the typology to the most illustrious, if not the most deserving, member of a dynasty".[319] We shall now take a closer look at this Akkadian corpus of "pseudo-autobiographies" to investigate further the nature and extent of its comparability with *Qoheleth*. This genre is represented by four main texts, one of Naram-Sin, another concerning a king of the dynasty of Isin, and two others of Sargon.[320]

A. The Cuthaean Legend of Naram-Sin

Of the many ancient stories of Naram-Sin, the Cuthaean Legend is said to reveal most about the character of this famous ancient king than any other text. In this particular inscription he is uniquely portrayed as "a man in introspection".[321] Based on the Neo-Assyrian copies of the text (i.e. the Standard Babylonian Recension) the legend is composed in the style of a first-person narrative framed by a prologue and an epilogue. In the prologue (ll.1-30), Naram-Sin introduces himself as the son of Sargon and proceeds to boast against the deeds of his royal predecessor

---

317 Finkelstein translates this word as "the element of the king's own instrumentality in bringing about the misfortune (by real or alleged misdeeds)" (1963, 467 n.23; as quoted by Evans 1983, 99). See also Finkelstein (1957, 88).

318 Ibid.

319 Evans 1983, 112.

320 Other minor texts which other scholars have placed under this genre classification include an unedited fragmentary text which is said to belong to an unidentified king of the Kassite period (Lambert (*CT* XLVI, nos. 49, 50) as cited by Lewis (1980, 90)), another Naram-Sin text (Grayson and Sollberger 1976, 103-28, as cited by Lewis ibid.), and another fragment of an Old Babylonian Sargon composition (Lewis 1980, 90, 116 n. 18). Westenholz has highlighted the difficulty in establishing the textual traditions behind the many fragments found, as "there are almost as many tales as there are tablets, with each tale witnessed by one manuscript only" (1997, 331).

321 Westenholz 1997, 264.

whom he identifies as Enmerkar. In the epilogue (ll.147-75) there are standard blessing oracles to future rulers, a call to read and adhere to the teachings of the text (which is his "stela"), a series of injunctions to be followed, and a final admonition to readers to leave their own stela so that posterity might similarly read and bless them. Qoheleth's introduction and epilogue reflect a similar theme and function although they do not together represent a parallel framework.

The events in the main narrative of Naram-Sin are to do with a devastating attack on the land by hordes of subhuman warriors ("warriors with bodies of cave-birds and faces of ravens").[322] Naram-Sin decides to confront the assailants and asks for an omen from the gods. Despite receiving a negative sign, Naram-Sin in his hubris launches an attack and as a result of his foolish action all of his armies are killed. In the aftermath of the battle, depressed and filled with self-doubt, Naram-Sin questions his worth as king. Naram-Sin eventually receives help from Ea who rescues the tragic hero by suggesting that he seeks further counsel from the gods. Naram-Sin follows the advice and proceeds with another attack on the enemy and is successful. The text then concludes with a series of admonitions to future rulers.

Whilst the details of the Naram-Sin legend are far removed from Qoheleth's narrative, there are several broad similarities to be observed between the two texts. First, there is the autobiographical style of narration with an introduction and epilogue, and the boasting over his predecessors. Second, there is arguably a similarity in the dialectic nature of both narratives where in the Naram-Sin text, as Westernholz notes, themes are found placed in "binary oppositions", such as warfare and peace, action and non-action, divine and human, and human and animal. This might be said to broadly parallel Qoheleth's dialectic manner of testing wisdom where contrasting wisdom truths appear to be juxtaposed to each other throughout his

---

322 Both Forrer and Gurney see this as a fanciful description of the human warriors who were led into battle by the historical King Annubanini of the Lulubi. See Gurney (1955, 95-7).

narrative.[323] The most striking similarity between both compositions, however, is the image of the despondent and resigned royal narrator who, in both texts, is regularly found in a pessimistic and reflective mood, brooding over his lack of power to influence dire events and circumstances. We find, on a few occasions, Naram-Sin in self-dialogue ("I spoke in my heart") and in a pessimistic mood.[324] In Naram-Sin's "second reaction" to the aftermath, for example, we hear the protagonist confessing his state of helplessness:[325]

> 88. I was bewildered, confused, *sunk in gloom*, sorrowful, exhausted.
> 89. Thus I spoke in my heart, these were my words:
> 90. "What have I left to the reign (i.e. for my successor)?
> 91. "I am a king who brings no security to his country,
> 92. "a shepherd who brings no security to his people.
> 93. "How am I to *proceed* and *keep myself out of trouble?*"

A similar sense of helplessness pervades Qoheleth's narrative. Upon reflecting on his inability to effect a positive change to the ongoing "vanities" of life Qoheleth succumbs to feelings of despondency and pessimism. This pessimistic mood, which often follows Qoheleth's observations of injustice and moral disorder, finds its clearest expression in his trademark cries of "vanity" and "chasing of wind". In Naram-Sin's "third reaction" a pensive mood is again discerned and the phrase "Thus I spoke in (to) my heart" is used.[326]

Naram-Sin's encouragement to adopt a policy of passive resistance in the face of attack from potential assailants also finds an interesting parallel in *Qoheleth*:[327]

> 154. Be not bewildered, be not confused,
> 155. be not afraid, do not tremble,
> 156. stablish thyself firmly,
> ...
> 164. Though he wander through thy land, go not out to him,
> 165. though he *slay* thy cattle, go not nigh him,
> 166. though he eat the flesh of thy...

---

323 See Chapter 4 for the discussion on the (dialectic) dynamics of Qoheleth's discourse.
324 See ibid., 317 l.79, 319 l.89.
325 Gurney (1955, 102-3 ll.88-93); (1956, 164). Italics his.
326 Ibid., 104-5 ll. 124-5.
327 Ll.154-6, 164-72, Gurney (1955, 106-109); see also ll.157-63.

167. though he ...
168. be meek, be hum[ble],
169. answer them (!) "Here am I, my lord",
170. respond to their wickedness with kindness,
171. to kindness with gifts and *exchanges*,
172. but do not go forth before them.

This advice, to apply calm before a threatening ruler, is similar to Qoheleth's admonition in Eccl. 8:3 and 5a:

8:3   Do not hurry to leave from his presence. Do not persist in an unpleasant matter for whatever he pleases he does.

8:5a Whoever obeys a commandment will not experience harm.

Another exhortation, placed somewhat unusually at the end of the text (in line 157) in the collection of didactic advice, finds a parallel saying in *Qoheleth*:[328]

157. enjoy thyself in the bosom of thy wife

Eccl. 9:9aα Enjoy life with the wife whom you love all the days of your vain life which he has given you under the sun.

Overall, there are quite a number of notable thematic similarities between *Qoheleth* and the pseudo-autobiography of Naram-Sin. To repeat the point made above, the more significant parallel lies in the typological image of the despondent royal narrator who, through his autobiographical narration, shares his past negative experiences for the purpose of instructing his audience.

B. The Text of a King of Isin

The second pseudo-autobiographical text concerns the legend of a king from the second dynasty of Isin. A portion of the surviving fragment (of the Neo-Assyrian copy) describes, in an autobiographical manner, the terror of the Elamite enemy on the people of Sumer and Akkad and how the narrator-king was overcome by fear and was reduced to "speaking (to himself) in panic, trouble, and despair".[329] On the reverse side of the frag-

---

328 Ibid., cf. Hoffner (1970, 18-9).
329 Lewis (1980, 89-90) quoting Tadmor (1958, 139 r. 6).

ment, the king tells of leading his troops into battle against the Elamites, but is soon forced to flee as they are stricken by a plague sent by their own god Nergal. The king then prays to Enlil to relent and to be of help to them. (Both Lewis and Longman have pointed out that this theme, of the king struggling against a superior enemy who is aided by their own god, is also found in the Cuthaean Legend.) Upon the initial defeat, the king falls into despair and mourns his plight.[330] However, upon supplication to his god, he eventually is victorious (this last part is only presumed for the Isin text). Lewis speculates that the original text must have had a framework of prologue and epilogue, but evidence for this suggestion is absent. Despite our limited knowledge of the original text, it may still be said that the autobiographical style of the work and the motif of the protagonist king in mourning and despair find a parallel in *Qoheleth*.

C. A Sargon Autobiography

The first Sargon text, a Sargon Autobiography, is unfortunately too fragmented and the surviving inscription does not seem to yield any comparable content with *Qoheleth*. Comprising only six legible lines, the text is written in the form of a first-person narration and is an Old Babylonian composition.[331] Not much may be observed of the text which has, in its introduction, the formulaic 1cs independent personal pronoun followed by the royal name: *a-na-ku sa-ru-ki-in* ("I am Sargon"). The lengthy royal titulary, as commonly evidenced in the ARI, is noticeably absent in this fragmentary text, which suggests that it is possibly not part of an official royal inscription.

---

330 Lewis (1980, 90); Longman (1991, 195).
331 Grayson 1975, 8, n.11b; chapter III, n.18.

D. The Sargon Legend

The second Sargon text, more commonly known as the Sargon Legend or the Sargon Birth Legend, consists of four surviving fragments which make up what appears to be the beginning two columns of the work. The first column consists of a prologue which tells the story of the birth of Sargon up to his ascension to the throne and is composed in the form of a first-person narrative. The story continues with the description of Sargon's heroic deeds and concludes with a challenge to any future king to emulate his extraordinary achievements. There is found, in one of the fragments, the formulaic royal self-introduction which identifies the composition with its narrator-king: *LUGAL.GI.NA (sarrukin) LUGAL (sarru) dan-nu LUGAL (sar) a-ga-de a-na-ku* ("Sargon, strong king, king of Agade, am I").[332] A second column, which is found in only one of the four fragments, has held scholars in puzzlement as it consists of a series of rhetorical questions which show no clear connection to the narrative in the first column. Lewis acknowledges the possibility that both works may not be related and may have coincidently been copied onto the same tablet, as is sometimes evidenced in other inscriptions.[333] This second portion of work is a didactic composition although there is no identification of its writer (whether Sargon or anyone else) or its audience. Interestingly, the sayings revolve around the theme of futility and there is also the repeated mention of "the wind". If this portion of text is indeed connected to the first column of text, then what we have here would be a most extraordinary paralleling with Qoheleth's favourite theme and motif of הֶבֶל "vanity" and וּרְעוּת רוּחַ "chasing of wind".

> 51. The ewe ran about in the steppe, why not...?
> 52. And the gazelle driven by the wind, the stag...by...
> 53. The screech owl which kept crying out...
> 54. For all its crying, what did it achieve?
> 55. The wind blew...
> 56. The onager constantly running about, where is...?
> 57. The wind blows in the steppe...
> 58. The onager constantly runs about, he twitches in the steppeland.

---

332 Lewis 1980, 24.
333 Lewis 1980, 11.

...
66. The wind..., human habitations...[334]

Westenholz comments, "The seemingly obvious message to be read out of the text is a commentary on the futility of all human effort. The relationship of this section to the story of Sargon is unfortunately not clear. It could contain his reflections at the end of his life. On the other hand, it may describe a tragic cataclysm at the end of his reign."[335] Lewis does not venture to make a link between the two columns of work except cautiously to note the probability of the connection, like Lambert.[336] He does not speak further about the second column of the work except to speculate that thematically the work may be "a prelude to an adventure story or a hunting motif".[337]

The general style and content of the Sargon Legend is considerably different to *Qoheleth* although there are a few similarities to be found. For example, the text is written in an autobiographical form and there is a description of Sargon's achievements as king, and the work is in semi-poetic language. Further, there is a set of prologue and epilogue, which frames the main body of narrative.

How do these Akkadian pseudo-autobiographies, as a genre, collectively compare with *Qoheleth*? In order to help answer this question, we turn to Lewis's identification of the key characteristics of this Akkadian corpus to see how well these match *Qoheleth*.

E. Key Characteristics of the Corpus

Lewis has drawn a list of distinguishing characteristics for this genre of "Akkadian pseudo-autobiography". Lewis's list is interesting in that all the characteristic features, which he notes of this corpus, appear to fit *Qoheleth*, with the exception of one

---

334 Westenholz (1997, 44-7); cf. Lewis (1980, 28-9).
335 Ibid., 36.
336 Ibid., 92.
337 Lewis 1980, 96.

(i.e. the seventh point). The following is his list of significant features of the Akkadian pseudo-autobiographies:[338]

1. The texts concern the figure of a great king and record either significant events or unusual experiences during his rule.
2. They are pseudepigraphical and purport to be genuine royal inscriptions.
3. They are written in the first person in the style of an autobiography.
4. Following the pattern of the royal inscription, they are constructed with a prologue, narrative, and epilogue.
5. The prologue begins with a self-presentation and may include information concerning the king's origin or the cause of the predicament he faces in the narrative section.
6. The narrative is devoted to a specific episode in the life of the king.
7. The narrative contains a message for future kings expressed in the form of a blessing, oracle, or curse formula.
8. The texts are didactic in nature; there is a moral to be learned from the personal experiences of the king that can be acquired by reading his "stela".
9. They are written in a poetic or semipoetic narrative style.

The characteristics listed by Lewis are derived from the shared features of all the texts under this genre. The Cuthaean Legend of Naram-Sin, being the most complete work of all, contains all of the above characteristics. That the list may be seen to fittingly describe *Qoheleth* suggests that a similar genre description could perhaps be also used for our Hebrew work. By comparing *Qoheleth* with the texts of this Akkadian genre we have come to appreciate better how certain passages in *Qoheleth* (viz. his teaching on the proper behaviour and actions before the king, e.g. 8:2-5; 10:20) need not be seen as being incongruent to a royal voice but rather in support of it, and that there is an overall good case for arguing that the royal fiction is integral to the composition of *Qoheleth* based on the similarities that it has with the Akkadian corpus of royal pseudo-autobiographies.

F. Summary

Our examination of the Akkadian corpus of royal pseudo-autobiographies has been fruitful. We saw how this group of

---

338 Ibid.

literary texts bears a remarkable likeness to *Qoheleth* with their pseudonymous first-person narratives which describe the life and experiences of famous kings. We noted initially that Longman's suggestion of a parallel between *Qoheleth* and his collection of three Akkadian works, based on a perceived similarity of structure, was unconvincing. Instead, a different corpus of "pseudo-autobiographies" (to which one of Longman's suggested three texts also belongs), was seen to bear striking typological similarities with the Hebrew composition. The comparable literary features which we noted include the use of the first-person narrative to describe the lives of the illustrious heroes and legendary kings of Akkad, such as Sargon and Naram-Sin. We also observed how the autobiographical narrative typically describes the narrator's past experience and observations as king, using these as examples for instructing his audience on how to make right decisions and for encouraging the inculcation of proper behaviour. Readers are also frequently warned not to neglect their religious duties and obligations, lest this leads to defeat in battle, and to heed one's advisers and diviners, which can bring about good consequences. The didactic aim of these fictional autobiographical texts is clear. Some Assyriologists see these texts as works meant to instruct future kings, although a more general audience might possibly be envisaged as well. These characteristic features, which we have observed of the Akkadian corpus, are also shared by *Qoheleth*, who similarly adopts the persona of Israel's famous wise king, Solomon, to present his teachings which arise from his observations and experience in life. The argument for the similarity between *Qoheleth* and the Akkadian corpus finds further support in the remarkable way in which eight of the nine features, which are noted by Lewis as characterizing the broader Akkadian corpus of "royal" pseudo-autobiographies, fit *Qoheleth*. Overall, our investigation has not only highlighted the parallels between *Qoheleth* and the Akkadian pseudo-autobiographies, but has further shown the possible links the Hebrew composition might have with the literary traditions of the ancient Semitic world. Our investigation has demonstrated the possibility that *Qoheleth* might have been written as a Solomonic pseudo-autobiography.

To conclude, it appears that in the ancient Semitic world of literary compositions, the lives and experience of famous royal personalities provided the inspiration for many literary-didactic works, created to teach and entertain.[339] As Liverani points out, whereas the "official" royal inscriptions were mainly celebratory in aim, the pseudo-royal compositions functioned primarily as tools for instruction.[340] Grayson similarly saw the Akkadian pseudo-autobiographies as primarily didactic in intent.[341] From the striking parallels noted between *Qoheleth* and the Akkadian corpus it is possible to suggest that the Hebrew work reflects the form of a royal pseudo-autobiography.

VI. Egyptian Instructions

In Chapter 2, mention was made of the suggestion by Perdue and others before, that *Qoheleth* follows the form of Egyptian Royal Testaments. We will now investigate the suggested comparability between these works, along with the two other Egyptian wisdom genres of "Instruction" and "Lament".

---

339 Scholars today generally acknowledge the close parallels between the Gilgamesh Epic and *Qoheleth* (e.g. Barton (1908); Loretz (1964); Brown (2000)). The thematic similarities between the two works are striking and include e.g. Gilgamesh's lament over the futility of humankind's toil, the *carpe diem* exhortations, and a similar use of the numerical proverb of the cord (Eccl. 4:2). Like the parallels between the Akkadian corpus of pseudo-autobiography and *Qoheleth*, a similar typological parallel may be seen between the Hebrew composition and Gilgamesh in that both bear descriptions of a famous royal persona whose life experience is used for a didactic purpose. In Gilgamesh, we have the portrayal of the legendary ruler of Uruk who fails in his quest for immortality despite his great wisdom and ability. In the epic, readers are led to share in the lessons that emerge as the narrator tells of the protagonist's journey and his encounters in his search for the secret to immortality. Interestingly, the experiences of Gilgamesh are more negative than good. I will not be discussing Gilgamesh here because of the clear difference in literary form (i.e. third-person epic narrative). Lambert's (1960, 50) comment that the epic reflects a common literary convention whereby the stories of the wise and foolish deeds of famous past kings were played out and transferred between royal characters provides a useful insight to the understanding of *Qoheleth* in that it helps us understand the sort of literary traditions with which the author of the Hebrew composition would have likely been acquainted and with which a work such as *Qoheleth* would have been in good company. See also Oppenheim (1964, 255).

340 Liverani 1995, 2364.

341 Grayson 1975, 8.

A. Royal Testaments

Behind Galling's argument that the author of *Qoheleth* wrote his work as a Royal Testament (*Königstestament*) in the manner of the Egyptian Royal Instructions (*Königslehre*) was his attempt to understand the use of a perfective verb in Qoheleth's opening introduction ...אֲנִי קֹהֶלֶת מֶלֶךְ in 1:12. Disagreeing with Delitzsch who interpreted the use of the perfective הָיִיתִי as an indication that it was the spirit of Solomon speaking, "resuscitated by the author of the book, who here looks back on his life as king",[342] Galling argued that the verse, and *Qoheleth*, was best understood against the background of the Egyptian Royal Testaments which often either reflected a change in government or the death of a ruler. Through a comparison with the Instruction for Merikare, he explains:[343]

> Zieht man nun zum Vergleich die ägyptischen Weisheitslehren heran, dann verliert das hjjtj mlk ("ich bin König gewesen") seine Absonderlichkeit. Der Typus der Königslehren wird auf den Tag des Regierungswechsels datiert. Bei der Lehre für den König Merikare ist das ganz deutlich die Sterbestunde des königlichen Vaters.

According to Galling, this would explain the use of the perfective verb and the other passages in *Qoheleth* which describe scenes of political oppression and great social changes.

Loretz, in response, has argued that Galling's suggestion of a similarity between the works is incorrect because firstly, the Instruction for Merikare is not a set of instructions given by a dying king to his succeeding son but rather a political declaration and a literary fiction and hence is not, in the true sense of the word, a *Königstestament*.[344] Loretz contends that the Instruction for Merikare was probably written either by King Merikare himself, or by his officials with his cooperation, and that it was a public declaration by a new king who was seeking to propagate his new brand of politics. Loretz argues that the new policies to be introduced by the new king Merikare were diametrically opposed in many important respects to those of his father. Thus

---

342 Delitzsch 1891, 226.
343 Galling 1932, 298.
344 Loretz 1964, 59.

in order to claim greater authority, a declaration of Merikare's new brand of politics was presented as originating from the mouth of his deceased father as a royal teaching.[345] Loretz, however, points out that the author of *Qoheleth* did not write the work with "half-hidden political objectives" (and as a political *Streitschrift*) nor is there any indication that Qoheleth intended to be portrayed as speaking from the dead, or that his instructions were meant for his successor.[346] Loretz argues that the only similarity between *Qoheleth* and the Egyptian Royal Testaments is that they are both literary fiction, although they both serve a different purpose.[347] Finally, Loretz points to the difference in worldviews, namely in relation to the deeds and speeches of the deceased, which effectively puts an end to Galling's suggestion of a similarity.[348]

Loretz is correct to point out that the political motive which underlies the Egyptian Royal Testaments is clearly absent in *Qoheleth*. In fact, it is this political aspect of the Egyptian Testaments that separates them from the closely associated Egyptian Instructions, even though the Royal Testament texts carry a similar "Instruction" (*sb3yt*) title.[349] Loretz is correct to argue against Galling's suggestion of a parallel as it is doubtful that Qoheleth's narrative was composed as a Royal Testament for

---

345 Ibid.

346 Ibid, 61. "Das Buch Qohelet ist auch nicht für den Nachfolger auf dem Königsthron verfaßt. Die Lehren Qohelets richten sich an alle. Im ganzen Verlauf seiner Darlegungen findet sich deshalb kein Hinweis, daß Qohelet seine Lehren als Testament verstanden wissen wollte. Qohelet geht ferner jede politische Zielsetzung ab, die den behandelten ägyptischen Texten zugrunde liegt." (ibid., 62).

347 Loretz was more keen to see the literary influence on *Qoheleth* as coming from Mesopotamia than from Egypt.

348 "Die Unterschiede zwischen Qohelet und den ägyptischen Schriften sind so groß und tiefgreifend, daß die jeden Vergleich vereiteln. Denn während die ägyptischen Dokumente die ägyptischen Anschauungen über das Fortleben der Toten zur Voraussetzung haben, vermissen wir bei Qohelet jedweden Hinweis auf den nahe bevorstehenden oder bereits eingetretenen Tod des Königs. Den König Qohelet vollends als Toten aus dem Jenseits herüber sprechen zu lassen, liegt außerhalb des hebräischen Gesichtskreises. Der Tote konnte nach dem Glauben der Hebräer von drüben her nicht mehr eingreifen..." (ibid., 62). Communication between the dead and the living, as reflected in written works, was considered normal in ancient Egypt (Parkinson 2002, 242).

349 Lichtheim 1996, 243.

those reasons which he has mentioned. Furthermore, we might recall from our earlier discussion, on the use of perfective verb to describe Qoheleth's kingship, that Qoheleth's reign should be interpreted as a present rather than a past reality.

To conclude, there are no good grounds for suggesting a similarity between *Qoheleth* and the Egyptian Royal Testaments based on the reasons mentioned above, and in particular, when we see up close that Galling's interpretation of the perfective verb, which first brought about the suggestion for a comparison with the Royal Testament, is no longer tenable. However, aside from the element of political motivation, there are some literary parallels to be observed between the works. We will examine these further in our following analysis of the Instructions since the Royal Testaments also bear the title of "Instruction" (*sb3yt*) and their literary forms are broadly similar to this major wisdom genre which we will examine next.

B. Royal Instructions

It is often suggested that there are many striking similarities between *Qoheleth* and the Egyptian Instructions, but a closer look at both reveals that there are also some important differences to be observed. To begin with, it is important to note that Egyptologists generally agree that within the corpus of Instructions itself there is a notable lack of uniformity in that there is a general absence of strict adherence to any known classical forms.[350] It is further said that the creative use and adaptation of the principal forms of Instruction, particularly from the Middle Kingdom onwards, suggests that the compositions were originally works of fiction which possibly could have belonged to "the same literary context of entertainment as the tales and reflective discourses".[351] The issue of the lack of uniformity among the Instructions perhaps warrants closer attention since they appear to hold helpful clues to our understanding of *Qoheleth*. Parkinson points out several significant observations

---

350 Kitchen (1979, 243, 259); Baines (1996); Loprieno (1996).
351 Parkinson 2002, 235.

about the Instruction genre, to do with this issue, which are particularly insightful. Firstly, he writes that although the teachings of the Instructions are "injunctions to perfection" in some cases (e.g. Merikare and Amenemhet) the narrator, rather than being the ideal exemplar of wisdom himself, is the exemplar by virtue of "speaking Ma'at".[352] A similar situation is arguably reflected in *Qoheleth* where the "wisdom" of Qoheleth is not to be found in his life and living (which in retrospection was deemed a vanity) but rather in his instructions and counsel. Hence it is his advice and admonitions, and not his life, which is "wisdom" to be listened. Secondly, the authorial figure of the narrator-king provides a broad sense of unity to an otherwise assorted collection of sayings. As king, he stands as the ideological centre to the whole culture, teaching both a wide audience and humanity as well.[353] Thirdly, the royal instructions are not exclusively didactic as they claim and often the main contents of the text do not link up with the intentions of the author as elucidated at the beginning of the work. Parkinson notes, for example, that in Amenemhet there are no specific teachings on how to carry out the role of king even though this objective is described in the opening words of the composition, and neither are the admonitions exclusively for the royal household.[354] Similarly in Merikare, the narrator's aim of giving the laws of kingship, as mentioned at the start of the text, is not found in the body of instructions.[355] These observations show that the Instructions have some measure of incoherence which, by contrast, helps to support the integrity and unity of *Qoheleth*.[356] Fourthly, the Royal Instructions are both reflective and

---

352 Ibid., 237-8.
353 Ibid., 238. Parkinson points out that the Instructions are often considered "authoritative" rather than "authorial" (see also Loprieno 1996, 46) and even in the teachings there is often a tension "between the ideology and its individual embodiment. Although the compositions deal with the ideal of wisdom, and have appropriate settings in the past or in the reign of an unspecified king, they formulate the interplay of ideal and actual in terms of personal conduct and ethical choices, and the settings act as fictionalizing devices" (ibid.).
354 Ibid., 238.
355 Ibid.
356 The issue of the coherence and unity of Qoheleth's narrative flow in relation to the presence of didactic material will be discussed in Chapter 4.

didactic.[357] Moreover, the didactic elements are occasionally found clustered at different points of the text for no clear and specific reason.

We shall now examine the literary similarities which *Qoheleth* is often said to share with the Egyptian wisdom genre of Instruction.

1. Fictional Authorship

Egyptologists generally agree that the royal ascriptions commonly found in the Royal Instructions are likely to be pseudepigraphic and fictitious rather than genuine in view of the apparent fictional nature of the compositions.[358] For if these works were indeed genuinely authored by the named king, then one would be obliged to contend with the possibility of much earlier texts having survived the process of being altered, translated, and transmitted over great periods of Egypt's history and time (e.g. in the case of Kagemni and Ptahhotep, from Old to the Middle Kingdom).[359] Such a scenario is clearly doubtful. The non-propagandistic nature of this corpus, with the occasional descriptions of the king in lament or expressing a weakness, further argues against the possibility of a genuine royal authorship. This latter image stands in contrast to the hyperbolic descriptions of the king's omniscience and omnipotence which are typically found in royal edifices and official monumental inscriptions. The "mainstream" texts are seldom explicit in revealing the weaknesses of kings nor do they describe the marginalization of the kingship as this was not the norm among

---

357 Parkinson comments, "in many places are didactic by example, through implication, and by extension rather than directly" (ibid.).   For example, Merikare and Amenemhet are both more descriptive and discursive than didactic in style.

358 Parkinson raises the pertinent point that the issue of fictionality or historicity may require more than a deciding between two separate dichotomies and that there is a possibility that a composition may have rewritten a historical event with some measure of creative and artistic freedom, e.g. Amenemhet (Parkinson 1996, 311).

359 *AEL* 2, 6-7. There are others who recognize an authentic authorial ascription in a few of the works, e.g. Amenemhet (see e.g. Kitchen 1977/8, 94-5).

public works.[360] However, in the rare instance where they are
spoken of explicitly, it is legitimized and put to the outer realm
of the gods.[361] Experts believe that the royal attribution, where it
is used, is possibly part of a literary strategy aimed at facilitating
the social reception of a primarily "unsanctioned" work (cf. the
"mainstream" official texts and inscriptions).[362] Most scholars
agree that this same intention lies behind the Solomonic fiction in
Qoheleth and the title of the work. Both Qoheleth's royal self-
introduction and the superscription introduce the author
Qoheleth as king. The title, in its reference to Qoheleth as בֶּן־דָּוִד
"a son of David" (which is not repeated in Qoheleth's self-
introduction in 1:12), clearly alludes to Solomon. The royal
ascription of 1:1 and Qoheleth's self-representation as king in
1:12 are to be seen as fictional. From a study of its language, it is
doubtful if the piece did originate from Israel's most famous
wise king himself.

2. Title

The title is the most basic literary feature of the Instruction
corpus and is found in nearly all the texts. This literary item
finds a parallel with the superscription of Eccl 1:1.[363] In its very

---

360 Silverman points out an exception, where Ramses II is described as a fallible
   human being in an inscription on a temple wall, which of course is meant to last
   forever. He suggests that the mention of the ruler's weakness in this occasion is
   likely to serve the broader literary purpose of heightening the dramatic effects
   of the more glorifying events to follow (1995, 51).

361 Baines 1996, 374-7.

362 Lichtheim observes that the didactic texts are primarily aristocratic until the
   New Kingdom period when they gradually became more "middle class". She
   notes that from the form that is adopted (i.e. the author speaks as a minor
   official and dispenses his advice in the form of a father-son instruction), the
   works are most likely meant for the "average man". She comments that the
   New Kingdom instruction "is suited to the thinking of anyone who possessed a
   modicum of education and of material comforts. Thus there is nothing
   specifically aristocratic about the values that are taught" (also Baines 1996).
   This development was likely a reflection of the growth of the middle class
   during a particular period of Egypt's history (*AEL* 2, 135).

363 Kitchen makes the observation that the title of *Qoheleth* is formulated
   substantivally (cf. verbal) and that this manner of formulation is common to
   both Egyptian and other West Semitic works (e.g. Ahiqar) but not to

basic form, the title comprises the keyword "Instruction" (*sb3yt*) (or "Teaching" in the later demotic works) which is followed by the title and personal name of the author expressed in the third-person.[364] Compared to *Qoheleth's* superscription, the Egyptian titles are more informative, often disclosing the name, rank, and position of the author and a description of its audience.[365] The author of the instructional texts is also always identified and never anonymous, although any attribution to a royal figure or a sage, as mentioned above, is likely to be fictitious.[366]

3. Framework

Fox has recently argued that Qoheleth's use of "an anonymous third-person retrospective frame-narrative encompassing a first-person narrative or monologue"[367] follows the compositional style of many Egyptian wisdom texts. However, although the majority of the Egyptian Instructions have prologues and epilogues framing the main body of texts (where they have survived), which are narrated in the third person, the same may not be said of *Qoheleth*.[368]

The prologues to the Egyptian works, where they are found, function like the epilogues in exhorting listeners to heed and obey the teachings given by the aristocratic or high-ranking author. There is no comparable form of this kind in *Qoheleth*.

Mesopotamian compositions (e.g. Sumerian, Akkadian), (1977/8, 77-8; 1979, 243-4).

364 Kitchen 1979, 243-5. For more a detailed discussion see Kitchen 1977/8.

365 Kitchen notes that, whilst the length of the titles vary within all periods and regions and may also include claims for the aims and value of the work (e.g. Ptahhotep, Amenemope; 1977/8, 76) or any other literary embellishments, the name of its author is always identified even in the most basic of titles (1979, 244).

366 Kitchen 1977/8, 93-5, 97.

367 Fox 1977, 91.

368 Kitchen, in his extensive comparison of the literary forms of Egyptian and Western Asian didactic treatise, concludes that there is a "relative consistency" of the use of prologues throughout all periods (1979). An exception is seen in Merikare. Parkinson argues in Merikare's case that the narrative framework was probably not needed since its readers would have easily recognized the genre from seeing the king's name and consequently would have understood its literary context and fictitious nature (2002, 249).

Fox, in arguing for the presence of a parallel framework in the Hebrew composition, is in fact referring to Qoheleth's superscription rather than a separate internal prologue within the work (some commentators view Qoheleth's opening poem as a poetic prologue, but this is a different issue from our argument at hand). There is clearly some confusion surrounding the use of the term, which may have caused Fox to incorrectly suggest a similarity. Kitchen has shown that not all Egyptian Instructions have prologues and that many of the works begin right after its title. It is clear that in Qoheleth there is an absence of a comparable prologue at the start of the work, and Fox's argument that the title should be considered a comparable counterpart to the prologues of the Instructions is both inaccurate and misleading.[369] (Qoheleth's superscription (1:1) may be said to better parallel the Egyptian title.) The frameworks in the Egyptian Instructions are generally viewed as part of the original text and integral to the rest of the composition. In contrast, the title and the epilogue of Qoheleth appear to be the work of a later editor(s).[370] It might be argued that the epilogist of Qoheleth, who was responsible for these editorial additions, was seeking to imitate the Egyptian Instructions genre by providing a broadly comparable "framework" made up of Qoheleth's title (1:1) and an epilogue (12:9-14), and a further aesthetic framing comprising the thematic motto of "vanity of vanities" in 1:2 and 12:8.

There is, however, a further observable similarity between the epilogues of Qoheleth and the Egyptian Instructions. The epilogues of the Egyptian texts, where they are found, often contain specific descriptions of their audience and context (e.g. in the Instruction to Kagemni the speaker's children are described as the audience, who are being taught in a classroom).[371] The same is true of Qoheleth's epilogue which describes Qoheleth's role as sage and teacher in what appears to be a formal context of instruction (Eccl. 12:9-10). The epilogues in the Egyptian texts lend encouragement to the learning of the materials given (with

---

369 Fox in fact argues that the superscription and the formulaic vanity call in 1:1-2 represent the corresponding "prologue" in Qoheleth.

370 See Chapter 1, pp. 19-23.

371 Kitchen 1979, 246.

their occasional exhortation to comply)[372] as does *Qoheleth*'s epilogue. There are, however, differences to be observed between the works as well. *Qoheleth*'s epilogue carries a further and unusual purpose of guiding the interpretation of the main message of the book, as seen in the epilogist's admonition "to fear God and obey the Torah", which is placed as the final and concluding remark of the book. Although the epilogues of the Egyptian texts do not offer interpretative guidelines they are nevertheless similar to *Qoheleth* in their endorsement of the message and contents of the main text.[373] Another interesting parallel is the "titular interjections" whereby the author is re-introduced further on in the work (e.g. Ptahhotep, Ani).[374] A similar occurrence is seen in Eccl. 7:27 where Qoheleth is re-introduced in the third-person.

Other minor similarities to be observed from the Egyptian Instructions include the oratorical style and personal tone of the texts, which are characteristically composed as first-person narratives. Johnson, in his comparative study of gnomic sayings in biblical and ancient Near Eastern wisdom literature, observes that the didactic sayings, in both *Qoheleth* and the Egyptian Instructions, appear to be organized around key words and themes.[375] Johnson further observes that, within the larger collections in both works, the smaller clusters of sayings sometimes show no clear connection to each other.[376] This was pointed out earlier by Kitchen in relation to the Egyptian texts.[377] Another

---

372 An exception to this general function of the epilogue is Ani, where there is a description of the voicing of the son's objection to his father that the teachings are too difficult to understand and obey.

373 In this respect, the epilogues of the Instruction to Kagemni and the Instruction of Ani come closest to *Qoheleth*. The former confirms the reliability of the sage's spoken words whilst also warning the reader against going beyond and not heeding the instructions given (cf. 12:11, 13-14). The Instructions of Ani similarly affirm the spoken instructions and urge the audience ("son") to pay attention to the words, though they may be difficult to understand and obey.

374 This is another "optional" literary device in the Instruction genre (Kitchen 1979, 246).

375 Likewise Kitchen (1973, 265), (1979, 280).

376 Cf. Ankhsheshonq's collection of 37 sets of maxims which as Lichtheim describes "do not amount to a comprehensive moral code, nor are they strung together in any logical order" (see *AEL* 1, 61-2).

377 Kitchen describes that the writers are sometimes found to "pass freely from one subject to another, without any special order of topics, perhaps even reverting

similarity, which Johnson notes, is the way in which the narrator's experience is used to validate the truths of the individual and longer series of sayings and how conversely the sayings are also used to confirm the conclusions reached through his observations and reflections.[378] Johnson also points to a few significant differences between *Qoheleth* and the Egyptian Instructions. Firstly, he argues that there is an absence of the imperative call to attention (e.g. "hear these words") in *Qoheleth* which is frequently found in the Egyptian works. Johnson contends that whereas the Instruction "most certainly is a direct address", *Qoheleth*, he argues, is not a speech as there is no indication of the intended audience or occasion to the writing or the use of typical phrases such as, "my son, your time is at hand".[379] Johnson further argues that the purpose of the Egyptian Instructions is "narrowly didactic, to provide specific moral guidance" whereas Qoheleth's aim lies in his examination and evaluation of the assumptions and conclusions of traditional wisdom.[380] These latter arguments of Johnson are clearly flawed for two reasons. Firstly, although Qoheleth presents his message as primarily an autobiographical monologue, the presence of second-person address (e.g. 2:1; 4:17; 5:1, 4-5, 7; 7:16-17, 21-22; 9:7, 9-10; 11:2, 5-6), didactic admonitions, and exhortations in the work clearly implies that external readers, as indirect addressees of the narrative, are also involved. Moreover, there is ample evidence of Qoheleth's use of the imperative (e.g. 4:17; 5:5; 7:14, 17, 21; 8:2; 9:7, 9-10; 10:4, 20; 11:1, 6, 10). Johnson's argument of the absence of stereotypical phrases of admonitions is superficial. Johnson's last argument is also erroneous as the purpose of *Qoheleth* is indeed to provide moral guidance, as is seen in his exposition of traditional wisdom topics such as wisdom and folly, death, fate, and the fear of God, to name a few.

---

to matters already touched on" (1979, 280). He adds that while in certain texts the sayings may be found grouped according to a certain theme or topic, others may include a miscellany of topics (e.g. Ani) which bear little or no connection to their particular segment (ibid.).

378 Johnson 1973, 265.
379 Ibid., 265-6.
380 Ibid., 266, 289.

There is ample evidence to support the argument of a similarity between *Qoheleth* and the Egyptian Instruction. There is the parallel use of a fictitious royal ascription and the presence of a framework (comprising *Qoheleth*'s title and epilogue) which surrounds a main body of text that is written predominantly in the style of a first-person narrative. Both *Qoheleth* and the Egyptian Instructions hold large collections of didactic sayings. There are, however, a few marked differences to be observed, such as the different topics explored in the individual texts, and there is also Qoheleth's peculiar style of argument. It should be said that the argument for a similarity of form between *Qoheleth* and the Egyptian Instructions ought to be qualified as experts note that even within the literary tradition of the Instruction corpus there is a general lack of an adherence to known classical forms.[381] Baines, for example, comments that the style of the Middle Kingdom Instructions lacks general uniformity and shows considerable fluidity in their range of use and adaptation of the smaller literary forms and devices. Kitchen similarly writes that the consistent yet flexible use of the basic conventions of the genre by the individual authors-compilers shows that the ancient writers were "masters of their craft, and not slaves of mechanical laws of a genre".[382] This observation of literary creativity and fluidity, which we have also encountered earlier in our investigation of the Assyrian corpus of pseudo-auto-biographies, may lend us a clue on the unique nature of our Hebrew text. Perhaps Qoheleth was also expressing considerable flexibility and freedom in his composition which nevertheless show some broad affinities with a number of the ancient Near Eastern literary texts and compositions.

There are a number of themes and motifs that are found in both *Qoheleth* and the Egyptian Instructions. These include the topics of court protocol, general moral conduct, observance of temple worship, world weariness, the reversal of fortune, the call to take the opportunity to enjoy life in the face of trouble, the incomprehensible ways of the gods, and the use of popular

---

381 Baines 1996.
382 Kitchen 1979, 259.

aphorisms in instructing the right way to live. We will look briefly at three of these themes.

4. Themes and Motifs

a. The Call To Enjoy Life

The call to "follow your heart" is a common theme found in many of the Instructions. The Admonitions of Ipuwer, in particular, carries the call to enjoy one's food in the face of distress with the further remark that such opportunities for enjoyment are only given to the one who is favoured by god. The advice on merriment closely resembles Qoheleth's counsel of the same in Eccl. 2:24-26a and 9:7.

> Lo, a man is happy eating his food. Consume your goodness in gladness, while there is none to hinder you. It is good for a man to eat his food. God ordains it for him whom he favors.[383]

> Eccl. 2:24-26a There is nothing better for a man than that he should eat and drink and find pleasure for himself in his work. This too, I saw, is from the hand of God; for who can eat or who can have enjoyment apart from me? For to whoever pleases him, he (God) gives wisdom, knowledge and happiness...

> Eccl. 9:7 Go eat your bread with enjoyment and drink your wine with a happy heart, for God has already approved your deeds.

Parkinson points out that the element of entertainment is a common feature in the Egyptian Instructions. Parkinson writes, "Ptah-hotep celebrates 'following the heart' (186), as does Merikare (30a-d). The Loyalist Teaching concerns the proper enjoyment of life and rewards, and even Amenemhet is concerned in part with regaining the 'happy hour'."[384] In many of the Egyptian texts (including Ipuwer, Merikare, Amenemhet), the advice to enjoy life is given against the background of chaos and distress. This is similarly observed in *Qoheleth* where the *carpe diem* counsel to seek enjoyment often emerges out of

---

383 *AEL1*, 157.
384 Parkinson 2002, 239-40.

Qoheleth's pessimistic musing on life's absurdities of which God stands very much in the centre.[385]

b. The Reversal of Fortune

It is commonly acknowledged that the descriptions of national chaos in the Egyptian Instructions are likely to be fictitious literary *topoi* rather than real depictions of historical events and situations. This would explain the use of heavy hyperbolic language to describe the social chaos, some of which are contradictory (e.g. in Ipuwer, the land is on the one hand described as being totally desolated while on the other the poor are said to have become rich, wearing fine linen and inheriting the wealth of their masters).[386] As Lichtheim explains, these pessimistic themes were probably employed to achieve the literary effects of glorifying the author who, because of his wisdom and capability, is able ultimately to overcome the sufferings described. In Ipuwer, the scene of the reversal of the social classes is repeatedly described, an example of which is repeated below:[387]

> See now, the transformations of people,
> He who did not build a hut is an owner of coffers.
> See the judges of the land are driven from the land,
> \<The nobles\> are expelled from the royal (10) mansions.
> See, noble ladies are on boards,
> Princes in the workhouse,
> He who did not sleep on a box owns a bed.   (cf. Eccl. 10:5-7)

Against this background of anarchy, Ipuwer advises his listeners to enjoy their meal as their god so allows (see a. above). The extreme extent of the national chaos is pictured in the cry of young children who are seeking death as a means of escaping the misery of their sufferings:

---

385 Fox writes, "When Qohelet's frustration at human helplessness peaks, he advises pleasure. It is almost a counsel of despair" (1989, 75).

386 *AEL* 1, 150.

387 *AEL* 1, 156.

Lo, great and small <say>, "I wish I were dead,"

Little children say, "He should not have made me live!" [388]

There is a similar yearning for a respite in Eccl. 4:2-3 (cf. 6:1-6):

So I praised the dead who already are dead more than the living who are still alive. Better than both of them is the person who has never lived, who has not seen the evil deeds that are done under the sun.

Qoheleth's call to "eat, drink, and be happy" often emerges from his pessimistic musings. His message to rejoice almost always comes as a counterpoint to his unhappy contemplations of humankind's helplessness and God's deterministic action.

c. Divine Determinism and the Hidden Ways of God

In the Instructions of Ani and Amenemope the themes of divine determinism and the incomprehensible and hidden ways of god are explored explicitly, more so in the latter than in the former (cf. Eccl. 3:11; 7:13-14; 8:16-17). In Egyptian Instructional texts, the reversal of fortune is often attributed to the work of the gods. In Amenemope the theme is developed from "action and success… towards contemplation and endurance" to make the point that listeners ought to embrace the disciplines of self-control, quietness, kindness, and humility before their god.[389]

Man does not have a single way,
The lord of life confounds him.
                    The Instruction of Ani[390]

There is no ignoring Fate and Destiny;
                    The Instruction of Amenemope 7/11[391]

Don't tease a man who is in the hand of the god,
Nor be angry with him for his failings.
Man is clay and straw,
The god is his builder.
He tears down, he builds up daily,

---

388 Ibid., 153.
389 *AEL* 2, 146.
390 Ibid., 142.
391 Ibid., 152.

He makes a thousand poor by his will,
He makes a thousand men into chief,
When he is in his hour of life.

The Instruction of Amenemope 24/11-17[392]

In the Late Period texts of Ankhsheshonq and Papyrus Insinger, the reversal of fortune between the wise and the fool (cf. Ani's rich and poor), which confounds man's understanding, is similarly attributed to the works of fate and fortune which are sent by god and are part of the divine order.[393] However, Lichtheim observes that in these demotic compositions, the authors show a more sophisticated interest in the moral order of the world as evidenced in their more thoughtful reflections on the cause-and-effect relationship between the activities of human beings and the world.[394] Lichtheim notes that, in Ankhsheshonq, a new interpretation is given to the concept of the "undeserved and unpredictable" reversal of human fortune, which is no longer seen as a result of a man's character and reason but rather is attributed to divine intervention.[395] In Insinger, this concept of fate is further "elaborated and systematized".[396] More importantly, the concept of fate (*shay*) is further developed to stand for "an unpredictable course of life governed by change".[397]

There is imprisonment for giving life.
There is release for killing.
There is he who saves yet does not find profit.
All are in the hand of the fate from the god.

Ankhsheshonq 26/5-8[398]

---

392 Ibid., 160.
393 *AEL* 3, 185. This theological explanation is missing in Ipuwer. Zimmerli observes that there is, in Insinger 35 (13), a reference to itself as a "royal book" (1962, 151). This is not noted in Lichtheim's translation (*AEL* 3, 213).
394 Lichtheim 1979, 294.
395 Ibid., 295.
396 Lichtheim describes the three lessons on fate as found in Insinger's paradoxical sayings as: (1) fate may be a result of man's own good character and reason, (2) fate is an unpredictable and constant master of human affairs, and (3) fate may favour the foolish or evil man (1979, 295-6).
397 Ibid., 296.
398 *AEL* 3, 179; Lichtheim (1979, 295).

There is one who does not know, yet fate gives (him) wealth.
        7/14[399]   (cf. Eccl. 2:18-21)

The fate and the [fortune] that come, it is the god who sends them.
        7/19[400]   (cf. Eccl. 2:26)

He lets the destiny of those on earth be hidden from them so as to be
unknown.
He lets the food of the servant be different from that of the master.
He lets a woman of the royal harem have another husband.
He lets the stranger who has come from outside live like the citizen.
There is no fellowman who knows the fortune that is before him. [401]
There is he who follows his counsel, yet he finds a slaying in it.
There is the wrong which the fool commits, yet he has success with it.
        32/18-24[402]

Fortune, blessing, and power are by his (the god's) command.
        The Ninth and Twenty-Fourth Instruction of
        Papyrus Insinger[403] 34/18[404]

Interestingly, Lichtheim points out that in addition to a similarity
of themes, some of the paradoxical sayings of Insinger share a
similar syntax with the sayings of *Qoheleth* (i.e. those with a
thesis/antithesis construction, e.g. Eccl. 7:15).[405] Although both
works dwell on the themes of injustice and disorder, Qoheleth's
perspective is significantly different to that of Insinger.
Qoheleth's philosophical arguments are far more sophisticated
and nuanced and go beyond Insinger's plain observations of the
unpredictability of the reversal of the right moral order, in terms
of the way Qoheleth leads his readers to see how humanity can
best deal with life's vanities and absurdities. More will be said of
this in Chapter 4.

---

399 *AEL* 3, 191; Lichtheim (1979, 296).
400 *AEL* 3, 191.
401 Cf. Eccl. 8:17; 9:1
402 *AEL* 3, 211.
403 *AEL* 3, 191, 209-11.
404 *AEL* 3, 211.
405 Lichtheim 1979, 301.

C. Summary

There appears to be a number of observable similarities between *Qoheleth* and the Egyptian Royal Instructions. These include the parallel use of a fictional royal ascription and a framework, and the presence of aphorisms and gnomic sayings in an predominantly autobiographical styled narration. A number of parallel themes were noted also between the works, such as the complaint of social upheavals and disorder, divine determinism, and Qoheleth's favoured *carpe diem* admonition. These thematic parallels could be due to Qoheleth's access to a stock of common wisdom sayings circulating within the various wisdom traditions of the Near East. Finally, Qoheleth's more reflective style of narration is not shared by the Instructions although Egyptologists have observed that in Amenemope, whose predominant style, in contrast to the other Instructions, is one of contemplation, there is an unusual quality of "inwardness".

VII. Pessimistic Reflective Discourses

A. Royal Laments

Scholars have previously pointed out the thematic similarities between *Qoheleth* and the Egyptian corpus of "reflective discourse". This genre is sometimes referred to as the "Lament".[406] The texts under this genre are often found to express grievance over the evil condition that the country has fallen into, hence are often pessimistic in tone. Though adopting real historical settings and royal associations in some cases, these texts are, like the Instruction, ultimately fictional literary creations. The descriptions of national distress and social calamity are commonly understood to reflect the author's particular choice of literary *topos* rather than a particular historical reality. This is because the descriptions of national chaos are often too vague and rhetorical to suggest seriously that the author is actually observing and experiencing the situation

---

406 Lichtheim (1996); Parkinson (1996, 305).

described in the text. Moreover, Egyptologists note that the historical contexts and period portrayed in the Laments, which are placed roughly in the period of the Eleventh to the Twelfth Dynasties, were not particular periods of national chaos.[407] Thus the themes of social distress and chaos in works such as the Prophecies of Neferti and Complaints of Khakheperresonb were made up in order that the kings may in the end be seen to be successful and triumphant.[408] The oratorical style of the Laments, which often reflect the form of a personal discourse or a dialogue, holds a clear similarity with *Qoheleth*. Lichtheim points out that this style of discourse, especially the dialogue with the heart, eventually evolved to a form which was subsequently used in early Egyptian autobiographical tomb inscriptions.[409] Another interesting characteristic of the reflective texts is their mixed use of genres and composite nature.[410] In the Complaints of Khakheperresonb, for example, there is a mixed use of metaphors and rhetoric, whilst in Ipuwer there is extreme hyperbole and a "fictional mythologic-messianic", and in Neferti there is the use of the pseudo-prophetic form.[411]   Like the Laments, *Qoheleth* may be argued to contain a "mixed" use of forms, namely, the autobiographical narration and didactic

---

407 *AEL* 1, 134-5. Similarly with The Admonitions of Ipuwer, whose description of chaos, scholars point out, is inherently contradictory (ibid., 150). Some specialists are of the opinion that the allusion to social disorder and national distress, though described in a general manner in most cases, could refer to specific periods of ancient Egypt's history, namely the "intermediate periods", rather than to any contemporary situation. During the intermediate periods, Egypt's institution of kingship was known to have suffered the loss of power, authority, and prestige and was significantly made weaker through civil wars, divided kingship, and climatic disasters. Some scholars posit that episodes from these difficult periods were treated discreetly by later and perhaps sectarian scribes in their recording of their own version of history in contrast to official texts and records which described the ideals of society. Hence to some, the Egyptian wisdom literature was revealing the historical reality while the major classical works looked to mask it – this is a possibility since dissent within society and in relation to the king is not a subject that is often shown in public.

408 Lichtheim argues that *Nerferti* was probably written by loyalists who were keen to depict the king as the guardian of order and justice despite the troubles that beset the nation (*AEL* 2, 134).

409 Lichtheim (1988); also (1996, 253-5).

410 Parkinson 2002, 226-32.

411 *AEL* 1, 149-50.

instruction. I shall now turn to examine The Complaints of Khakheperresonb for any possible similarity with *Qoheleth*. This particular text is the most relevant for comparison as its narrator, who is a sage, carries in his name the prenomen of a king.[412]

Khakheperresonb and the Theme of Social Disorder

The theme of social disorder, which is present in nearly all the Egyptian reflective texts, is found also in both Khakheperresonb and *Qoheleth*. In the Egyptian Reflective Discourses there is often the airing of grievances against the socio-political changes and upheavals of the time. In Khakheperresonb, the author is seen to lament over the observed injustices in the market square and bribery in the establishments, as well as the reversal of the fortunes of the social classes, all of which echo Qoheleth's own distress over the social disorder which he too observes (e.g. 3:16-18; 4:1-3; 5:7-8; 8:11-17). The reflective style of Khakheperresonb, which is written as an internal dialogue between the author and his heart, finds another parallel with *Qoheleth*. The pessimistic sentiments expressed in the Egyptian writer's observations of social disorder, which are described in general terms, further matches Qoheleth's negative mood. Like Khakheperresob, Qoheleth similarly does not reveal the specific historical details of the distress described. The following is a passage from Khakheperresonb:[413]

> (10) I meditate on what has happened,
> The events that occur throughout the land:
> Changes take place, it is not like last year,
> One year is more irksome than the other.
> The land breaks up, is destroyed,
> Becomes [a wasteland].
> Order is cast out,
> Chaos is in the council hall;
>
> I cry out about it,
> My limbs are weighed down,
> I grieve in my heart.

---

412 Ibid., 145.
413 *AEL* 1, 147-8.

Come, my heart, I speak to you,
Answer me my sayings!
Unravel for me what goes on in the land,
Why those who shone are overthrown.   )   cf. e.g. Eccl. 10:6-7
I meditate on what has happened:
While trouble entered in today,
And turmoil will not cease tomorrow,
Everyone is mute about it.
The whole land is in great distress,   )
Nobody is free from crime;   )
Hearts are greedy.   )   cf. Eccl. 5:7b, 8(?), 9
He who gave orders takes orders,   )   [ET 5:8b, 9, 10]
And the hearts of both submit.   )
None is wise enough to know it,   )   cf. Eccl. 8:1, 17

B. Summary

The similarities between *Qoheleth* and the Egyptian Laments lie mainly in their pessimistic reflective style of writing and their reflections on the theme of social chaos. The Egyptian Laments, however, lack the structural similarity that the Instructions broadly share with the Hebrew work. Further, the Laments do not generally hold collections of gnomic sayings.

VIII. Concluding Remarks

The chapter began with the examination of West Semitic and Assyrian royal inscriptions and their formulaic self-introductions and pattern of royal boasting and found that these bore remarkable syntactical and thematic similarities to Qoheleth's self-representation and boast of achievements in 1:12-2:26. Undoubtedly Qoheleth would have been aware of these ancient royal inscriptions and consequently their literary characteristics. The investigations above suggest that Qoheleth is likely to have imitated the forms and styles of these royal Semitic inscriptions in order to be identified with them and to add authenticity to his royal guise. Our comparative study also confirms that Qoheleth's use of הָיִיתִי to describe his kingship in his opening self-introduction should be understood as referring to an existing rule rather than a past fact. This conclusion is based on the observation of a similar use of the perfective verb, in the West Semitic royal texts, to indicate a ruler's ongoing reign. That Qoheleth did adopt the style and literary conventions of ancient Semitic royal inscriptions for his own composition is possible and this would further suggest that the common formula used in the writing of the ancient royal texts were current and circulating throughout the ancient Near East, and that the kings, of whose inscriptions we have knowledge, as well as the author of *Qoheleth*, all drew upon these in different ways and for different compositional purpose.

Longman's claim of a structural similarity between *Qoheleth* and his newly created genre of "fictional Akkadian autobiography" was found, on closer examination, to be unconvincing as was his analysis of the Hebrew and Akkadian texts which had problems of inaccuracy. *Qoheleth*, however, was instead found to have very close thematic parallels with the Akkadian corpus of "historical-literary" texts known also as the "pseudo-autobiographies" of the kings of Akkad. Seven out of the total eight distinguishing characteristics of this corpus, which Lewis drew for the pseudo-autobiographies, were found to closely match *Qoheleth*. The most significant parallel observed between *Qoheleth* and this corpus is the autobiographical style of composition where the narrator-king is found sharing his observations and personal experience of events and incidences (which are significant and often negative) with his listeners. Admonitions and exhortations to learn from his success and mistakes are given at the end of the texts. It was particularly helpful to see how the Akkadian royal pseudo-autobiographies often describe the errors and the weaknesses of the king, turning them into lessons for the benefit of future rulers and possibly to a wider audience as well. Assyriologists have also pointed out that the pseudo-autobiographies were likely created as models of instruction for future kings through the description of the past actions and decisions of the kings. Unlike the "official" and "non-fictional" royal inscriptions which were written to celebrate the king's achievements in public, these fictional royal compositions were likely to have been written to instruct future kings and perhaps were even created to entertain the common people with stories written in the memory of famous heroes of the past. They were composed with a pedagogical aim and were often based on the legendary lives of famous kings. Further, these fictional compositions are known to imitate the literary styles and stereotypical features of official royal inscriptions, in a manner similar to *Qoheleth*'s adoption of the style and literary conventions of ancient royal inscriptions. The above investigation into this Akkadian corpus and its characteristic features has not only supported my argument for a coherent and sustained reading of the royal voice in *Qoheleth*, but has also raised the possibility of the use of a Solomonic persona for his literary purpose and has presented his message in the form of a royal discourse, similar to the Akkadian genre of royal pseudo-autobiography.

Overall, the above analysis of comparable ancient texts has been helpful in demonstrating that it is possible to see the royal fiction in *Qoheleth* as being pervasive and integral to the entire narrative and that it is further possible to appreciate *Qoheleth* as a self-contained literary work of royal fiction when viewed against the background of ancient Near Eastern literature.[414] *Qoheleth* also appears to bear a close similarity to the Akkadian corpus of pseudo-autobiography, not least in the pessimistic character of its narrator-king.

---

414 Similarly von Rad 1972, 227.

Chapter 4

Qoheleth as Royal Autobiography

At this point of our study, it appears that there are good grounds
to continue with the argument for a pervasive royal voice in
Qoheleth, as first supported by the investigation into the allegedly
"anti-royal" passages and, subsequently, from the analysis of
comparable ancient Near Eastern texts and compositions. So far
in our study, a variety of descriptions for the royal material in
Qoheleth have been used. From the ancient Near Eastern materials analysed in Chapter 3, we had "fictional auto-biography",
"pseudo-autobiography", "testament", "instruction", "pessimistic reflective discourse", and "lament"; when talking of the royal
voice, Chapter 2 used "guise" and "persona". My suggestion is
that a more precise and instructive term to describe *Qoheleth* is
"royal autobiography". In this final chapter, I shall argue that the
autobiographical narrative is the predominant style in the work
and that it pervades the entire composition and helps to give it
unity. I shall investigate the function of the wisdom sayings and
their relationship to Qoheleth's I-narration, to see if their
presence does pose a challenge to the unity and cohe-rence of the
work. I shall also discuss the style and dynamics of Qoheleth's
discourse and will argue that a careful identification of his
peculiar manner of thought can help explain the contra-dictions
and inconsistencies traditionally found in the book as well as
provide a key to understanding his message and relationship
with wisdom tradition.

I. Autobiography as a Wisdom Form

The "autobiographical narrative" is a well-recognized literary
form that is commonly used in biblical wisdom literature. Also

described as "confession" and "I-narration", it is found in all the biblical wisdom books and is distinguished by their first-person narration and the author's use of phrases such as "I saw", "I have seen", "I considered", and expressions which reflect his dialogue with himself (e.g. "I said to my heart"). The I-narration is a popular and main wisdom form which aims to show that the lessons taught are rooted in the personal observations and perception of the teacher, and that the words spoken are borne out of his own experience.[415]

In the book of *Job*, the autobiographical narrative is most notably seen in Chapters 29 to 31, where Job delivers an extended confession on his own. Ample examples of this literary form may also be found in the dialogue sections of the book, for example, in Eliphaz's accusation of Job that his misfortune is a result of his own sin and folly, which Eliphaz supports with his own observation of the doctrine of natural retribution:

> As I have observed, those who plough evil and those who sow trouble reap it.   *Job* 4:8

> I myself have seen a fool taking root, but suddenly his house was cursed...   *Job* 5:3

In the book of Proverbs, in 24:30-34, the lesson on how the lazy reaps poverty (vv.33-4) comes out of the context of the teacher's own observation of the undesirable state of the lazy and foolish men's estates:

> I passed by the field of a lazy man and by the vineyard of a foolish man. Thorns had come up everywhere, the ground was covered with weeds, and the stone wall was in ruins. I applied my heart to what I observed and learned a lesson from what I saw: A little sleep, a little slumber, a little folding of the hands to rest, and poverty will come on you like a bandit and scarcity like an armed man.

---

415 The autobiographical narrative is also used in the apocryphal wisdom books of Ben Sira and Wisdom of Solomon. The prologue of Ben Sira contains a personal testimony of the author, in which his identity and the description of his personal involvement in the collection and writing up of the wisdom contained in the book are spoken of, which are reiterated in the epilogue (50:27). The author's personal involvement in the attaining of wisdom is also repeatedly mentioned throughout the work, e.g. 39:12, 32, and the autobiographical poem of 51:13-30 found near the end of 11QPsalms[a] (also known as 11Q5) columns XXI-XXII. In Wisdom, the writer uses reflective poems and a confessional style of narration to instruct his listeners in the way and truths of wisdom.

The autobiographical narrative, which is commonly used for moral instruction, is also found in the wisdom psalms – which often speak of the actions and destiny of the righteous and wicked – where the lessons are typically set in the context of the psalmist's own experience and observation. For example, in Ps. 37:35-6, the psalmist speaks of his personal observation of the destiny of the wicked:

> I have seen a wicked and ruthless man flourishing like a green tree in its native soil, but he soon passed away and was no more; though I looked for him, he could not be found.

A few verses before (vv.25-6), he speaks, albeit hyperbolically, of his general experience and observation of the blessing of the righteous and their family:

> I was young and now I am old, yet I have never seen the righteous forsaken or their children begging bread. They are always generous and lend freely; their children will be blessed.

The autobiographical narrative, as used in wisdom compositions, is commonly recognized as a literary form with an inherently persuasive quality. As von Rad describes it, its confessional style "enlivens" the presentation of the teaching thereby enhancing the effectiveness of the instruction.[416] Von Rad further explains that the autobiographical narrative creates the impression that the teacher is imparting his personal experience whilst also "making himself personally responsible for the perception which is presented" both of which helps to enhance the validity of the truth taught.[417] This literary form is also widely used in ancient Near Eastern wisdom literature, particularly, in texts which are purportedly authored by king or beings of high authority. It has been said that the autobiographical style of wisdom composition originated from Egypt,[418] and is most closely associated with the genre of Egyptian Instructions.[419]

Many commentators recognize the use of the autobiographical narrative in *Qoheleth* and see it as integrally linked to the royal guise which together are said to be limited to

---

416 von Rad [1972, 38]; "um den Unterricht zu beleben" (1970, 56).
417 Ibid.
418 Crenshaw 1974, 256.
419 Lichtheim 1988.

Qoheleth's introductory passage of 1:12-2:26.[420] As I have argued in the earlier two chapters of this study, there appear to be good grounds for recognizing the pervasiveness of Qoheleth's royal voice in the main body of work, both from my comparative analysis of ancient Near Eastern wisdom literature, and from my arguments against the suggestion of the presence of "anti-royal" passages in the work. In contrast to the ancient literary compositions examined in Chapter 3, *Qoheleth* gives a further impression that the author's genuine experience is being spoken of, and that the work appears to reflect a genuine autobiography, rather than a formulaic work which is composed according to clear literary conventions. *Qoheleth* exudes a personal mood and exhibits a peculiar and individualistic style of narration. Furthermore, compared to some of the ancient compositions (e.g. Egyptian Instructions) Qoheleth's narrative shows more coherence and unity. Loretz, however, has vehemently rejected the possibility that the work might be in any way a genuine confession and Qoheleth's personality historical.[421] He further rejects any attempt to understand the personality of the author. Loretz argues that the entire composition is purely a work of literary fiction and that the author was merely using a well known literary form to deliver his message to great effect. According to Loretz, there is no genuine impression of the author to be found in the work. Loretz is clearly reacting in an extreme postmodern mode with his denial of the possible presence of a genuine personality in the work.

In contrast to Loretz, Höffken has argued for a genuine autobiographical voice in *Qoheleth*. Höffken contends that there are two separate "egos" ("I"s) present in the narrative.[422] The first is the "completely nonfictive I" (*ein völlig unfiktives Ego*) which belongs to the author who, in the text, is critically reflecting and comparing his own experience with the teachings of the wisdom tradition.[423] His presence is clearly detected in those passages which describe the narrator's personal

---

420 Crenshaw (1987, 30); Seow (1997, 48); Brown (2000, 7-8).
421 Loretz 1963.
422 Höffken 1985, 125-6.
423 Ibid., 125.

observations and experience and which are marked by phrases such as "I saw" and "I thought/said". The second "I", for Höffken, is the "fictive I" which is the Solomonic persona behind whom the author is hiding his own personality. Höffken argues that the Solomonic guise is used because it is indispensable for any wisdom composition in view of Solomon's "good reputation" in Israel's wisdom tradition. Furthermore, the Solomonic persona is necessary for a critical work such as *Qoheleth*, as it affords the sage a safe place from which he can challenge traditional wisdom. Like many commentators, Höffken argues that the use of the Solomonic persona is only temporary and limited to 1:12-2:11. Höffken also contends that the Solomonic fiction in *Qoheleth* is radically against the Solomonic tradition of wisdom since, unlike Israel's wisest king who praised wisdom and was able to receive knowledge through prayer, Qoheleth rejects wisdom's benefits and contends that wisdom and knowledge are both unattainable.[424]

Höffken, in his argument for the two kinds of I's in the text, recognizes that there is a genuine revelation of the author's self in the work as is most clearly observable in Qoheleth's description of his personal experience and observations (which, Höffken argues, only appear after the fictitious Solomonic introduction of 1:12-2:11). Höffken's dichotomy of the fictive and nonfictive "I", along the lines commonly suggested (that is, at the 2:11 or 2:26 mark), is, however, unpersuasive in view of my earlier arguments that the royal voice may indeed be heard in a consistent manner throughout the work. Furthermore, I do not agree with Höffken's view that the work is subversive and anti-royal and that Qoheleth is radically against traditional wisdom in his testing of wisdom's validity and worth. I shall say more about this latter issue in my concluding chapter.

Höffken's description of the author's self-expression in terms of the two "egos" is also unconvincing as is his suggestion of a strict dichotomy of the fictive and nonfictive "I" in *Qoheleth* along commonly argued lines. This latter argument of Höffken's is clearly too simplistic as it ignores the complex nature of an

---

424 Ibid., 127.

author's self-expression in an autobiographically styled work.[425] Höffken does not explain whether the boundaries between his suggested "I"s are strictly maintained or whether they might be crossed during the autobiographical act of writing; whether there might be further versions and combinations of the author's self in the work than the two that he suggests; and whether the "nonfictive I" could also be a fictive altered ego. In contrast to Höffken's thesis I would argue instead that the author, as Qoheleth, takes on the royal persona of Solomon as a channel with which to share his personal experience (whether real or imaginary) which clearly pervades his narrative. Thus, where Qoheleth is writing from his personal experience it is not to be distinguished from the royal persona. Höffken's error lies in trying to separate the two (if not more) "personalities" in the work which are inseparable. Thus, to modify Höffken's argument, I suggest that the character of Qoheleth in the work represents a mixture of the Solomonic persona and the natural self of the author (which includes both his "true" and "fictive" self); how much or how little, and when or where these portions are at work in the text cannot be determined and is beyond the scope of this study to pursue further.

II. The Autobiographical Character of *Qoheleth*

As has been seen in Chapter 3, the striking similarities between *Qoheleth* and the Akkadian pseudo-autobiographies provide good grounds for describing the Hebrew composition as royal autobiography. However, there is clearly more to Qoheleth's narrative which would support this literary description than that which has been derived from my previous comparative study. In particular, *Qoheleth* appears to hold certain literary features which are characteristic of genuine autobiographies. I shall examine, in the coming sections of this chapter, a few of these

---

425 Literary critics of the autobiography genre continue to discuss and debate over the issue of the truth and fictive nature of the self in an autobiographical narrative with majority agreeing that there are possibly multiple egos to be found in any autobiography, and that these may be "fictional" (yet also "true") to any degree. See e.g. Pascal (1960, 16); Starobinski (1971, 287); Eakin (1985, 3).

key features of autobiography, which include the basic element of Qoheleth's I-narration, the personal and revelatory nature of his discourse, and the presence of a coherent personality behind his peculiar yet consistent style of narration.

An "autobiography", by definition and to go by the elements of the compound word, is an account of an individual's life (*bios*) written (*graphein*) by the individual himself (*autos*).[426] Although *Qoheleth* is notorious for not disclosing any clear historical information about its anonymous author, it may still be said that readers are able to capture some aspect of Qoheleth's personality from his narrative which expresses vividly his intellectual and emotional struggles with wisdom in his experiment and quest for the meaning of life. Although there is hardly any biographical details of Qoheleth to be found in the book, it is still possible to deduce some aspect of his theology and psyche from the content, style, and delivery of his narrative[427]; thus many have been able to say that, at the end of the work, they have met with the narrator.

The autobiographical nature of *Qoheleth* is in fact well recognized by scholars even if they do not use the term "autobiography" to describe it. Braun, for example, admits to the very individualistic nature of Qoheleth's pondering, whilst Fox has argued that there is a unity to the book which comes from sensing "the constant presence of a single brooding consciousness".[428] Many commentators today readily speak of the "personality" behind the work and the "sensing" of the spirit of Qoheleth between the pages. Hengel, for example, writes, "even if we have no more external data about his person... one can still

---

426 Although "autobiography" is a Greek term, literary critics of the genre generally regard Augustine's *Confessions* as marking the beginning of the genre. See further discussion on pp. 154-156. It is presumably possible that Qoheleth may have known about the emergent genre (if we are to accept a fourth to third century date for the book) but it is more likely that his style of writing did not yet have a name.

427 Modern literary critics generally see the particular "style" which an author adopts for his or her autobiographical work as a natural part of the author's autobiographical act of self-description, giving insight to readers of the author's character and therefore it is to be valued as a constituent of autobiographical content. See Starobinski (1971, 285); Eakin (1985, 23).

428 Braun (1973, 170); Fox (1989, 159).

speak of a marked 'individuality' of authorship".[429] As early as the turn of the nineteenth century, Bishop Lowth in his comment on the autobiographical trait of *Qoheleth*, noted that the style of the work was "singular" even though the language appeared "frequently loose, unconnected and approaching to the incorrectness of conversation".[430] Whybray similarly observes that one of the most remarkable features of the book is its strongly personal tone and that it "has a unity of thought and expressions which marks it out... as the highly individualistic work of a single mind".[431] Whybray further argues that Qoheleth "fills his work with claims that he has made his own personal assessment of the state of the world" and that "these claims are made so frequently in the book that they may be seen as a *leimotif*".[432] Many scholars of *Qoheleth* today readily admit to an awareness of "the man behind the book" and have used the perceived unity of the author Qoheleth to argue for the integrity and unity of the composition.[433] This is in clear contrast to earlier interpreters who saw the work as self-contradictory and containing inconsistent viewpoints, which many went on to solve through attributing the problematic passages to the hands of external interpolators or Qoheleth's dialogue partners or simply through tricky methods of exegesis.[434] Other modern scholars who admit to the autobiographical "feel" of the book include Lauha, who contends that although the book has no logical plan it nevertheless expresses a unity of style and thought and that the observations which Qoheleth makes are derived from his "real and painful

---

429 Hengel (1974, 116).
430 Lowth 1815, 342-3. Others who note the individuality in the work include Whybray (1989, 35-40), Braun (1973, 170), and Gordis who went as far as to write a chapter on the personality of "the man Qoheleth", speculating on his personal details, such as his bachelorhood, success in academia, and his financial security (1968, 75-88).
431 Whybray 1974, 67.
432 Ibid., 239-40.
433 Even Wildeboer, writing at the end of the 19th century, remarked, "Unser Buch ist keine logisch fortschreitende philosophische Abhandlung... Es bildet ein Ganzes, aber die Einheit liegt hinter den Ausführungen im Geiste des Schreibers" (1898, 111).
434 See discussion on the early interpretations of *Qoheleth* in Chapter 1.

life".[435] Brown makes a similar comment, "As I read Ecclesiastes, I am struck by the book's intensely personal style, subtle argumentation, and prescriptive power, despite what appears to be a rambling and circuitous manner of presentation... filled with personal experiences and lessons, the book comes as the distillation of an investigative journal, the notebook of a resigned cynic."[436]

The main reason behind my suggestion for viewing *Qoheleth* as an autobiography is the observation that the first-person narration pervades the book and that there appears to be a coherent personality behind the work who is recounting an aspect of his personal life to his readers, and using his personal observations and experience to impart some sort of instruction. Like a genuine autobiography, there is an observable consistency to Qoheleth's revealed personality in the work. There are also other literary elements present in *Qoheleth* which give the work the character of an autobiography. These features, which literary critics of autobiography also see as characterizing the genre, include the author's retrospective assessment of his life and personality,[437] the presence of a coherent story which expresses a

---

435 "Obgleich man seinen Ich-Reden keine autobiographischen Hinweise entnehmen kann..., sind diese Aussagen mit ihren rhetorischen Fragen dennoch nicht einfach kühle Feststellungen, sondern in ihnen stecken Beobachtungen aus wirklichem, schmerzhaftem Erleben" (1978, 9). By "autobiographical references" Lauha is probably referring to the disclosure of more specific and particular details relating to Qoheleth's own (historical) context. In an earlier article, Lauha also spoke of the coherence of the book that comes from the sensing of a personality behind the composition, "Es handelt sich darin (im Buch Qohelet) vor allem um eine strukturelle Eigenschaft der Persönlichkeit und um eine bestimmte Verhaltensweise der Religion gegenüber" (1955, 183).

436 Brown (2000, 17).

437 Starobinski 1971, 285. This phenomenon, of the multiplicity of the writer in a work, is commonly acknowledged by the literary critics of the autobiography genre as a characteristic feature of genuine autobiographies in general. However, the definition of the nature and function of the various projections of the author in autobiography is variously interpreted by the literary critics. Usually, the character version of the author is distinguished along the lines of fiction/nonfiction, and present day/younger author, or a combination of these. In fact, many interpreters of *Qoheleth* have already identified an old and present Qoheleth and a younger Qoheleth of the past who is spoken of in retrospect in the work (e.g. Gordis (1968); Fox (1993)). Whilst the notion of the doubling of the autobiographer in an autobiography and in *Qoheleth* cannot be denied, there is no need here to explore further this interesting issue.

certain consistency of relationship between the author's self and the outside world,[438] and the presence of a self-searching quest which most literary critics argue underlie all genuine auto-biographies.[439] A further characteristic of a genuine auto-biography, namely of the confessional kind, is its inherent didactic purpose.[440] I wish to argue that all these features are found in *Qoheleth* and shall discuss these key points of Qoheleth's autobiography later in this chapter.

Although my discussion here has focused on the auto-biographical trait of *Qoheleth*, I suggest that the book should be identified more precisely as a royal autobiography. As Whybray quite rightly points out, Qoheleth's royal persona, although not always expressly spoken of, is integrally connected with the "I"s in the narrative.   And as Christianson similarly argues, Qoheleth's royal voice may be said to implicitly reassert itself with every self-reference that he makes throughout his discourse.[441] Following Whybray and Christianson's arguments, it may be said that Qoheleth's royal presence may be sensed throughout the narrative, through every self-reference that he makes, which implicitly reminds readers of his royal persona. This argument is reasonable since, as was seen earlier, the arguments for the presence of "anti-royal" passages in the book are weak and inconclusive.

In defining the use of the term "autobiography" I have not unduly sought to rely on the insights of modern literary criti-cism. Besides not reaching a consensus on the definition of the genre,[442] modern critics of autobiography also carry a bias in their discussion of the genre in their belief that autobiography came into existence only with the western conceptualisation of the individual, the effable self. Literary critics of the genre hold

---

438 Pascal 1960, 5, 9.

439 Olney 1972, 30.

440 See e.g. Starobinski (1971, 288-9); Weintraub (1978, 21) for discussions on the didactic element in Augustine and Rousseau's *Confessions*.

441 Whybray (1989, 46); Christianson (1998, 147 n.61).

442 Olney, who represents the more conservative of the new literary critics, laments at the difficulty of defining the genre: "indeed, definition of autobiography as a literary genre seems to me virtually impossible, because the definition must either include so much as to be no definition, or exclude so much as to deprive us of the most relevant texts" (1972, 38-9).

that Augustine's *Confessions* marks the first in this line of literary tradition and that essentially there were none before.[443] This, coupled with their increasing focus on psychological interpretations, renders much of their discussion incompatible with my purpose of studying a text such as *Qoheleth*.

III. The Pervasive Presence of Qoheleth

A. The Prevalent "I"

As I have just noted, many commentators today subscribe to the view that there is a coherent personality to be found in *Qoheleth*, which arises from the observation of a consistent tone to the work and the repetition of particular phrases and expressions which give the impression that there is a single author behind the work. Loretz's analysis of Qoheleth's language, namely his tabulation of Qoheleth's use of words, themes, and phrases reveals some interesting results which could be used to support the argument for the unity of *Qoheleth* and a singular authorship to the book. For example, of the 2643 words used between 1:4 and 12:7, Loretz describes 562 as being the author's "favourite".[444] This translates to 21.2% of the total vocabulary in the book. Loretz's research also reveals that, apart from the first and last chapters, the proportion of Qoheleth's favourite words per chapter ranges between 14.3% to 29.1% for the chapters

---

443 See for example, Misch (1950, 3-4). Lichtheim complains against this bias and especially of the use of Augustine's *Confessions* as the starting point for the study of the history of the genre saying, "*Confessions* is a mountain of an autobiography, to be sure, and one which appears to be blocking the view into the two millennia that preceded it" (1992, 2). Although most historians of the genre do not deny that the concept of the self would have existed before Augustine's *Confessions,* they nevertheless argue that these tended to be written in a restricted and conventional way. Weintraub, for example, contends that all autobiographical writings prior to *Confessions* were written in more restricted forms such as *res gestae,* memoir, diary, which are clearly in contrast to the fifth-century work as "none opened up their souls in the inwardness of genuine autobiography" (1978, 1). I believe that my findings in *Qoheleth* clearly prove this perception wrong.

444 Loretz 1964, 179. See also ibid. p. 178 for other statistical data on Qoheleth's vocabulary.

between 2 to 11.[445] Although these findings are suggestive of the unity and integrity of the text, most scholars continue to express puzzlement over the disjointedness and the lack of flow of Qoheleth's narration and the alleged elusiveness of his character in the work. To investigate further this latter issue, I shall now carry out an examination and analysis of Qoheleth's use of self-referencing verbs as a means of determining the pervasiveness of the "I-narration" in the book.

In Hebrew, the first-person subject may be expressed in a number of forms and a variety of ways such as through the use of the first-person personal pronoun, the first-person verb, and other verbal forms which, when used in connection with first-person pronouns and verbs, give a clear indication of their subject. Since the verb in the Hebrew language stands at the core of the expression of predication, and because it has the greatest "multifunctionality" of all the word classes in Hebrew, I have chosen to focus on the verbal form for my following investigation.[446] My purpose here is to tabulate the frequency and distribution of all the self-referencing verbs found in *Qoheleth* – not just the 1cs verbs to which commentators usually refer when discussing Qoheleth's first-person discourse in 1:12-2:26, but also other verbs which clearly have Qoheleth as their referent subject.

My investigation reveals that there are a total of 92 verbs that are used to represent the self-narrating voice of Qoheleth in the book.[447] This total is made up of 78 1cs verbs and 14 non-1cs verbs which nevertheless have Qoheleth as their subject. This latter group of verbs, which are listed below, consists of (1) three infinitive absolutes (4:2; 8:9; 9:11) and three participles (2:18; 7:26; 8:12) which either follow or are followed by a first-person singular verb or the first-person independent pronoun אֲנִי, and (2) eight third-person verbs which are connected to first-person

---

445 Ibid.

446 Waltke-O'Connor 1990, 343-4.

447 1:12, 13, 14, 16 (4x), 17 (2x); 2:1, 2, 3, 4 (3x), 5 (2x), 6, 7 (2x), 8 (2x), 9 (3x), 10 (4x), 11 (3x), 12, 13, 14, 15 (3x), 17, 18 (3x), 19 (2x), 20 (2x), 24; 3:10, 12, 14, 16, 17, 18, 22; 4:1 (2x), 2, 4, 7 (2x), 15; 5:12, 17; 6:1, 3; 7:15, 23 (3x), 25, 26, 27, 28 (4x), 29; 8:9 (2x), 10, 12, 14, 15, 16, 17; 9:1, 11 (2x), 13, 16; 10:5, 7.

suffixed nouns or prepositions (e.g. לִי , יָדִי , עֵינִי , לְבִּי) where clearly Qoheleth is the subject (1:16; 2:7 (2x), 9, 10 (2x), 11; 7:28).

1:16	וְלִבִּי רָאָה
2:7	הָיָה לִי (2x)
2:9	חָכְמָתִי עָמְדָה
2:10	שָׁאֲלוּ עֵינַי and לִבִּי שָׂמֵחַ
2:11	שֶׁעָשׂוּ יָדַי
2:18	אֲנִי עָמֵל
4:2	וְשַׁבֵּחַ אֲנִי
7:26	וּמוֹצֶא אֲנִי
7:28	בִּקְשָׁה נַפְשִׁי
8:9	(רָאִיתִי) וְנָתוֹן
8:12	יוֹדֵעַ אֲנִי
9:11	(שַׁבְתִּי) וְרָאֹה

אֲנִי עָמֵל in 4:8 is excluded because it is part of a hypothetical quotation by Qoheleth and is strictly not in reference to himself.[448]

Converting the data into a chart we have the following.

Absolute frequency

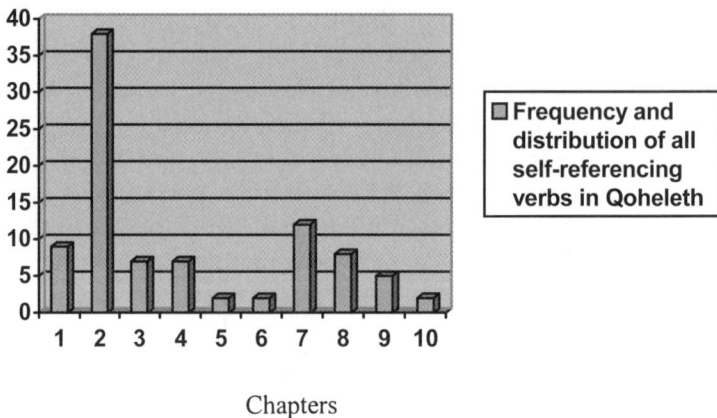

Chapters

---

448 Cf. Gordis (1968, 97).

The above diagram reveals that the self-referencing verbs are found in every chapter from the first to the tenth, but not in the eleventh and twelfth chapters.[449] Despite the fact that the chapter divisions are questionable in some cases,[450] and the lengths of the individual chapters not wholly uniform, it is still helpful to observe that the self-referencing verbs make their first appearance in 1:12 and are still found after the first two chapters of the book. They appear in every chapter from the start of Qoheleth's self-narration in 1:12 until Chapter 10 (10:7). It is also interesting to note that Chapter 10 ends with a warning against speaking ill of the king. We further observe that there is a heavy concentration of self-referencing verbs in the first four chapters of the book as well as in Chapters 7 to 9. This finding challenges those arguments which see the autobiographical narration as limited to Qoheleth's introduction or the first half of the work. It further demonstrates that the collections of sayings in Chapters 4, 7, and 10 do have portions of I-narration in them and are not completely free of the autobiography motif. This set of results is very similar to Isaksson's tabulation of the frequency and distribution of all the first-person independent pronouns in the book, with the exception that there is no occurrence of the pronoun in Chapters 6 and 10.[451] That both analyses reveal a similar pattern is not surprising in view of Qoheleth's tendency to use the 1cs independent pronoun in a pleonastic manner, that is, to accompany verbs which already have a clear first-person subject referent. In conclusion, the above analysis has helped to demonstrate and affirm the limits as well as the pervasiveness of Qoheleth's I-narration, which is being suggested in this study, in objective terms. I shall now turn to examine the nature and function of sayings in *Qoheleth* and the issue of unity.

---

449 This supports the limits to Qoheleth's narrative as described in Chapter 1, pp. 19-24.

450 E.g., the division between Eccl. 5 and 6 comes in the middle of the thematically coherent unit 5:7-6:9 [ET 5:8-6:9].

451 Isaksson 1987, 142-4.

B. The Second-Person Address and the Issue of Unity

The function of didactic sayings in the book of *Qoheleth* and their relationship to the "I-narration" portions will now be examined in order to see whether it lends support to my argument for the autobiographical character of *Qoheleth*.

A glance through *Qoheleth* would suggest that there is no observable pattern to the distribution of gnomic sayings in the book. As I have clarified in Chapter 3, Longman's argument that the didactic sayings are found exclusively in the second half of the book is incorrect. It is, however, correct to say that they are found in greater numbers towards the end of the book, namely in Chapters 5, 7, and 10. Such a description should not be taken to suggest that there is a discernible pattern to the occurrence of the sayings in the manner posited by Longman. It is also often observed that the pockets of wisdom sayings, which interrupt the flow of the autobiographical narration, appear occasionally to have no clear and direct relationship with their surrounding contexts, and in some cases even appear to contradict other parts of the narrative. In order to help us determine if Qoheleth's switching between a narrating and didactic posture is a matter of a change in narrative style (i.e. reflecting a switch in the mode of presentation), or a change in perspective (i.e. reflecting the work of a different author) I shall need to examine the purpose and use of the sayings in the book. As far as the charge that a few of the admonitions are "anti-royal" in message or sentiment is concerned (with the implication that they indicate a change in perspective, e.g. from royalty to subject) my investigation of this in Chapter 2 reveals that this is not necessarily so.

1. Qoheleth as Narrator and Teacher

The change from first-person discourse to second-person address in the book was noted early on by Gunkel who argued that the switching reflected the dual role of Qoheleth and was not to be regarded as evidence against the unity of authorship. Gunkel suggested that at the start of the work the author had preferred to express his personal opinion and experience through the use of the I-narration, but after awhile, the author fell back to the more common didactic form of wisdom instruction, and proverbial sayings were consequently spoken without having any clear connection between them.[452] It might be said that this style of instruction, into which Qoheleth regularly switches and which is intricably connected to the author's didactic role, is consistent with the purpose of the work as a wisdom composition. As Whybray writes, "That Qoheleth's purpose was an educative one is supported by stylistic considerations. Especially in the second half of the book he makes frequent use of the proverb style – that is, especially of the 'sentence' (*Aussagewort*) which succinctly describes a key aspect of life, the admonition (*Mahnwort*) which equally succinctly gives advice, and the so-called '"better"-proverb', which states what is preferable to something else."[453] Whybray adds, "It is reasonable to suppose that his purpose was to make his views known to others in order to persuade them of their truth: in other words, he was, in some sense of the word, a *teacher*, and one who wished to point out certain errors in the current beliefs and teaching of his day."[454] Kroeber likewise sees Qoheleth as taking up the mantle of a teacher in the "you-speeches" (*Du-Rede*). He makes the comment that Qoheleth's didactic role is undeniable,[455] although part of his instruction takes a different style to that of the conventional teachers of wisdom (cf. Proverbs) with the use of the I-narration (*Ich-Rede*). According to Kroeber, the use of the more personal style of I-narration merely reflects Qoheleth's realization of the limits to his understanding of wisdom, as he lets his listeners share in his observations and in his thinking as well as in the open questions with which he finds himself confronted in his intellectual struggle for the meaning of life.[456] Galling, Hengel,

---

452 *RGG¹*, 1407.

453 Ibid, 241-2.

454 Whybray 1998, 241.

455 "Zwar ist er Lehrer und will Lehrer bleiben. Sein Buch sähe anders aus, wenn er nur betrachtend für sich selbst geschrieben hätte. Es findet sich die Du-Rede, mit der er sich an einen Belehrung suchenden Hörer wendet" (1963, 35).

456 "Er fühlt sich nicht mehr als der Belehrende über den Hörenden, sondern sieht sich neben ihnen in der Solidarität des Nichtwissens und in der Preisgegebenheit an ein unberechenbares Schicksal. Das Einzige, was er tun kann, ist dies, daß er die Menschen teilnehmen läßt an den Wegen seines

and many others have similarly argued that the changing and interchanging between Qoheleth's narration and "instruction" is no barrier to accepting the unity of authorship, especially since a coherent picture of Qoheleth's personality (and his message) may still be discerned by the reader at the end of the work.[457]

Bratsiotis[458] in his comprehensive study of all the monologues in the Old Testament argues that *Qoheleth* reflects a "mixed form" monologue, where the narrator is speaking both to himself and to external readers whom his instructions are for.[459] Bratsiotis further describes Qoheleth's narrative as a "Denkspruch-Monologe" (which, he adds, is also found in the wisdom psalms), which is typically used to teach wisdom topics.[460] Hence, according to Bratsiotis's argument, there is good reason to treat the gnomic and aphoristic sayings in *Qoheleth* as belonging to the greater narrative and also to Qoheleth's purpose of investigating and testing wisdom. As Bratsiotis points out, the second-person address is not necessarily incompatible with, but may be viewed as integral to the rest of the composition and complementing the author's use of the "autobiographical monologue" as an alternative means of delivering his wisdom and instruction.

Thus, the presence of the sayings and maxims amidst Qoheleth's autobiographical narration need not be viewed as awkward, just as Qoheleth's didactic role should not be treated as incompatible with his narrating function. As the scholars

---

Denkens, an dem geistigen Ringen eines langen Lebens, und sie so teilhaben läßt an seinen letzten Erkenntnissen, die doch meist nichts anderes sein können als offene Fragen. Dieser Haltung entspricht die Ich-Rede, in der Qoheleth zugleich rückwärts schauend seinen Lebensweg betrachtet" (ibid.).

457 E.g. Hengel (1974, 1:116-7). Polk similarly writes, "one of the most conspicuous features of Ecclesiastes is its pervasive use of the first person. Where explicit first person references are absent, one finds admonitions couched in direct address, or descriptive data, often in proverbial form, which bear directly on a personal stance toward life and in which one clearly recognizes the voice of Qohelet, just as if the frequent "I have observed" were present" (1976/77, 5).

458 Bratsiotis 1961.

459 Bratsiotis suggests that there are three major forms of monologue: the exterior monologue (where the object of the speech lies outside or beyond the narrator himself), the interior monologue (where the narrator is holding the speech with himself), or a mixed form monologue (which is a combination of the other two) (ibid., 37-9).

460 Ibid., 41.

mentioned above have also noted, Qoheleth's adoption of a double role of autobiographer and wisdom instructor is not unfamiliar in wisdom compositions. His frequent changing of roles in the work should therefore not be taken as *prima facie* evidence against its unity. A more appropriate way of determining this latter issue would be to investigate more closely the nature and function of the sayings in the work, a matter to which we shall now turn.

2. The Use of Sayings in *Qoheleth*

Qoheleth's frequent shifting between his didactic and narrating positions may be ascribed to his peculiar and non-systematic way of thinking, as reflected also in his frequent weaving between themes and topics. Examples of Qoheleth's erratic pattern of thought may be observed in the introductory passage of 1:12-2:26, where we find two proverbs (1:15, 18) embedded in the first-person discourse. In 1:18, which is usually thought of as a quotation of a proverb, the presence of the causative כִּי, which demonstrates a link with the previous verse, indicates that the verse is an extraneous explanation of what has just been said. Similarly, 1:15 rounds up Qoheleth's preceding remarks on the futility of trying to discover, by wisdom, the system of moral law in the world.[461] We see this saying repeated (with the use of the same two verbs) in 7:13. In some cases, it is not difficult to discern the connection between the quoted proverb and the narrative context in which the sayings are expressed (e.g. 3:15). Qoheleth's views are sometimes conveyed in different literary forms. For example, his conviction that human beings cannot know their fate and the events of the future, which Qoheleth conveys in the form of an admonition four times in 11:5-6, is found expressed elsewhere as a plain statement (e.g. 3:11; 8:16, 17; 9:1) and a rhetorical question (e.g. 2:19; 6:12 (2x); 8:1, 7). Whilst certain individual sayings of Qoheleth may be explained in this manner, the more sustained use of the didactic forms of instruction in the book requires further investigation. To this

---

461 Whybray 1989, 50.

end, I shall now turn to look at the theories of Gordis and Whybray, and the form-critical analysis of Johnson on the nature and function of sayings in *Qoheleth*.

a. Gordis's Theory of Quotations

Gordis suggests that there are at least four main purposes behind Qoheleth's quotation of short pithy sayings, from the old wisdom tradition, in his narrative.[462] First, Qoheleth cites a proverb in order to express directly his point of view without any further explanation or comment. This is seen, for example, in 10:18, 11:1, and also 7:3, where it is used to express Qoheleth's own pessimism. Secondly, a proverb may be used, despite being irrelevant to its immediate context, for the sake of completing another proverb to which it is connected and which is used to support Qoheleth's general argument, e.g. 5:1-2 [ET vv.2-3], where the end saying ("as dreams come with many concerns, so the fool speaks with many words") is added for the sake of completeness. According to Gordis, there are ample examples of such usage in Egyptian literature (e.g. in the Admonitions of a Prophet).[463] Another example of this in *Qoheleth* is in 11:3-4. The third purpose behind Qoheleth's quoting of wisdom sayings is to enable him to offer his own comments on the subject of the sayings. Gordis points to the collection of *ṭôb* sayings in 7:1-14 as an example of where Qoheleth adds his own point of view, distinguished by his peculiar style of argument and pessimistic perspective, after quoting traditional proverbial truths. 7:2b is another example where Qoheleth offers his morbid comment on death and the living after citing a traditional proverb on the subject in 7:2a. Other examples are 8:5a ("whoever keeps his command will experience no trouble") which repeats his preceding advice to submit oneself to political authority, and 8:12b-13 ("it will be well in the end with those who revere God and fear Him and it will be far from well with the sinner, who, like a shadow, will not long endure, because he does not fear

---

462 Gordis (1949). See also (1939).
463 Gordis 1968, 101.

God") which, as Gordis argues, is a quotation of a traditional view on divine justice with which Qoheleth disagrees in the surrounding sustained commentary in vv.11-14. Another example of this usage is found in 9:4 ("He who is attached to the living still has hope, for a live dog is better than a dead lion"), which is a traditional proverb that affirms the value of life. Qoheleth uses this proverb cynically to counterbalance his own argument about the futility of living in vv.5-6. Gordis points out that this manner of use is not unique to *Qoheleth* but is also evidenced in other ancient Near Eastern texts such as the Babylonian Koheleth (ll. 69-71, 215f.) where a proverb is sometimes quoted for the purpose of refuting or discussing the topic further.[464] The fourth purpose behind Qoheleth's quotation of proverbs is for emphasizing the multifaceted nature of truth. This usage is also evidenced in other biblical wisdom books (e.g. Prov. 26:4-5; Job 12:12f.), where diametrically opposite sayings may be deliberately juxtaposed next to one another in order to highlight the fact that empirical truths are often too complicated to be expressed in only one alternative. The clues for discerning which proverb reflects the views of the writer are often easy to find. In Qoheleth's case, his views and sentiments are often marked by his trademark cries of "vanity", "meaningless toil", and "the chasing after wind". Examples of this include Eccl. 4:5-6; 9:16, 18. In 4:5-6, Qoheleth shows his preference for the second pair of contrasting proverbs by adding his characteristic phrase "vanity and chasing after wind" in v.6.

Fox, however, disagrees with Gordis's theory of quotations and has expressed his unease over the inference of quotations in the absence of any clear structural markers.[465] Fox's concern is not so much over the impossibility of Gordis's suggestion as it is over the range of possible interpretations for the text should this theory be sanctioned. Fox argues, for example, that 8:11-12a and v.14 (cf. 8:12b-13 which Gordis sees as the quoted views of others) could just as well belong to a pupil of Qoheleth whose idea the narrator is quoting to reject.[466] I do not see Fox's concern

---

464 Ibid., 105-6.
465 Fox 1989, 26-8.
466 Ibid., 26-27.

as a serious challenge to Gordis's theory of quotations. The only concern with Gordis's argument, as I see it, is where a particular clause or verse, which purports to be a quotation, might be ambiguous. Thus, for example, it might be said that Gordis's interpretation of 7:3 as a quotation of a proverb is arguable as the phrase could also belong to Qoheleth, though spoken or thought of in the form of a quotation.[467] However, Gordis does admit to the ambiguous nature of some of these verses and is careful to describe the purported quotations as "virtual". Furthermore, Gordis does not deny that all the suggested quotations could be original epigrams of Qoheleth as well. Thus he makes the comment that the collection of sayings from 10:2 to 11:6 could all be either original proverbs of Qoheleth or traditional proverbs which he cites to support his own view and sentiment. Gordis's theory of quotations, in my view, provides a viable answer to the question of contradictions and a more suitable alternative to the theory of massive interpolation and gloss. The persuasiveness of Gordis's theory of quotations lies partly in the general observation that many verses do have a ring of conventional or proverbial wisdom in them.[468] Gordis, however, does also recognize that his theory is difficult to verify as there is no way by which the genuineness of the purported quotations may be determined.

Building on Gordis's theory, Whybray has gone on to compare the purported proverbs in *Qoheleth* with the "older" sayings in Prov. 10-19, and, on the basis of form, content, and language, Whybray has identified what he believes are eight "traditional" wisdom sayings in the work.[469] After analysing the function of the sayings in relation to their surrounding context, Whybray concludes that the sayings are used in one of two ways. First, some sayings are quoted to express or support

---

467 For a book which is notoriously enigmatic and ambiguous in many areas, all theories of interpretation for *Qoheleth* can begin only on a set of presuppositions which can rely, for their strength, only on the reasonableness of their assumptions. In comparison with Gordis's theory of quotations, Fox's argument for a single authorship to the book (i.e. from 1:2-12:14) is even more speculative. Furthermore, Fox's thesis requires the "intuitive sensing" of the presence of the "frame-narrator" in the text (1977).

468 Similarly Murphy 1992, xxxiv.

469 Whybray 1981.

Qoheleth's view on a particular matter. These sayings may be quoted with or without further comments or elucidation from Qoheleth. For example, in 10:3 and v.13 Qoheleth affirms, with his comments, the sayings presented earlier in verses 2 and 12. In the case of 7:5-6, both sayings are likely to be traditional proverbs which he cites and with which he agrees – as evidenced by the "vanity" judgment following the sayings. Secondly, the sayings are also used to prove the relative nature of certain truths (e.g. on wisdom and folly, the wise man and the fool, the meaning of toil, e.g. 2:14a; 4:5-6; 9:17). Whybray, however, contends that Qoheleth never cites traditional wisdom in order to contradict or refute it completely. Whybray notes further that whenever a saying presents the two ways of living – that of the wise man and the fool – Qoheleth's comment, where it is added, always refers only to the fool.[470] Qoheleth also seems to prefer using older wisdom to support his arguments and sentiments where it relates to the frustrating effects of folly in the world. Whybray writes:[471]

> Qoheleth valued these older sayings, then, not because they teach, by contrasting two modes of conduct, that one can be happy if one wishes by choosing wise conduct rather than foolish, but because they offer evidence congenial to his own view, that the world is at least as full of fools as it is of wise men. *"This"*, he says, *"is vanity"*. In other words, Qoheleth has completely reinterpreted the wise-foolish contrast of the older sayings, seeing in them a meaning quite different from that which we are accustomed to see in them. For him they express not an optimistic teaching but a pessimistic one: the presence of folly in the world is – to use his own imagery – the fly in the ointment (x 1) which makes ineffective the wisdom existing in the world, which if only it existed without the counterweight of folly would make it a good world.

Whybray argues that this peculiar tendency of Qoheleth highlights his frustration with the "predominating" and "tragic" nature of folly.[472] More will be said about Qoheleth's views on wisdom and folly later in this chapter.

Gordis and Whybray concur that the sayings in *Qoheleth* function to elucidate or qualify older or traditional wisdom, but

---

470 Ibid, 447.
471 Ibid.
472 Ibid.

never to disagree with it completely. The theory of quotations supports the argument for the coherence and integrity of Qoheleth's message and offers a tenable solution to the problem of contradictions in the book. It provides us with a better understanding of the nature of Qoheleth's relationship with tradition, namely that Qoheleth does not reject it completely, but rather, is keen to draw out its limitations to which his own experience attests. With great erudition and skill Qoheleth challenges tradition with its own forms[473] to make the point that life is more complex than what many believe tradition has made it out to be. To be sure, Qoheleth's testing and interaction with wisdom follows in the way of Israel's sages of old and is very much in keeping with wisdom tradition's own enterprise. The theory of quotations helps us see more clearly the lines of thought behind Qoheleth's discourse, revealing, in particular, his mature relationship with tradition. The presuppositions of the theory are reasonable and the persuasiveness of it is further enhanced by Gordis's argument that the suggested phenomenon is well attested in other biblical and extra-biblical literature.[474]

b. Johnson's Form-Critical Analysis

Johnson's detailed form-critical study represents a different approach to the examination of the nature and function of the sayings in *Qoheleth*. In his work, Johnson identifies two principal contexts in which the "sayings"[475] appear, and analyses the

---

473 Cf. Dell (1991, 138-47).

474 Michel (1989) offers a different version of the quotations theory which is unconvincing. Michel posits that Qoheleth first lays down his philosophy on humanity's ambitious pursuit of gain in life in 1:3-3:15. Qoheleth subsequently interacts with the opinions of others and with his own observations on this subject. Michel argues that where the material in the discourse differs from the philosophy expressed in 1:3-3:15 (which is not particularly distinctive from the rest of Qoheleth's narrative) it is to be attributed to the opinions of others, and where it resonates with the views expressed in 1:3-3:15, these differences are to be seen as occasions where Qoheleth is quoting himself (*Selbstzitate*). See also Murphy's comment (1992, xxxvi-ii).

475 By this Johnson means "a brief, one or two line utterance on a particular theme, which usually has attained (or is intended to attain) some circulation among one or more groups within a society for one or more reasons, i.e., utility, aesthetic appeal, profundity" (1973, 52). This term also covers various other

meaning and purpose of the sayings in relation to these contexts. The first group of contexts comprises first-person reports,[476] paraenesis,[477] and commentary,[478] in which Qoheleth's own comments and arguments are also to be found; the second consists of collections or series of other sayings.

Johnson concludes, from his analysis, that the sayings which are juxtaposed with first-person narrations and third-person commentaries function in one of three ways: (1) to introduce a unit of thought (4:9, 13; 6:7; 10:4; 11:7), (2) to conclude a unit of thought (1:15, 18; 4:5-6, 12b, 17b; 5:2, 6; 6:9), or (3) they are cited within a unit of thought to form part of that thought (2:14a; 3:20b; 8:5; 9:4b). The first two purposes are straightforward enough. As for the third, Johnson points out that the grammatical construction of the units of thought, in all the examples, is clear and the sayings may be seen to be linked to its immediate context either asyndetically or by the use of a conjunction. These sayings are quoted by Qoheleth either to confirm or disagree with the conclusions reached in his observations and reflections (or conversely, he uses his experience to validate or qualify the truth of a saying).[479] For example, the proverb of 3:20b which speaks of the end sum of the nature of humankind, that they are dust and will return to dust at death, complements the thought in 3:19a that human beings and animals share the same fate. As for 8:5, this is a moral sentence which not only supports the paraenesis of 8:2-4, but also confirms both the rhetorical question and saying of 8:1a and v.1b on the advantages of wisdom, namely that it gives the wise the knowledge and ability to adapt and survive in any particular situation in which they may find themselves. Similarly, Qoheleth's belief in the value of life and living in 9:4a is reasserted in the moral sentence of 9:4b. I add to these examples,

---

subgenres such as the proverb, moral sentence, paraenetic saying (i.e. admonition and exhortation), and other sayings (ibid., 64-70).

476 This refers to texts which report an observation in the form of a first-person speech (Johnson 1973, 76).

477 Johnson defines a "paraenesis" as an instruction with an accompanying reason (ibid., 52; see p. 70 for examples).

478 This refers to a discourse which is written in the third-person and which holds both conventional and sceptical thinking (ibid., 76).

479 Johnson 1973, 197, 265, 275.

2:14a, which provides an interesting situation in that the moral clause serves a dual purpose. 2:14a firstly affirms Qoheleth's initial observation in 2:13 – that the wise man is better off than the fool – but this is subsequently dismissed by Qoheleth in a moment of self-reflection in 2:14b, where he speaks of a different experience encountered which questions the truth of his first observation. Johnson's conclusion on the function of the sayings in relation to its surrounding narrative contexts are similar to that of Gordis and Whybray. All three studies agree that the sayings in *Qoheleth* bear some connection to the narrative contexts with which they are juxtaposed or in which they are embedded.

As for the lengthier clusters of sayings, Johnson distinguishes between those sayings that belong to a "collection" (i.e. where the sayings make their own individual point), and those that are part of a "series" (i.e. where the individual sayings are grouped according to a particular principle and make a single point).[480] Johnson identifies fourteen groups of "series" in *Qoheleth* and has analysed how these are organized and the relationship between the individual sayings themselves (5:9-11; 7:1-4, 5-7, 8-9, 10-12, 19-21; 8:1a-1b; 9:17-10:1; 10:2-3, 8-9, 10-11, 12-15, 16-20; 11:1-4). From his examination of the meaning, location, and function of the sayings within a series, Johnson concludes that the indivi-dual sayings are likely to be part of the original composition as they appear closely connected to each other with their shared keywords (e.g. 7:10-12), themes, and subjects (e.g. 5:9-11; 7:2-4, 19-21; 8:1-2; 10:2-3, 8-9), and they collectively form a logical argument (e.g. 7:5-7; 9:17-10:1).[481] Both these points are widely assumed by commentators.

A more important conclusion which Johnson arrives at regarding the function of the sayings in the book is that some of the series of sayings do no more than present "conventional values" and "generally accepted conclusions" (e.g. 7:8-9; 7:10-12; 7:19-21). Johnson contends that in some of the series of sayings, a clause, which he believes was probably not part of the original sayings, is added in order to make a point or to help form the

---

480 Ibid., 197-8.
481 Ibid., 265, see also 198.

series into a logical argument (e.g. 5:9b and v.10b to vv.9-11; 7:1b, 2, 3 and 4 to 7:1-4; 7:6b to vv.5-7; 9:18b and 10:1 to 9:17-10:1; 10:14b to vv.12-15).[482] These added clauses, Johnson argues, are distinguishable by their peculiar vocabulary and motifs. Thus, to continue with examples from Eccl. 7, in the passage of 7:1-4, Johnson sees verses 3 and 4 as having been added to 7:1-2 to increase the effect of the paradox created by the series of sayings with their assertion that "a sober recognition of man's existence is better than blissful ignorance". Johnson points out further that vv.1b, 2, 3, and 4 all reflect the same pessimistic mood.[483] In 7:5-7, Qoheleth's added expression of "this too is meaningless" in 7:6b challenges the universal distinction between the wise man and the fool, as reflected in the preceding verses, for even the wise man can also turn into a fool (7:7). The end saying of 7:7, which according to Johnson is another added clause to the series, distinguishes itself as Qoheleth's opinion and helps to form the series into a logical argument.[484] Johnson, like Gordis and Whybray, admits that it is impossible to determine whether these sayings belong to Qoheleth, particularly those which are found embedded in the discourse sections and appear to reflect the form and style of traditional sayings. Johnson believes that it is possible that some of Qoheleth's brief observations, particularly those which reflect the style of a saying (e.g. 4:17; 5:2, 6; 8:5), may not be originally his.[485] Johnson concludes his investigation of the series of sayings with two observations about their "pattern of arrangement". First, Johnson suggests that the series of sayings reflect Qoheleth's dialectic approach to understanding reality, holding various comparative truths about a single subject without necessarily aiming to provide a resolution to the tensions observed.[486] Secondly, the grouping together of similar sayings is to help emphasize the author's

---

482 Ibid., 199. However Johnson's interpretation of a few of the clauses are debatable, e.g. 5:9-10, which is admittedly ambiguous.

483 Ibid., 199 cf. Gordis who reads 7:4-5 as Qoheleth's commentary on the sayings.

484 Ibid., 199.

485 Ibid., 65, 199.

486 Ibid., 141.

point by means of repetition. It also reflects his deeper understanding of the topic at hand.[487]

Johnson also points out that there are places where the sayings appear to bear no relation to another neighbouring series, but upon closer look may be seen to belong to the wider group of themes and topics which Qoheleth discusses elsewhere in the book. He argues that this same lack of continuity between sayings is also evidenced in the book of Proverbs and the ancient Near Eastern didactic compositions which he discusses.[488]

Johnson's analysis enable us to draw two important conclusions about the location and function of the sayings in *Qoheleth*. First, Johnson's conclusions, based on careful form-critical analysis, support the argument that the didactic sayings in *Qoheleth* form an integral part of the larger narrative. This is unsurprising since the sayings are necessary to the purpose of Qoheleth's experiment (which is the testing of traditional wisdom). Secondly, Johnson's work confirms again that Qoheleth is not rejecting tradition but merely testing wisdom to draw out its limitations.[489] From observing his skilful use of wisdom forms in the work, there is no doubt that Qoheleth is well educated in the tradition, which he now tests and questions reusing its own forms and techniques.

Finally, it may be said that Qoheleth's use of sayings helps to characterize him as a wise man. Whybray makes the interesting observation that the random variety of sayings, even within a series of sayings, "recalls the behaviour of 'Solomon' in 1:12-2:26 when he tries one thing after another".[490] I should add that Qoheleth's expert use of gnomic and aphoristic material readily reminds readers of Solomon and his patronage over collections of didactic material (e.g. Prov. 1:1; 10:1; 25:1). The royal charac-

---

487 Ibid.
488 See ibid., 201-268, 269-289.
489 Murphy points out that the sayings in Eccl. 7 are more tight-knit than those in Proverbs (1992, 62). He also points out that even the aphorisms in Proverbs have been shown by Plöger (1984) and van Leeuwen (1988) to contain subtle connections, namely through the use of catchwords, cf. Heim (2001).
490 Whybray (1989, 118). Whybray also adds that "the conclusion reached in 7:13-14 is similar to that reached by 'Solomon'"(ibid.). Jastrow suggested further that the sayings were "scattered" throughout the book for the purpose of strengthening the plausibility of a Solomonic authorship (1919, 76).

terization of *Qoheleth* is further enhanced by the nature of Qoheleth's experiment which, according to wisdom tradition itself, falls within the purview of royalty (Prov. 25:2).

IV. The Dynamics of Qoheleth's Narrative

Many commentators have described Qoheleth's narrative as a continuous "rambling" with no clear progression of thought. Neverthless for a number of them this peculiarity is not a good enough reason for doubting the integrity and unity of the work. As Whybray comments:[491]

> ... the disjointed character of Qoheleth's book, the reason for which is not clearly known, does not in my opinion preclude the reader from perceiving that it has a unity of thought – a perception that has emerged to some extent from Qoheleth's constant repetition of key phrases, but more than that: despite some contradictions, which may well point to tensions in Qoheleth's thought (and there are, it should be noted, such tensions also in the *Pensées*), there is sufficient consistency of thought displayed in Qoheleth's book to enable the reader to form a clear idea of his views.

Fox expresses a similar opinion in his description of the narrative flow of *Qoheleth*: [492]

> ... the territory with all its bumps and clefts... they are not mere flaws, but the essence of the landscape.

Whilst I subscribe to the view that there is no discernible design to Qoheleth's narrative as a whole (except perhaps in a broad sense that Qoheleth's narrative has an introduction (1:12-2:26) which sets out the details to his quest and pursuit, and which forms the background to the rest of his discourse[493]), I do nevertheless believe that there is, on the level of the individual units of thought, an identifiable pattern to his arguments.[494] We

---

491 Whybray 1998, 241.
492 Fox 1989, 28.
493 I would further add that Qoheleth's advice in 11:1-6 reflects an appropriate conclusion to the main body of narrative.
494 There are those who argue that *Qoheleth* follows the form of early Greek speech (e.g. Backhaus, Schwienhorst-Schönberger) or diatribe (Lohfink) and thus posit that there is a discernible pattern of development in Qoheleth's discourse.

shall now turn to look at two theories which suggest that there is a noticeable system of structure, albeit at a micro-level, to Qoheleth's narrative which relates to his thought pattern and to his manner of testing wisdom.

A. Loader's Theory of Polar Tensions

The suggestion that the contradictions traditionally identified in the book might be reflecting Qoheleth's dialectic debate with wisdom tradition was posited early on by Müller, and Loader has since argued it in greater detail.[495] Loader contends that the tensions and contradictions in the book represent the dialectic debate that Qoheleth is having in his mind with conventional wisdom, where in his evaluation of traditional wisdom, Qoheleth challenges its truths and teachings with other wisdom sayings or with his own opposing experience of it. Loader argues that in Qoheleth's dialectic with traditional wisdom, opposing thoughts to general wisdom are juxtaposed to each other, proceeding from thesis to antithesis over several themes and subject matters until it culminates in the conclusion of הֶבֶל "vanity". According to Loader, all the contradictions can be explained as the author's deliberate juxtaposing of opposing thoughts in his evaluation of traditional wisdom; they are "nothing other than intended polar structures" of the debate.[496] These polar structures are also linked in form and substance. Loader further suggests that the entire book is made up of an integrated system of polar thought-patterns and argues that there are sixty main units of these in the book.

Loader's argument is helpful in the way it highlights the dialectic nature of Qoheleth's thought and how these tensions are continuously maintained throughout the work. Loader makes the observation that unlike other "protesting" wisdom

---

These suggestions are not persuasive for the reasons given by e.g. Crenshaw (1980, 29); Murphy (1992, xxxi); Krüger (2004, 8).

495 Müller (1968); Loader (1979).
496 Loader 1979, 133.

works from the ancient Near East and in the Bible,[497] where the tensions which arise from the interaction between "dogmatized wisdom" and "protesting wisdom" are always resolved with either of the two winning the argument,[498] with *Qoheleth*, "the crisis never results in tension being discharged but always in its maintenance".[499] Loader's argument that the tensions are never resolved and are continuously held throughout the book indirectly suggests that there is no progression or pattern of development to Qoheleth's discourse.[500] Loader further concludes that Qoheleth does not totally reject traditional wisdom. Despite demonstrating the limitations of conventional wisdom and how its truths can sometimes be inapplicable in certain situations, Qoheleth's own observations and experience of the "absurdities" and "vanities" of life are still not enough to bring him to reject the authority and value of traditional wisdom. This affirms my contention that conventional wisdom is not completely dismissed by Qoheleth. Loader also points out that Qoheleth uses traditional religious vocabulary and conventional sayings to argue against traditional wisdom.[501] We have seen this previously in relation to Qoheleth's use of didactic sayings to test and question wisdom tradition itself. From this particular observation, Loader argues that Qoheleth "stands in solidarity with general hokmah" by the display of his competent knowledge of its forms and his use of it to protest against the dogma of "general hokma" itself.[502] This comment is both insightful and important as it helps to throw light on the matter of purported inconsistencies in the book which, Loader argues,

---

497 E.g. the Babylonian work of Ludlul and as several psalms and the book of Job from the Bible.

498 In Ludlul and the "theodicy psalms" dogma eventually triumphs whereas in Job, Loader claims, "the tension is discharged in favour of the protesting wisdom" (Loader 1979, 123). Loader's latter point finds support in the fact that the questioning of the principle of "just desert" in Job's circumstance does not ultimately receive an answer; see Dell (1991, 216); Lambert (1995, 33).

499 Loader 1979, 123.

500 Loader vividly describes the tension as follows: "When the two poles of doctrine and protest are counterpoised in the ancient Near Eastern wisdom, the headache is always followed by relaxation – but in Qohelet's head the migraine throbs continually" (ibid.).

501 Ibid., 115.

502 Ibid.

may be explained as Qoheleth's use of conventional forms – such as, the better-saying (6:3), truth-saying *(Wahrspruch)* (1:18), proverb (10:1) – for an unconventional purpose, which is to challenge, but never to reject completely, tradition itself.[503]

On closer examination, Loader's analysis has a few problems. For a start, Loader's system of categorizing Qoheleth's narrative into neat units of bipolar tensions is suspect. Not only is the suggested schema too complex to be convincing, but more importantly, Loader's structural analysis is also questionable at several places. For example, Loader's description of the peri-copes are at times inaccurate, such as his labelling of 1:12-2:26 as "the worthlessness of wisdom" which is clearly a vague generalization. Furthermore, whilst Loader is not totally wrong in claiming that there are polar patterns of thoughts in the book (the clearest being the poem on time in 3:1-8) many of the tensions which he identifies in the text have more than one corresponding point, some of which are found outside the unit. The nature of the tensions and poles are also sometimes unclear, and Loader's delineation of the text in some cases is, at times, forced.[504]

A specific interpretative problem that I should like to mention here is Loader's contention that Qoheleth denies all laws of retribution and rejects any link between right deeds and good consequences or wrong deeds and bad consequences.[505] In his analysis of 8:10-15 and 9:1-10, which he organizes under the theme "no retribution where expected", Loader notes that Qoheleth observes, in 8:10-15, that the doctrine of retribution does not operate in the cultic field, where it would at least be expected, and that he ironically quotes a traditional wisdom saying on retribution in 8:12b-13, before citing another example of a "vanity" of life. In 9:1-10, Qoheleth lists a series of observed examples where, according to Loader, God is indiscriminate

---

503 This observation is also made by Dell who argues that Qoheleth's reuse and occasional misuse of wisdom forms to attack the tradition is part of the author's paradoxical technique which contributes to the peculiar nature of Qoheleth's discourse (1991, 138-147).

504 See the criticisms of Fox (1989, 20-1, 115 n. 38); Whybray (1989, 21); Murphy (1992, xxxvii-viii).

505 Ibid., 98.

towards the pious and the wicked. I believe that Loader is wrong in his interpretation that Qoheleth has totally rejected the law of retribution because divine justice is not seen to be operating according to expectation. On the contrary, Qoheleth *does* believe in the doctrine of retribution and the reason why the tensions arise, and why Qoheleth is frustrated by the observed moral chaos in life, is because his belief in divine justice is not affirmed or met as expected. In fact, Qoheleth knows that God will judge (3:17) and that it will go well with the righteous (8:12b-13; contra Loader), but Qoheleth also realizes that God's ways are inscrutable and he is aware that he is confronted with a God who acts in freedom. Fox similarly points out that some of the tensions in the book arise because Qoheleth *"knows* that God will judge, but he also *sees* the injustice of undeserved fates and delayed retribution".[506] Qoheleth does not reject the doctrine of retribution; he merely surrenders to the fact that it is operating on principles that are clearly beyond human understanding.

Despite these flaws which do not override the more positive aspects of his arguments, Loader's theory of polar tensions has affirmed, once again, the nature of Qoheleth's discourse, namely that it does not hold any discernible pattern of development to the book, and that the composition essentially expresses Qoheleth's testing and debate with traditional wisdom which helps to explain the "contradictions" or "tensions" traditionally found in the book. There are, however, a few questionable elements in Loader's argument, particularly to do with the limits, description, and analysis of the units of thought, which I believe, do not invalidate the more helpful conclusions which he makes. Whilst Loader has helped to highlight the dialectic nature of Qoheleth's narrative, a further investigation into the author's style of argument would be helpful. I shall now turn to investigate this issue.

---

506 Fox 1998, 235. Italics his.

B. Qoheleth's *Zwar-Aber* Dialectic Style of Argument

Whilst Loader's theory of polar structures has helped to emphasize the importance of taking into account the dialectic nature of Qoheleth's discourse when attempting to understand the "contradictions" in the book, Hertzberg's theory of Qoheleth's *zwar-aber* style of argument has gone further in identifying more precisely the peculiar and intricate manner by which Qoheleth debates and delivers his point. Like Loader, Hertzberg's theory recognizes the dialectic pattern of Qoheleth's thought but goes further with its suggestion that the author's nuanced pattern of argument reflects a *zwar-aber* ("yes-but") sequence.

Hertzberg argues that the alleged contradictions in the work may be explained as Qoheleth's peculiar pattern of thought which reflects a *zwar-aber* style of reasoning. Although describing *Qoheleth* as "jerky" and not reflecting any logical progression at all, Hertzberg nevertheless argued that it clearly reflects the work of a single author.[507] He contends that Qoheleth's arguments follow a *zwar-aber* pattern, wherein a truth or fact would first be stated before Qoheleth proceeds to qualify or challenge it with his own view.[508] This *zwar-aber* dialectic style suits Qoheleth's purpose of testing traditional wisdom. Qoheleth also uses a variety of different wisdom forms to help make his point. Hertzberg's identification of the *zwar-aber* dialectic aptly captures the manner in which Qoheleth often counters one truth statement with a subsequent negating assertion. I may add further that this *zwar-aber* dialectic also occurs across passages of texts and in the reverse direction and at times consecutively for multiple units of thought in succession and may involve more than a single theme at a time. I shall now turn to analyse three passages of texts, i.e. 4:4-6; 9:11-12, 13-16, which I have organized according to their extent of intricacy, to illustrate the point. I shall attempt to draw out the message of these texts by paying close attention to the *zwar-aber* dialectic style of argument.

---

507 Hertzberg 1963, 29.
508 So also Zimmerli (1974, 130-1) and Krober (1963, 37-8).

1. 9:13-16: Wisdom's Subservience to Time and Chance

13 גַּם־זֹה רָאִיתִי חָכְמָה תַּחַת הַשָּׁמֶשׁ וּגְדוֹלָה הִיא אֵלָי:

14 עִיר קְטַנָּה וַאֲנָשִׁים בָּהּ מְעָט וּבָא־אֵלֶיהָ מֶלֶךְ גָּדוֹל וְסָבַב אֹתָהּ וּבָנָה עָלֶיהָ מְצוֹדִים גְּדֹלִים:

15 וּמָצָא בָהּ אִישׁ מִסְכֵּן חָכָם וּמִלַּט־הוּא אֶת־הָעִיר בְּחָכְמָתוֹ וְאָדָם לֹא זָכַר אֶת־הָאִישׁ הַמִּסְכֵּן הַהוּא:

16 וְאָמַרְתִּי אָנִי טוֹבָה חָכְמָה מִגְּבוּרָה וְחָכְמַת הַמִּסְכֵּן בְּזוּיָה וּדְבָרָיו אֵינָם נִשְׁמָעִים:

13 This too I have seen, (an instance[509] of) wisdom under the sun and it seemed great to me.
14 (There was) a little city with a few men in it, a great king came to it and besieged it and built against it great siegeworks.
15 In it was found a poor wise man and he could have[510] delivered the city by his wisdom but no one gave thought[511] to that poor man.
16 So I say, wisdom is better than strength, but the wisdom of the poor man is despised and his words are not heard.

It is often asked of this passage, whether the story is based on a past event (i.e., the poor man *did* save the city but was not remembered or rewarded) or whether it is a hypothetical case invented by Qoheleth (i.e., the poor man *would have* saved the city, but no one gave thought to him). The dialectic pattern is clearly at play in the details of this example story. Of the two possible interpretations, the latter is the more likely as it avoids getting into two further contradictions within its immediate context. Firstly, v.15b is best read as a conditional clause for there would be a contradiction if the poor wise man had delivered the city by his wisdom only to have Qoheleth follow with the saying in v.16 that "wisdom is better than strength, but the poor man's wisdom is despised and his words are not heard".[512] If the poor

---

509 Taking חָכְמָה in apposition to זֹה - GKC§131a, k, l; McNeile (1904, 108); Gordis (1968, 310); Whybray (1988, 147).

510 A number of commentators read וּמִלַּט־הוּא as hypothetical (see footnote 512). For the use of the perfective verb in this manner see GKC§106p. Also see the main discussion.

511 Or "remembered", cf. in 5:19 where it means "to pay attention to", "giving thought to".

512 Those who interpret וּמִלַּט־הוּא as hypothetical include McNeile (1904, 12-13); Ginsberg (1952, 56-7); Hertzberg (1963, 181); Kroeber (1963, 120); Scott (1965, 247); Galling (1969, 78); Lauha (1978, 177); Loader (1979, 58-60); Zimmerli (1962, 229); Isaksson (1987, 97) cf. Fox (1989, 263-4) and Murphy (1992, 100) who

man had actually delivered the city by his wisdom, then his wisdom was not despised and his words were heard. Secondly, this line of interpretation would avoid a further possible contradiction with v.17 which speaks of the occasionally unassuming appearance of wisdom – how easily the poor but wise man and the quiet words of the wise are overlooked. In this story, several of the book's key themes are brought into play again: the value of wisdom, its elusiveness, and the dictates of "chance". The story tells of a small city which was besieged by a powerful enemy, and there was a poor but wise man who, by his wisdom, could have saved it if only someone had remembered him. Using his peculiar *zwar-aber* style of argument, Qoheleth contends that wisdom is of value, and he states resolutely in v.16 that it is better than military power, although at times it is not given the chance to show its true worth. The poor but wise man could have saved the city as he had the potential to do so *but* he was overlooked by the people and was not given the "chance" to prove wisdom's power and worth (vv.15c, 16b). In this example story Qoheleth makes the point that wisdom is easily overlooked and often made "subordinate" to "time and chance".[513] Qoheleth uses the element of conditionality (the "but") to highlight the elusive nature of wisdom. This example story, which began with a focus on wisdom (of the poor man; cf. v.13), ends with the subject of "time and chance" to make the point that the destiny of humankind is determined by these twin powers. A similar point is made in the preceding verses 11 and 12 with which the example story shows a clear connection and with which it forms a coherent unit of thought and argument. I shall now examine 9:11-12 to observe another instance of Qoheleth's dialectic argument involving a similar collection of themes.

---

interpret it as a past event. This is not to deny that this event, or something similar, might have been witnessed by Qoheleth since the description given in the passage is fairly typical and even general in its record of the details. In the end, as Fox rightly points out, the factuality of the event is not as important as how it serves to illustrate Qoheleth's point (similarly Lauha 1978, 176f.)

513 Isaksson 1987, 98. The story could be read to make the obverse point about the fool, that is, while it is true that, but for the interference of "chance", the wise but poor man would have helped to save the city, in contrast, the fool will never be able to accomplish such a great deed, even if the opportunity arose for him to speak, for he lacks the necessary "wisdom".

2. 9:11-12: Fate, Time, and Chance

11 שַׁבְתִּי וְרָאֹה תַחַת־הַשֶּׁמֶשׁ כִּי לֹא לַקַּלִּים הַמֵּרוֹץ וְלֹא
לַגִּבּוֹרִים הַמִּלְחָמָה וְגַם לֹא לַחֲכָמִים לֶחֶם וְגַם לֹא לַנְּבֹנִים
עֹשֶׁר וְגַם לֹא לַיֹּדְעִים חֵן כִּי־עֵת וָפֶגַע יִקְרֶה אֶת־כֻּלָּם׃
12 כִּי גַּם לֹא־יֵדַע הָאָדָם אֶת־עִתּוֹ כַּדָּגִים שֶׁנֶּאֱחָזִים בִּמְצוֹדָה
רָעָה וְכַצִּפֳּרִים הָאֲחֻזוֹת בַּפָּח כָּהֵם יוּקָשִׁים בְּנֵי הָאָדָם
לְעֵת רָעָה כְּשֶׁתִּפּוֹל עֲלֵיהֶם פִּתְאֹם׃

11 Again I saw under the sun that the race is not to the swift, nor the battle to the strong, nor bread to the wise[514], nor wealth to the brilliant, nor favour to the learned, but time and chance happen to all.

12 For no one knows his hour. Like fish which are caught in an evil net, and like birds which are caught in a snare, so like them human beings are trapped at an evil time when it falls unexpectedly upon them.

Commentators are generally agreed on the point of these two verses, which is, that human beings do not have absolute control over their own destiny. They can never be completely sure that their natural strength, talent, or ability will bring about a successful outcome, because they are unable to predict the workings of "time and chance" which ultimately determine the events of the day. In making this point, Qoheleth is not discouraging ambition or hardwork, nor is he denying the effectiveness of the laws of deed and consequence either here or elsewhere. In fact, Qoheleth's use of this particular example suggests that he believes that there is a place for human aspirations and that one ought to also expect the law of natural retribution to be in operation in the world, which rewards and punishes the deeds and actions of humankind accordingly. For, as one can observe, the swift do usually win, the strong do usually conquer, and the wise, brilliant, and learned do usually succeed with their talents (cf. 8:14).[515] Neverthless, the point which Qoheleth makes here, like that of the example story of 9:13-16, is that "expected" outcomes sometimes do not turn out as they should because of the unpredictable visit of "time and

---

514 "Wisdom" here is likely to refer to skill and ability, cf. the skilled craftsmen of Solomon (1 Kgs. 5:18), so Zimmerli (1962, 228-9).
515 Zimmerli 1962, 230-1.

chance". The swift, strong, and wise can be successful in their tasks only if "time and chance" permit them to achieve their due results.[516]   Whybray puts it differently, that a man "does not know *when* in his case the normal operation of cause and effect will be suspended".[517] This is not to deny wisdom's worth since Qoheleth praises wisdom albeit implicitly in 9:16, 17, and 18 and more explicitly in 2:13-14a. Consistent to his *zwar-aber* pattern of argument, Qoheleth, in these verses and the passage following, is relativizing the value of human skill, ability, and strength. Qoheleth is seeking to highlight how life can sometimes be unpredictable as seen in the continual occurrence of unexpected events and outcomes. In verse 12, Qoheleth's point is extended and applied to the unexpected evil events which befall humankind. Qoheleth is not denying the value and worth of human talent and strength (and their potential to achieve positive results for those who possess them), but rather he is making the point that these qualities should not be seen as being beyond reproach. Qoheleth's dialectic treatment of a topic or theme is often not carried out systematically or completely at any one place in his narrative. Instead, he often picks up and continues with his argument at various points of his discourse.

Finally, I shall examine another passage which expresses the *zwar-aber* pattern of thought. In 4:4-6, we observe another of Qoheleth's dialectic argument which incorporates what appears to be two proverbial sayings.

3. 4:4-6: Competitiveness Versus Contentment

4 וְרָאִיתִי אֲנִי אֶת־כָּל־עָמָל וְאֵת כָּל־כִּשְׁרוֹן הַמַּעֲשֶׂה
   כִּי הִיא קִנְאַת־אִישׁ מֵרֵעֵהוּ גַּם־זֶה הֶבֶל וּרְעוּת רוּחַ:

5 הַכְּסִיל חֹבֵק אֶת־יָדָיו וְאֹכֵל אֶת־בְּשָׂרוֹ:

6 טוֹב מְלֹא כַף נָחַת מִמְּלֹא חָפְנַיִם עָמָל וּרְעוּת רוּחַ:

4 And I saw that all toil and all successful work come from a man's envy of his neighbour. This also is a vanity and a chasing after wind.

5 The fool folds his hands and ruins himself.

---

516 Isaksson 1978, 98.
517 Whybray 1989, 146.

6   Better is a handful of tranquillity than two hands full of toil and a chasing after wind.

In this passage, Qoheleth makes the observation that humans are often occupied with work which is marked by excessive striving and motivated by ignoble reasons (e.g. envy (v.4) and greed (v.8)). Such a preoccupation is "a vanity and chasing after wind" even though a temporary gain may indeed be made. The thought here complements Qoheleth's call, made elsewhere and throughout his narrative, to enjoy one's "lot" in life which is "given" by God, without not seeking to burden oneself further with greedy ambitions and work which would bring on unnecessary stress and striving (cf. v.8; 2:22-23; 5:16-17). Qoheleth's advice here is to avoid the life that is marked by "exaggerated and inappropriate effort".[518] Qoheleth warns elsewhere that such a (foolish) life, which anxiously strives to accumulate wealth, will expose the worker to added frustration and even illness (5:16 [ET v.17]), especially if another fool were to surpass him or her, thereby arousing further feelings of injustice (2:15). Qoheleth, however, is quick to qualify his words in v.4 (in typical *zwar-aber* style) with a proverb in 4:6a ("the fool folds his hands and ruins himself") to warn his listeners against taking the extreme opposite position of being unduly passive or lazy (cf. 10:18). We find a similar warning against inappropriate passivity in Qoheleth's concluding passage in 11:1-6 (viz. vv.4-6).[519] In the above text, Qoheleth gives his end thought in the subsequent second saying (v.6b) which advises that, a person who resolves to be content with the "portion" that God "gives" to him or her is ultimately better off than the one who strives to secure more than his or her "given lot" (and who may indeed be making gains). In the end, the contented person is the wiser and happier individual.

---

518 Levine 1990, 286-7.

519 In 11:1-6 Qoheleth advises that whilst is it important for people to understand that time and chance are predetermined by God, this truth should not lead them to the point of being immobilized by fear and dread, but rather to seek to live fully (a similar advice is found in 9:7-10). He calls on his listeners to be courageous to take the required measure of risk to do those positive and charitable actions as a means of making others happy, for it is in carrying out these deeds (of charity) that the benefactor will gain a sense of joy for himself whilst also creating the opportunity for other possible future rewards.

My examination of the above texts confirms that Qoheleth's *zwar-aber* pattern of thought works across units of passages and even between narrative and didactic materials. Qoheleth's *zwar-aber* style of testing wisdom often highlights the delicate nature of wisdom's influence and its limitations. In two of the above passages this thought (of the precariousness of wisdom) leads him to the conclusion that there are no guaranteed outcomes in life and that certain "natural" laws (e.g. of deed and consequence, and retribution), as traditionally taught, do not express fully the truth about the reality of the operations of moral order in the universe. Since nothing in life is guaranteed or permanent, "all" that an individual may possess (talent, ability, achievements, gains) is thus potentially worthless and a vanity (2:22-23). Thus, Qoheleth warns against being presumptuous about one's natural ability, talent, strength, wisdom, or skill for as he has observed of others, and of himself, these cannot be totally relied upon to secure, for the individual, a meaningful and lasting "gain". Qoheleth has found this fact of life frustrating and a cause for pessimism. Qoheleth makes a further point that the principle of deed and consequence does not appear to be always in operation in this world, as evidenced by the existence of injustice and evil. Applying the theory of Qoheleth's *zwar-aber* style of argument to our understanding of Qoheleth's narrative, previously assumed contradictions in the book may be explained as Qoheleth's attempts at highlighting the "absurdities" in life and how humankind's fate and destiny are ultimately determined by the dictates of "time and chance".

V. *Qoheleth* As Royal Autobiography

A. The Story of the Life of a King

I have thus far argued for the pervasiveness of Qoheleth's royal voice and the unity of his discourse and have gone further to suggest the identification of Qoheleth's narrative as "royal autobiography". My reading of Qoheleth's narrative as royal autobiography appreciates the work as being more than a treatise on wisdom themes and topics which are loosely held together. I maintain that there is a discernible royal context to Qoheleth's narrative which is composed in the style of a royal pseudo-autobiography after Solomon who, in his quest to discover the meaning of life, muses on the events and experiences from his past. I argue that Qoheleth's use of a royal persona is a deliberate attempt at affirming an essential continuity with a past tradition where wisdom was once associated with king and court. Furthermore, Qoheleth's use of a Solomonic guise was to help lend credence and authority to his message and teaching despite its heavy questioning of traditional wisdom.

As was shown in my earlier investigation of the main evidence of Qoheleth's royal voice in Chapter 2, there are many allusions to Solomon in Qoheleth's narrative which are found beyond the introductory passage of 1:12-2:26. We have seen phrases used in Qoheleth's narrative which clearly echo those that are used to describe Israel's famous wise king in the Solomonic narratives in the books of Kings and Chronicles. In fact, many of the situations described in the Solomonic narratives in the book of Kings could serve as possible background to Qoheleth's feelings of insecurity and his musings on the issues of injustice and the meaning of life. For example, that Solomon's rule was never perceived to be totally secure is clear from the Deuteronomic passage of 1 Kgs. 11:14-26 which describes the ongoing threats of incursion and rebel attacks from within as well as outside his kingdom. Like other rulers, Solomon's regular exposure to political threats would provide a suitable context to Qoheleth's musing on the issue of oppression (4:1-3) and even successorship (2:17f.). The Deuteronomist's description of Solomon's failure to keep God's commandments which incurs the punishment of a future divided kingdom (e.g. 1 Kgs. 11:6, 9-13) provides another fitting background to Qoheleth's warning against taking a casual attitude to God (4:17f [ET 5:1f]), and conversely, his advice to take one's vows before God seriously (5:3-6 [ET vv.4-7]).

In addition to these allusions to Solomon in *Qoheleth*, my examination of ancient Near Eastern texts in Chapter 3 also reveals that Qoheleth's narrative bears a remarkable affinity, in terms of form and content, with the Akkadian royal pseudo-autobiographies. Using Lewis's list of the characteristic features of this Akkadian corpus, we see many points of similarity between the ancient corpus and *Qoheleth*. These include the manner in which the Hebrew work is written as a pseudepigraph purporting to be a genuine royal composition. (The author's use of the pen name "Qoheleth" and the lack of a more direct association with Solomon hint at the author's pseudonymous intention.) Formwise, like the Akkadian royal pseudo-autobiographies, Qoheleth's narrative begins with a formulaic self-presentation and an introductory narrative which provides the background to the rest of his narrative.[520]

It is not difficult to appreciate *Qoheleth* as reflecting an episode in the life of Solomon who, in a private moment of reflection, shares his thoughts on the "vanities" of life and reveals his anguish over his inability – despite being the nation's exemplary wise man and chief dispenser of justice – to resolve the many "inconsistencies" of life from which he is not exempt. The awareness of the limitations which he faces as king despite his talent, resource, and achievements fuels his pessimism and is that which moves him to test wisdom's own limits in order to search out the deeper question of the meaning of life. That Solomon could have mused on such issues is entirely possible in the light of the fact that, like the rest of humankind, he too is not exempt from the vanities of life.

Another element of similarity between *Qoheleth* and the Akkadian royal pseudo-autobiographies is the way in which the Akkadian texts usually describe an "unusual" experience of the king. In the case of *Qoheleth* this lies in the unexpected vulnerability of the Solomonic persona, as he is seen to be unable to cope with the injustices that surround him, despite his wisdom and power. Like the Akkadian corpus there are also moral lessons to be learned from both the personal experiences of Qoheleth the protagonist as well as the didactic sayings which he dispenses in his narrative.

It is not difficult to see how the royal autobiography form suits the purpose of a composition which seeks to test and debate with conventional wisdom in order to expose its limits.

---

520 This pertains to points 1, 5, and 6 on Lewis's list.

Qoheleth's appeal to personal experience and observations as a means to illustrate and elucidate his teaching helps to enhance the persuasiveness of his message. Similarly, by setting his instructions in the form of a direct speech of a king, Qoheleth's message is given added authority. Finally, the royal autobiography motif is, as we have seen, a well-recognized wisdom form and its use by Qoheleth strongly supports with its didactic purpose.

B. Qoheleth's Quest for the Meaning of Life

Qoheleth's narrative is an account of a man's quest to discover the meaning of life in a world that is full of observable inconsistencies and absurdities. Using the literary form of a royal autobiography, Qoheleth tells of his philosophical attempts at understanding his observations of social injustice and moral disorder around him (1:14) and to discover how best human beings should live in a world where events and situations are never entirely predictable (1:13; 2:3b). Of special concern to Qoheleth is the issue of wisdom (1:17) and work (2:3b); namely whether they are to be actively pursued even though there is no certainty as to their reward.

The quest to find meaning and to make sense of one's world lies very much at the heart of wisdom tradition. Wisdom, in a broader and intellectual sense, may be defined as a particular spirit of enquiry into the "understanding of reality".[521] Like the sages of old, Qoheleth shares in this same pursuit of seeking to formulate a worldview which will enable him "to understand and interpret, to articulate and organize, to synthesize and

---

[521] Von Rad [1972, 6]; "Wirklichkeitsverständnis" (1970, 7). Murphy has some qualms about using the term "order", as does von Rad though to a much lesser extent (1990, 157). I believe that the use of the term "order" in our discussion is justified. Of course, we are not speaking of a fixed order, as if these perceived patterns of experiences, which appear to replicate themselves in a general way, are always entirely predictable. There are, clearly, certain "regularities", as Murphy also recognizes, which are discernible in the world which Qoheleth similarly notes (e.g. in Eccl. 3) and other ancient wisdom traditions have also discerned and taught, such as the ancient Egyptian wisdom concept of Ma'at.

universalise his human experience".[522] This search for a satis-
factory paradigm with which to understand one's universe (1:12)
represents a universal and basic need of humankind which is
shared by everyone in every successive generation.[523]

Qoheleth's search for order emerges from his observation of
the inconsistencies and absurdities of life, of the social injustices
and moral chaos which are found in the political and court
contexts as well of the world and humanity in general. From the
passages examined earlier in Chapter 2, it has been seen how
Qoheleth speaks of his awareness of corruption in the human
system of justice and how human beings are inevitably flawed
(3:17). Oppression (4:1), corruption (5:7-8 [ET vv.8-9]), miscarriages of justice (3:16), promoted in part by incompetent
leaders occupying positions of authority (10:5-7), the reversal of
societal norms (10:5-7) – these and others, Qoheleth concludes,
represent the universal failings of humankind, which no single
ruler in relation to his land (5:8 [ET v.9]) nor any successive
generation of leaders is able to control, much less prevent. More
depressing to Qoheleth is the discovery that all humanity is
corrupt (7:20) and that there is a perverse tendency in human
beings to inflict harm and evil on others, and that those with
power often use it to oppress others (4:1). Another conclusion
which Qoheleth arrives at from his observations is that there are
plenty of fools in the world, the presence of whom is an
abomination to God (5:3 [v.4]; as well as to other human beings!)
and whose foolish actions and work contribute to the chaos in

---

522 Cassirer (1944, 221) as quoted by Olney (1972, 8). It is interesting to note that
     modern literary critics of the genre of autobiography also point out that a
     personal quest for order lies behind all genuine autobiographies. It is said that
     the autobiographical act of writing comes at a point when the author manages
     to reduce his or her cosmos to order and is able to see his or her life as
     something of a unity (e.g. Pascal 1960, 9).

523 Einstein, in his autobiography, similarly observes this universal longing in
     humankind: "Man tries to make for himself in the fashion that suits him best, a
     simplified and intelligible picture of the world; he then tries to some extent to
     substitute this cosmos of his for the world of experience, and thus to overcome
     it. This is what the painter, the poet, the speculative philosopher, and the
     natural scientist do, each in his own fashion. Each makes this cosmos and its
     construction the pivot of his emotional life, in order to find in this way the
     peace and security which he cannot find in the narrow whirlpool of personal
     experience." Einstein (1962, 225) as quoted by Olney (1972, 8).

the world. They turn the status quo of the world on its head by assuming positions of authority and power (10:5-7) and by perpetuating chaos. They are a testing to the wise and their presence can sometimes defy or even override wisdom (10:1). All this and more, Qoheleth sees as part of the universal and inevitable moral failings of humankind – the "vanities" of life – which contribute to the futility of living "under the sun". Qoheleth's pessimism is a result of his frustration at life's injustices and absurdities, which even he, as king, for all his wealth and power, is unable to control, much less influence. The only solace, as he sees it, lies in humanity's hope in God, in the One who alone can resolve the universal moral chaos once and for all, although the time and day of reckoning remains a mystery to them (3:17). However, behind Qoheleth's frustrations as an ineffectual king lies a deeper cause for his anguish and pessimism, which is his inability to fully understand God at His work. Qoheleth's philosophical struggle to comprehend principally the operation of "chance", which he sees as responsible for determining the destiny of humanity, is representative of wisdom tradition's higher intellectual enquiry. And it is this challenge to understand wisdom at a metaphysical level which leads Qoheleth to search and test conventional wisdom for its truths concerning the perceived moral order in this world. [524]

Qoheleth's philosophical quest is concerned with the search for the knowledge of divine action in the created world which, as he already recognizes, is partly revealed in the ordering of the seasons and nature's timing (3:1-8). Yet Qoheleth yearns to discover more fully the mind and purpose behind the universe in order that he may be able to predict and ultimately control his own destiny. Knowledge of how and when God operates in the world would enable human beings to predict future events and consequently to make "gains" and "profit" from it (8:7-8). In fact,

---

524 Von Rad speaks of the "supra-personal" aspect of the autobiography form of wisdom composition, which, he argues, often aims to present the truths in commonly encountered realities which readers can then readily identify thereby elevating the content of the instruction onto the level of truth. However, he further argues that these fictitious autobiographical observations "in themselves... possessed no personal note" [1972, 38, 24].

it might be said that this desire is an inherent characteristic of humankind and emerges out of our dislike for second-guessing and surrendering to a world of probability. Such a pursuit is representative of humanity's desire to have a world that is clear and determined, where human beings can know exactly what lies ahead in order that they may be able to plan for their future. As it is a universal human condition, Qoheleth's search for a paradigm of clarity is also a pursuit shared by everyone. The quest to catch God at His work, as it were, assumes that there is a system of principles, law, or order which determines the outcome of every event and situation which occurs in the world. This constant search for an understanding of the way in which the universe operates constitutes a basic need of humankind. However, as Qoheleth discovers, wisdom is elusive and not only are God's ways incomprehensible, but He is also responsible for hiding it from humanity.

It is also clear that Qoheleth understands that the world and its daily operation are not the result of blind chance, but that God is in charge and actively involved in maintaining the order of the universe, even though this is not always easily discernible by human beings.[525] Qoheleth's belief in the existence of order in the universe is seen in his poem on time (3:1-8) which he interestingly begins with the acknowledgement that "all" events and situations (לַכֹּל , לְכָל־חֵפֶץ "for everything" and "for every activity") surrounding humankind are not so much determined by the people who are in them as they are by the divine being who stands apart from them.[526] Later in his discourse, Qoheleth extends the concept of order and timing to the topic of wisdom, for example, in his advice on the value of right timing (10:11) and appropriate behaviour (8:3-6).

Many commentators have argued that Qoheleth rejects the doctrine of retribution and some argue further that his work represents a break with tradition and possibly even reflects his loss of religious faith.[527] However, as I have discussed above,

---

525 Von Rad 1972, 85.

526 Lohfink 2003, 59-60.

527 Lauha (1955, 186); Müller (1978, 238); Crüsemann (1984, 61); also Schmid (1961); Gese (1963).

such a notion is unconvincing since there is good evidence to show that, although Qoheleth is testing wisdom, he does not ultimately reject its truths and purpose, the latter of which is evidenced in his attempts at inculcating moral behaviour and in his encouragement of the pursuit of wisdom, all of which betrays a belief in the existence of the doctrine of retribution. Qoheleth's continual belief in the doctrine is further attested by his acceptance of the fact that the total grasping of the workings of this principle is out of the reach of humankind (and that wisdom can also be elusive). Loader is right to point out that there is no resolution to Qoheleth's debate and testing of conventional wisdom in that his search ultimately reveals several disappointing truths about humanity's relationship with the world and God. Like his *zwar-aber* style of argument, Qoheleth finds that, although there is a basic sense of order to be observed in the world, a precise understanding of the nature of its operation is elusive. Its principles of action, though stable, are never absolute; they are predictable, yet never enough to enable human beings to make lasting gains from it. Qoheleth eventually discovers that behind the element of uncertainty lies the work of "time and chance", which ultimately holds the power to affect the conditions surrounding events and their final outcomes.

Because Qoheleth is king, his conclusions, which proceed from his quest, carry added authority and validity for the rest of humankind for, if he, as the nation's wisest man, in all his wisdom and wealth has discovered that God's ways in the world are inscrutable how much less will others succeed in the attempt. That Qoheleth offers himself in this experiment as leader and the model representative of humankind is clear from his rhetorical question in 2:25, "for who can eat and find enjoyment if not I"? Commentators who argue that the work is a satire often suggest that the royal fiction is only temporary because it would be ironic to have the character of Solomon fail in his quest, given his renowned sagacity. For Solomon was a king whose wisdom greatly impressed the wise men of the East (1 Kgs. 5:10-14 [ET 4:30-34]; 2 Chr. 9:1-12), and who was credited by the authors of the books in the Old Testament as responsible for the development of wisdom in Israel (1 Kgs. 5:12 [ET 4:32]; Prov. 1:1; 10:1; 25:1; Canticles 1:1). Furthermore, Solomon was renowned for his understanding of the natural world (1 Kgs. 5:13 [ET 4:33]) and for his ability to offer astute judgments in difficult situations (1 Kgs. 3:16-28). Yet, Qoheleth's choice of a Solomonic persona for his narrative is as necessary as it is deliberate; for Solomon, the wisest and most able person in the land, would have been readily seen to have the capability to carry out this most profound task of searching to understand the work of God. Moreover, Solomon's reputation as Israel's wise king *par excellence* would help to lend support and authority to Qoheleth's pessimistic conclusions.

C. Qoheleth's Conclusions and Advice

From his careful testing of wisdom against itself and his own experience, Qoheleth concludes that any attempt to "work out" the operations of moral order in the world (which would consequently enable human beings to be in better control of their life) is a misdirected effort and a vanity. Qoheleth acknowledges, with resignation, that God is sovereign and inscrutable (cf. 3:11; 6:10; 7:13, 23, 24; 8:17), and human beings can neither find out what they are to do (cf. 6:12a; 7:29; 8:16, 17) nor know what will come after them (cf. 6:12b; 9:11-15; 10:14; 11:4-6). Humankind will always have to contend with God who acts by His will and pleasure. As Zimmerli puts it, in Qoheleth's quest to understand the operations of moral law in the universe, he "meets with a reality that is determined and cannot be apprehended" and "(b)ehind all this determination and all this ability not to be apprehended it is God, who cannot be scrutinized, who is free, who never reacts, but always acts in freedom".[528] Even if a person may claim to know the timing of the seasons yet עֵת ("proper time") remains at God's disposal (11:4-6). In the light of the frustrating limits that are imposed upon humanity's attempts at discovering the *modus operandi* of God, Qoheleth advises that humans can do no better than to make full use of "what God gives in every moment and be glad of the portion that God

---

528 Zimmerli 1964, 156.

gives".[529] They can do no better than to surrender to God's ways in the world because the opportunities for enjoyment in life – for which everyone looks – also comes from Him.

In regard to the extent of God's sovereignty Qoheleth discovers that even the personal emotions of human beings are dependent upon Him who holds the power to affect the emotional condition of individuals (2:26; 5:19; cf. 6:2; 9:7, 9). Qoheleth realizes that human beings cannot hope to find enjoyment apart from divine empowerment (2:24, 26; 5:19; 9:9) for even happiness (i.e. the deep-seated state of consciousness[530]) and the ability and opportunity to experience it, are brought about by God. The destiny of humankind ultimately lies in the hands of God.

There is, however, a further truth which Qoheleth discovers, that is, those who "please" God (2:26) and whose deeds are "approved" by Him (9:7) will receive satisfaction and enjoyment in their work. Qoheleth contends that the righteous are indeed favoured by God (8:12) although there are also times where there does not seem to be a proper distinction between them and the wicked (e.g. where the righteous get what the wicked deserve and vice versa (8:14)). These exceptions are incomprehensible to Qoheleth and constitute a part of the overall observed chaos in the world and are a further cause for pessimism. Qoheleth further discovers that work which stems from a desperate desire to secure a lasting profit is "a vanity and chasing of wind" for its promise of gain is illusory (2:11). Humans should instead seek to participate fully in life, taking up those opportunities for happy experiences which are ordained by God (3:22; 5:17-19 [ET v.18-20]; 9:7-9). The key to overcoming the "vanities" in life lies in being contented with one's lot and enjoying those positive moments in one's life as they are given by God.

Aware of the limits that God has placed on humankind's quest for knowledge concerning their future and destiny, Qoheleth advises his listeners to accept their life as given and governed by God with all its complexities, sorrow, and joy (7:14).

---

529 Ibid., 157.

530 For a helpful discussion on Qoheleth's use of the words שָׂבַע ,שָׂחַק ,טוֹב ,שִׂמְחָה and their nuances, see Fox (1989, 64-7).

Qoheleth concludes that the key to surviving this world, with all its inconsistencies and absurdities, is for human beings to actively engage with life, not to be manipulative or assertive, but to seek enjoyment in all that they do, treating each task that they find themselves with as a gift from God.[531] To be precise, the kind of pleasure which Qoheleth recommends is not hedonism. It is not laughter without limits, nor merriment without restraint, for such hedonistic behaviour belongs to the fool who acts without self-control or discipline.[532] The fool lacks knowledge and ignores the moral boundaries to his own detriment (7:4 cf. 2; 10:16 cf. 17). Rather, the joy which Qoheleth encourages others to seek is that which comes from an energetic pursuit of life.[533] Life is to be lived and enjoyed, for, as Qoheleth discovers, it is in celebratory living that everything else has its place.[534] As Good puts it, "The joy 'attends you' in toil. It makes relative wisdom useful. It renders the puzzles of life bearable."[535] Yet Qoheleth is aware that the happiness which God gives to human beings in order to lend significance to their lives must also have its ingredient of sorrow.[536] Moreover, those positive moments in life are only given as a חֵלֶק "portion" (2:10, 21; 3:22; 5:17-18 [ET vv.18-19]; 9:6, 9).[537]

It is clear that Qoheleth's advice presupposes a belief in the doctrine of divine retribution and his invitation to actively "live life" is thus directed to the righteous and those whose deeds are

---

531 Good 1965, 194.
532 Qoheleth can be seen on several occasions to warn rulers, officials, and those in positions of authority to be responsible in effecting their duties, and to avoid slack attitudes and indiscipline (e.g. 10:16-17), warning them of the disillusionment which accompanies all ill-gotten gains (5:9-11 [ET vv.10-12]; 2:26) and the possibility of their removal by others (4:13-16) and by God (2:21, 26; 8:13; 9:12). Whilst Qoheleth clearly encourages the enjoyment of life, he does criticize immature and self-indulgent behaviour. Whilst Qoheleth does encourage the pursuit of pleasure, he makes it clear that it is to be sought within the confines of proper contexts (9:7-9) and with responsibility.
533 Good (1965, 192). Gordis describes it as, "a full-blooded and tangible experience, expressing itself in the play of the body and the activity of the mind, the contemplation of nature and the pleasures of love" (1968, 129).
534 Good (1965, 194).
535 Ibid.
536 Ibid., 193.
537 Zimmerli 1964, 158.

accepted by God (9:7). They are the ones to whom God would give happiness and satisfaction in their toil (2:24, 26; 5:18-19[ET vv.19-20]). This would be consistent with Qoheleth's explanation that, in contrast to the wise and righteous, the fool is the one who strives to make great gains only to end up in frustration, illness, and resentment (5:16 [ET v.17]), without any reward of satisfaction or joy, for God does not enable him to enjoy his work and wealth (2:26b; 6:2). Qoheleth's invitation to pleasure then is clearly not meant for fools.

VI. Qoheleth's Thoughts on Wisdom and Folly

Given the traditional classification of *Qoheleth* as a wisdom book and seeing as the wisdom element is an essential part of Qoheleth's autobiographical narrative, I shall now examine Qoheleth's treatment of the primary theme of wisdom and folly. This investigation will help to determine Qoheleth's wisdom credentials in relation to mainstream wisdom tradition.

Accepting the fact that the law of moral order is beyond the comprehension of human beings and any attempt to prove otherwise is but "a vanity and a chasing after wind" (8:16), Qoheleth nevertheless advocates the pursuit of wisdom and emphasizes the importance of being able to weigh situations wisely and to make the right decisions. For everyone will have to make choices in life which involve the recognition of alternatives, the exercising of options, and the evaluating of contingencies and probabilities.[538] And there is advantage in being able to do so wisely hence Qoheleth's concern for teaching others the value of wisdom and how to live as a wise person. Consistent with his self-portrayal as king, Qoheleth draws examples for his advice from the court context, for example, listeners are warned to guard their behaviour in court so as to keep themselves from potential harm (8:2-6). There is the admonition to obey and be loyal to the monarch (8:2-5) and to avoid any possibility of being implicated for seditious activities (10:20). There is also a warning against taking a casual approach

---

538 Levine 1990, 288.

to God (4:17-5:6). As I have argued in Chapter 2, these passages are not incompatible with a royal voice but rather may be seen to support it.

The suggestion by a few scholars that Qoheleth denigrates wisdom is to be dismissed as Qoheleth never rejects wisdom totally, nor does he ever commend folly as an option.[539] That Qoheleth condemns folly is clear from his repeated warnings against it throughout the work (e.g. 3:11; 4:13; 5:1, 3, 4; 6:11f.; 7:13; 8:17; 10:2, 12-15; 11:5). Qoheleth, however, does recognize that the value of wisdom is relativized in certain situations. A little folly can outweigh wisdom (10:1), and a wise man may turn into a fool through extortion and bribery (7:7). Wisdom is inconspicuous at times (e.g. the wise but poor man, 9:15) and it is also never a permanent virtue (4:13-16). Nevertheless, Qoheleth believes that wisdom is of value and is to be pursued because ultimately it is in the individual's best interest to avoid being a fool. To those who argue that such a pursuit would be pointless in the light of the inevitability of death, Qoheleth has this to say: despite the fact that death awaits everyone irrespective of their moral sensibilities (2:14), and however transitory life may be, it is still advantageous to be wise, for "wisdom preserves the lives of those who possess it" (7:12); it guides the wise man and saves him from harm (8:5), and wise words can win him favour (10:12). The same, however, may not be said for the fool whose speech is madness (10:13-14) and whose presence is irksome even to God (5:3b [ET v.4b]).[540]

Qoheleth's advice is personal and persuasive. Reflecting on his past life, Qoheleth admits that even this was partly spent as a fool (2:1-11) – a choice against which he is now keen to warn others. Qoheleth points out that no one is indeed protected from acting like the fool (7:20), not even a king. In fact, everyone is naturally born without knowledge (11:5). Nevertheless, for each individual there is the potential to become wise and there is

---

539 Levine writes, "Despite his repeated *caveat lector* that available knowledge is limited, Qoheleth is the Bible's most militant advocate of wisdom and most strident critic of folly" (ibid., 278-79). See also Murphy (2003, 18).

540 Thus Levine makes the comment, "whereas the Evildoer wrongs *others*, the Fool is *his own* worst enemy" (1990, 280). Italics his.

advantage and value in aspiring to grasp hold of wisdom.[541]
Qoheleth is also careful to warn that, just as it is possible for a
person to be wise, so it is equally possible that a wise person, if
unguarded, may turn into a fool (7:7). It is Qoheleth's deeper
understanding of the dangers of living the life of an ignorant fool
that colours much of the contemplation that is expressed in his
narrative, and his advice to pursue wisdom frequently emerges
out of his reflections on the foolish mistakes and tragedies
observed of others and himself. Qoheleth contends that the kind
of life to be avoided is that which is lived with "exaggerated and
inappropriate effort",[542] where a person strives at his work with
great anxiety (2:21-23) and for the wrong reasons (e.g. out of
envy and greed 4:4, 8), only to end up with frustration,
afflictions, and resentment (5:15-16 [ET vv.16-17]) as he over
expends himself (7:16-17; 10:15). His ignorance leads to the
awkward timing of his actions (10:10-11) and makes him the
laughable fool. Qoheleth also warns against challenging the
natural and moral boundaries which God has established (3:10-
22 viz. v.14),[543] and discourages any effort which seeks to achieve
that which is not "approved" by God (cf. 9:7) for this can only
lead to great frustration as all toil to this end is but a vanity (5:12-
16 [ET vv.13-17]; 6:1-2). Qoheleth concludes that no one can
achieve a full understanding of the work of God nor can anyone
know for sure "whether love or hate awaits the individual" (9:1)
for "all share a common destiny – the righteous and the wicked,
the good and the bad, the clean and the unclean, those who offer
sacrifices and those who do not" (9:2a). Thus, Qoheleth advises
that humans can do no better than to find enjoyment in all that
they do and not to apply exaggerated efforts in the hope of
securing that which is not "approved" by God.[544] Hence his
repeated recommendation to "eat and drink and find satisfaction
in all one's toil for this is the gift of God" (3:13; 4:6, 7-8; 5:19).
Qoheleth further encourages his listeners to actively participate
in life, although this may require some measure of risk-taking

---

541 Ibid.
542 Ibid., 287.
543 Ibid., 282-3.
544 Ibid., 285-6.

(cf. 11:1-6). His exhortation "live life" is heard most emphatically at the conclusion of his narrative in 11:4 where his listeners are urged to "go on and live"! "Invest in life"! Qoheleth's counsel clearly follows in the way of Israel's wise men who preached that the reality of existence lies in the here and now.[545] The sages taught that this is the world for which human beings are intended and they had better invest here for there is no better world.[546] Ultimately, the meaning of life is *life* in the here and now since, as Qoheleth discovers, there is no remembering of the past (2:16) nor can the future be secured (3:22 cf. 6:12; 7:14; 8:7; 9:10; 10:14).[547] As king, such truths are even more essential to Qoheleth as even he cannot look beyond life (9:10) nor claim to be able to secure any "gains" in this life as all that he has and will accomplish may yet be inherited by someone unworthy of receiving his achievements (2:18-21; 4:8; 5:12-16). Thus, in conclusion, Qoheleth recommends that the wisest action for any human being then is to make the most of life in the light of the limits that death sets to human aspirations (9:5).[548]

VII. Concluding Remarks

In this chapter I have taken my argument for the unity and pervasiveness of the royal voice in *Qoheleth* further by positing that Qoheleth's narrative is best described as having the form of a royal autobiography. This idea was prompted by the observation of the striking similarities between the Hebrew composition and the corpus of Akkadian royal pseudo-autobiographies. In this final chapter, I have gone further to show that this motif is indeed the dominant literary feature of

---

545 Brueggemann (1970).

546 As Brueggemann points out, the ancient sages believed that "There is no use waiting for better opportunities for our destiny is wrapped up with this ambiguous time and place, and it is here that we must work out our faith and our personhood." (ibid., 10).

547 Good (1981, 173-4). The "pleasure" and "life" which Qoheleth advocates are, of course, understood as one which is to be pursued within the parameters of God's commandments and laws (cf. 5:6 [ET v.7]; Murphy 1966, 13-14).

548 Ibid., 173-4.

the work and is that which gives unity and integrity to Qoheleth's narrative.

My argument began with the reiteration of the fact that the "autobiographical narrative" is a major wisdom form and indeed a prevalent one in biblical wisdom literature. An analysis of the self-reference verbs in *Qoheleth* demonstrated that Qoheleth's narrating voice permeates the work, namely from 1:12 to 10:7. I proceeded to argue that readers are able to discern a coherent personality in Qoheleth's narrative despite the lack of a clear structure to the work. The theories and studies of Gordis, Whybray, Johnson, Loader, and Hertzberg were convincing in their argument that the inconsistencies and self-contradictions traditionally found in the work may be satisfactorily explained as Qoheleth's quotation of traditional wisdom in order to debate with it. These works further confirmed that there is a consistency to Qoheleth's discourse which, upon closer examination, is dialectic in nature. An analysis of three passages to test the theory of Qoheleth's *zwar-aber* pattern of argument affirmed Hertzberg's argument that some of the "contradictions" in the text may be explained as reflecting the peculiar manner by which Qoheleth tests wisdom in order to draw out its limitations. This is what gives the work its protesting character, and which has also led many scholars to misinterpret the tensions in the text as reflecting Qoheleth's attack on tradition. Whilst not every theory and study examined was free from weakness, nevertheless, the main ideas expressed were found to be convincing and did provide strong support for the overall unity and integrity of Qoheleth's narrative and message. It was also demonstrated that the tensions in the text could also be explained as reflecting Qoheleth's personal struggle with the frustrating realities of life and the dilemma that he faces between the truths of traditional wisdom and his own experience in life.

We have also observed that Qoheleth is clearly well versed in the teachings and formulations of traditional wisdom as evidenced by his use of traditional wisdom forms, namely the didactic sayings, to refine, qualify, and show the limitations of the teachings of the tradition itself. We saw, through the theories and studies of Gordis, Whybray, and Johnson, that Qoheleth does not reject traditional wisdom but rather is keen to

reexamine its value and applicability. Despite his critical testing
of the wisdom tradition, Qoheleth's attitude towards wisdom is
essentially a positive one – he does advocate the pursuit of
wisdom and encourages wise living. It is clear that Qoheleth
remains very much in line with wisdom tradition in that he
examines and tests wisdom only ultimately to affirm many of its
truths and teachings, e.g. revering God (3:14; 5:6 [ET v.7],
keeping to cultic obligations (e.g. 5:3-4 [ET vv.4-5]), the value of
knowing about "appropriate" timing and behaviour, and the
operations of chance (e.g. 3:1-11; 9:11, 13-16) – truths which also
belonged to Israel's "older" wisdom (e.g. Prov. 15:23; 23:1-3;
25:11; 27:1, 14). Qoheleth's openness to new levels of
understanding bears the hallmark of wisdom's core belief and
enterprise. The argument that the work reflects a royal parody or
a subterfuge against God should therefore be abandoned and
seen as no longer tenable. Such a view is incompatible with
Qoheleth's continual support of traditional wisdom even though
he insistently warns of its relative value.

Unlike the more Stoic book of Proverbs, Qoheleth's
instructions do not come out of a fixed body of opinion, belief, or
procedure but rather emerge out of his interpretation of the
observed incongruencies in the world, the universal state of
human nature, and the received tradition of wisdom. Qoheleth's
instructions are uniquely presented in the form of an
autobiography of a king who is keen to share his philosophical
struggle and personal insights on these issues. That Qoheleth
chose to present his instruction in the form of an autobiography
is not wholly surprising in the light of our knowledge of
comparable forms of wisdom literature from the ancient Near
East and even within biblical wisdom itself.

Chapter 5

Conclusion

This study began with the purpose of testing the argument for the unity and pervasiveness of the royal voice in *Qoheleth*, whether it might have a more positive and integral role in the work, functioning not as a temporary literary artifice but as an overall organizing strategy for the main body of text in the book. It began with an overview of past interpretations of *Qoheleth*, focusing on the history behind the arguments for a Solomonic authorship and the issue of contradictions. It noted how in current scholarship there is a pervading sense of scepticism in the interpretation of the royal representations in the work which is complemented by the argument that the book is a subversive composition aimed against the institution of the monarchy and wisdom tradition. Against this present majority view of the royal fiction as merely a literary artifice which is limited to the first two chapters of the book, this study set out to test the pervasiveness and unity of the royal voice in the book.

The study commenced with an examination of the evidence for the royal voice in the first two chapters of the work (viz. 1:12-2:26), which are commonly regarded as representing Qoheleth's introduction. This was followed with an examination of the arguments of Perdue and Christianson for the pervasiveness of the royal voice. A closer look at their arguments revealed that they are both of the view that the royal elements carry a satirical purpose, with Perdue going further to suggest that the work is a subversive polemic against God. In order to test these arguments, which hold a sceptical view of the function of the royal voice in *Qoheleth*, eight passages, which are commonly regarded as being "anti-royal" in message and sentiment, were closely and carefully examined. These passages – Eccl. 3:16-17; 4:1; 4:13-16; 5:7-8 [ET vv.8-9]; 8:1-5; 10:5-7, 16-17; 10:20 – comprise general musings of injustice and exhortations which concern kingly rule and which most commentators attribute to the voice of either the powerless or the oppressed. Close analysis revealed that none of these texts were decisively "anti-royal"; instead, they were found to be compatible with a royal voice and clearly implied a court context as well. As a next step, the argument for the unity and pervasiveness of Qoheleth's royal voice was tested for parallels against compositions from the ancient Near East. With the ancient Semitic royal inscriptions a close similarity in the style and language of the works concerned were observed and which appeared to suggest Qoheleth's intent to identify his work as a royal text. The analysis of another comparable ancient corpus, i.e., the Akkadian royal pseudo-autobiographies revealed even closer parallels between the works. This latter corpus comprise didactic narratives that purport to be written by a famous king in the form of a first-person account. The structural and thematic similarities that it shared with the Hebrew composition led to the suggestion of identifying *Qoheleth* as royal autobiography. In the final chapter, the argument for reading *Qoheleth* as royal autobiography was advanced after further analyses on the spread of Qoheleth's "I"-narration and the function of the "sayings" in the work confirmed that this proposition was both valid and reasonable. Finally, an interpretation of the purpose and message of Qoheleth's narrative was forwarded. This was followed with an analysis of Qoheleth's treatment of the themes of wisdom and folly, the results in which his solidarity with mainstream wisdom tradition was confirmed.

The first and most obvious conclusion to be drawn from this study is that the prevalent view in *Qoheleth* studies, which argues that the royal voice is merely a temporary literary device limited to the first two chapters of the book and used for a satirical purpose, has considerable weakness in the light of my analyses. The investigations carried out in this study have shown that there are good grounds for seeing the royal voice of Qoheleth as permeating his narrative and that it may be further described as being presented in the form of a royal autobiography. This study has also shown how this motif gives unity to the main body of the book (1:12-11:6) and does not necessarily reflect a protest against kingship. The suggested royal context to Qoheleth's didactic wisdom composition is not far-fetched when viewed against ancient Near Eastern literature which do have wisdom compositions with comparable forms to *Qoheleth*. It is generally acknowledged that most ancient Near Eastern didactic wisdom texts are attributed to kings, a characteristic which is most clearly seen in the ancient Egyptian corpus. The Egyptian Instructions are well known examples of didactic literature supposedly written by kings and aristocrats. As was seen in the investigation in Chapter 3, *Qoheleth* does display a broad similarity of form to the Royal Instructions although *Qoheleth's* distinctiveness is also evident, most notably in its pessimistic and critical style of wisdom. A much closer parallel is seen in the Akkadian royal pseudo-autobiographies where the weaknesses of the royal narrator are sometimes exposed as part of its lesson to readers. My comparative analysis helped to establish further the argument for the coherence and unity of Qoheleth's royal voice (and indirectly and more generally the rest of his narrative) and has further highlighted the link between Hebrew wisdom composition and the Akkadian literary tradition of pseudo-autobiography in its use of a royal persona, portrayed at times in less than flattering ways, for a didactic purpose. Qoheleth's use of conventional wisdom forms (to question the tradition itself) and his adoption of a royal guise hints at the author's deliberate attempts at establishing the book firmly within wisdom tradition. And far from being a work belonging to someone on the edge of the tradition, it shows the author steeped in the tradition but wishing to take it further in the direction of a specific critique. Furthermore, within this context and by his use of the royal autobiography form, Qoheleth's narrative affirms and sustains the tradition of royal wisdom which Solomon represents and which he is also keen to continue.

There are those who have argued that *Qoheleth* represents a "crisis" in Israel's wisdom tradition (often citing Qoheleth's attack on wisdom and his theology of a distant and disaffected God as evidence[549]) and others who view the book as representing a later and evolved development in the wisdom

---

549 E.g. Gese (1963); Crenshaw (1988).

tradition.[550] Whilst it is beyond the scope of this study to explore this issue further, a few thoughts have nevertheless emerged from the above investigations which I wish to offer, which are relevant to the question of *Qoheleth's* place in the history of Israel's wisdom tradition. First, as Murphy aptly points out, compared to the confidence and optimism expressed in the instructions of Proverbs, wisdom in *Qoheleth* appears to be less assured of her claims.[551] Yet, as von Rad has also highlighted, earlier biblical wisdom has always been aware of the limits of her experience in the world as seen in the sayings in Prov. 16:1; 19:21; 20:24 and 21:30-31.[552] The sages of biblical wisdom were clearly aware of the paradoxical nature of humanity's quest for wisdom and the understanding of reality, that whilst human beings are to work towards being wise and gaining knowledge, they too should be aware of their limitations. Although we have observed the radical approach that Qoheleth takes in his teaching, which is in clear contrast to Proverbs' more mild and optimistic approach to life, my investigations above have revealed that Qoheleth's protests do not lead to the total rejection of the tradition but are only a critique of it. Qoheleth does no more than to continue the development of wisdom's own process with his examination and correction of wisdom's own principles.[553]

This study has demonstrated that the common argument that *Qoheleth* represents a total attack against traditional wisdom is overstated. Instead, it has been observed above that Qoheleth, though keen to make the point that "wisdom is a relative affair",[554] actually affirms the many wisdom topics that he touches on and encourages his hearers back to wisdom's central focus, which is the pursuit of wisdom and the enjoyment of life. Qoheleth's deliberate use of conventional wisdom forms and its truths to question tradition itself seems to hint at the existence of institutions and a milieu which may have continued to promote

---

550 Schmid (1966).
551 Murphy 1981, 236.
552 Von Rad 1972, 97-110.
553 Murphy 1981, 236.
554 Loader 1979, 122.

traditional wisdom (and which also would have been responsible for educating Qoheleth in the knowledge of its conventions and traditions) and one which Qoheleth was keen to challenge and develop. Again, those who have argued that the book reflects a "crisis" of wisdom have also said that it was against the established orthodoxy of tradition that Qoheleth was attacking from the sideline. Although this is a possible view it is nevertheless unlikely because of a further and more critical question which such an argument would raise, namely, why a radical work at the fringe of tradition which attacks established conventions would have been preferred and consequently preserved in the canon over works of a more traditional nature. I suggest that a more likely interpretation is that Qoheleth's protest is a development from within the confines of mainstream wisdom itself whilst remaining very much a part of it.[555] This notion finds support in Dell's suggestion that the "protesting" character of *Qoheleth* may be a reflection of mainstream wisdom which was also considered "orthodox" during the time of the writer.[556] This is not difficult to imagine since, as was seen above, Qoheleth is not totally rejecting wisdom but only testing it. This would serve as a good reason for its preservation and circulation and eventual entry into the canon. Dell further argues that by the time of the epilogist the concept of wisdom had changed. Thus, wisdom at this later period "was being judged by different standards of orthodoxy which related to harmonization with the Torah".[557] It was this later addition, that is, the provision of an

---

555 Crenshaw argues that sceptical thought which not only is evident in *Qoheleth* but also inherent in certain Israelite dogmas represents a natural development from within Israel's own religion (1980). Crenshaw, however, posits that *Qoheleth* represents a "crisis" in the wisdom tradition with its severe attack of it and God (1988).

556 Dell (1994). Cf. Schmid's (1966) theory of the evolution of wisdom, which he argued was observed in the traditions of ancient Egypt, Mesopotamia and Israel. Schmid suggested that, in its first and early phase, wisdom is flexible and relative and reflects more closely to reality. In the second phase, wisdom becomes dogmatic and begins to set hard and fast rules. The final stage is the "crisis" phase where the tradition itself is seen to protest against its own dogma. According to Schmid's model *Qoheleth* belongs to the crisis stage. One may posit further the return of wisdom tradition to orthodoxy following its phase of protest. See the main discussion above.

557 Dell 1994, 328.

orthodox interpretative context by the editor, which secured the book its place in the canon. Dell's argument could be taken one step further to suggest that the history of Israel's wisdom tradition may have developed in a *cyclical* manner, between periods of optimistic orthodoxy and protesting pessimism. Such a view is possible given that the wisdom of Ben Sira and the epilogue of *Qoheleth* are often said to reflect a similar brand of orthodoxy and possibly even share a similar period in wisdom's history of development.[558] Should this be the case then it would be possible to say that we have in the book of *Qoheleth* evidence of wisdom tradition from two different periods of its history (rather than the argument of *Qoheleth* as a non-mainstream wisdom text being aligned and reinterpreted by a pietistic redactor).[559] *Qoheleth* may thus be said to represent a *transitory* or *intermediate* period in Israel's history of wisdom tradition when protesting types of compositions were *en vogue* with their testing and questioning of wisdom's more confident and optimistic dogma. This idea could be tested further for compatibility with those studies which focus on sociological issues to try to determine the possible background which would have given rise to a general sceptical or pessimistic mood in Israel's history and hence influenced Qoheleth as well. Another possible area for future research would be to test this argument more fully against ancient Near Eastern wisdom literature.

The second conclusion to be drawn from this study relates to Qoheleth's use of royal fiction. Whilst commentators usually see Qoheleth's use of the royal guise as the most likely reason for the book's preservation and entry into the canon (a suggestion which is not improbable), this study has gone further to suggest

---

558 E.g. Sheppard argues that both Ben Sira and the author of the Eccl. 12:13-14 share the same ideology (1977, 182, 187-8).

559 Cf. Dell's suggestion on the possible reason why *Qoheleth* and not Ben Sira succeeded in entering the canon: "... the epilogue to Ecclesiastes functions to make a link between wisdom and torah and reflects an interpretation of Ecclesiastes as wisdom in a new sense that characterized the period of this redaction. I suggest that chronologically the epilogue to Ecclesiastes came to be written before Ben Sira and so represents a first stage in the development of this explicit wisdom/torah link. This would explain why Ecclesiastes is in the canon and Ben Sira is not, despite the fact that Ben Sira is more overtly torah-centred wisdom" (1994, 313).

that the royal voice has a more integral role in the composition reflecting the traditional link between the king and wisdom. From this study, it is possible to postulate that Qoheleth's use of a royal guise was part of his deliberate attempt at affirming an essential continuity with a past tradition where wisdom was once associated with king and court. Furthermore, Qoheleth's use of a Solomonic guise was to show that despite the heavy questioning and scrutiny to which conventional wisdom was subjected, the work was to be appreciated as mainstream wisdom.[560] I would like to suggest further that the pervasiveness of the autobiography motif may have been the key to the book's entry into the canon in that at the time of canonization, the Solomonic guise was seen as pervading the whole book and that it was not merely limited to its ascription and Qoheleth's introduction. The pervasion of the royal autobiography motif coupled with the book's inherently sapiential character may have been the decisive factors that finally ensured its entry into the canon.

In this study, we have seen that there are many example-stories in *Qoheleth* which carry heavy political and royal overtones and themes which may have been created to present an impression of a court background and suggest that Qoheleth's audience might have had close court connections, all of which would further support the traditional notion that wisdom was held under the patronage of the king.[561] It might also be said that *Qoheleth*, with its stated aim of testing and teaching wisdom, creates the impression of an audience which is made up of a classroom of students who are well-versed in the teachings of the tradition which are being put to the test in this work. This brings up images of a wisdom school setting with connections to the court. As the investigations above have shown, the allusions to

---

560 We might also add Childs's remark that Qoheleth's use of a Solomonic persona who is "the eponymic father of Hebrew wisdom, is specifically to guard the normative status of this message against ascribing it to the individual quirks of its author" (1979, 588).

561 Garrett, for example, believes that the implied readers were "people who were likely to have access to the king and to the circles of power. They were people for whom the pursuit of wealth was a real possibility and not just a fantasy and who had the leisure time for intellectual pursuits" (1993, 33).

Solomon are present and pervasive, and all of Qoheleth's examples and teachings could be viewed as having a court context. Whilst it is clear that the work cannot be dated to the time of the monarchy,[562] Qoheleth's use of a Solomonic guise appears to be aimed at recalling Solomon as the chief patron of wisdom, reaffirming wisdom as a court product and harking back to the golden era of the Solomonic Enlightenment when scribes were possibly working in schools at court and wisdom was taught there.[563] In his attempt to retroject the work into the time of Solomon and to create it as a retrospect of that earlier wisdom tradition, when wisdom flourished as never before or since, Qoheleth grounds his own reflections in that tradition. This further suggests that the accounts of Solomon's famed wisdom in the Bible might perhaps be more than a legendary embellishment of history.[564]

To conclude, this study, which began with the initial purpose of demonstrating the pervasiveness of the royal voice, has gone further to present a case for the identification of royal autobiography in *Qoheleth*. This study has argued that the autobiography motif gives unity to the book of *Qoheleth* and helps to explain and solve the problem of the contradictions of thought traditionally found in the book. It is likely that the autobiographical presentation of Qoheleth's narrative was a deliberate attempt to link up with royal wisdom of the pre-exilic period, echoing in particular the golden days of wisdom at the time of Solomon, and grounding the author's message in the heartland of the wise of the pre-exilic royal court. It is clear that this presentation took place in the post-exilic period when much of that royal context would have been lost. The optimism of the traditional wisdom quest as represented by Proverbs had passed and yet the author wanted to affirm an essential continuity with past tradition, even though he now needed to subject it to much questioning and scrutiny in the light of his own experience.

---

562 I accept the traditional fourth to third century dating of the work based primarily on arguments of language. See e.g. Schoors (1992).

563 Cf. von Rad [1970]; Heaton (1974).

564 For arguments in this direction see Scott (1976); Meade (1986, 48-51); Lemaire (1995).

Bibliography

Aharoni, Y., 1981. *Arad Inscriptions*. JDS. Jerusalem: Israel Exploration Society.

Avishur, Y., and M. Heltzer, 2000. *Studies on the Royal Administration in Ancient Israel in the light of epigraphic sources*. ACP. Jerusalem: Graphit.

Backhaus, F. J., 1993. *„Denn Zeit und Zufall trifft sie alle": Studien zur Komposition und zum Gottesbild im Buch Qohelet*. BBB 83. Frankfurt am Main: A. Hain.

Baines, J., 1991. "Society, Morality, and Religious Practice", in *Religion in Ancient Egypt. Gods, Myths, and Personal Practice*, ed. B. E. Shafer (London : Routledge), 123-200.

_____. 1996. "Myth and Literature", in *Ancient Egyptian Kingship: History and Forms*, ed. A. Loprieno (Leiden/New York/Köln: Brill), 361-78.

Barton, G. A., 1908. *A Critical and Exegetical Commentary on the Book of Ecclesiastes*. ICC. Edinburgh: T. & T. Clark.

Baumgartner, W., 1933. *Israelitische und altorientalische Weisheit*. SGV 166. Tübingen: Mohr (Siebeck).

_____. 1959. *Zum Alten Testament und seiner Umwelt*. Leiden: Brill.

Barucq, A., 1967. *L'Ecclésiaste*. Paris: Beauchesne.

Beckwith, R., 1985. *The Old Testament Canon of the New Testament Church*. Grand Rapids: Eerdmans.

Beentjes, P., 1998. "'Who is like the Wise?': Some Notes on Qohelet 8,1-15", in *Qohelet in the Context of Wisdom*, ed. A. Schoors (Leuven: Uitgeverij Peeters), 303-18.

Black, J., A. George, and N. Postgate (eds.), 1999. *A Concise Dictionary of Akkadian*. SANTAG AUK 5. Wiesbaden: Harrossowitz.

Borger, R., 1961. *Einleitung in die assyrischen Königsinschriften, Erster Teil: Das zweite Jahrtausend v. Chr.* HOE V/1/1. Leiden/Köln: Brill.

_____. 1964. *Die Inschriften Asarhaddons Königs von Assyrien.* AfO 9. Osnabrück: Biblio. Reprint, 1961.

Bratsiotis, N. P., 1961. "Der Monolog im Alten Testament", *ZAW* 73: 30-70.

Braun, R., 1973. *Kohelet und die frühhellenistische Popularphilosophie.* BZAW 130. Berlin: de Gruyter.

Bron, F., 1997. "Karatepe Phoenician Inscriptions", in *The Oxford Encyclopedia of Archaeology in the Near East*, ed. E. M. Meyers (Vol. 3; New York: Oxford University), 268-69.

Brown, F., S. R. Driver and C. A. Briggs. 1907. *A Hebrew and English Lexicon of the Old Testament.* Oxford: Clarendon.

Brown, W. P., 2000. *Ecclesiastes.* IBC. Louisville: John Knox.

Brueggemann, W. A., 1970. "Scripture and an Ecumenical Life-Style", *Int* 24: 3-19.

_____. 1990. "The Social Significance of Solomon as a Patron of Wisdom", in *The Sage in Israel and the Ancient Near East*, ed. J. G. Gammie et al. (Winona Lake: Eisenbrauns), 117-32.

Burkes, S., 1999. Death in Qoheleth and Egyptian Biographies of the Late Period. SBLDS 170. Atlanta: Scholars Press.

Caquot, A., 1978. "Israelite Perceptions of Wisdom and Strength in the Light of the Ras Shamra Texts", in *Israelite Wisdom: Theological and Literary Essays in Honor of Samuel Terrien*, ed. J. G. Gammie et al.(Missoula: Scholars Press), 25-33.

Childs, B. S., 1979. *Introduction to the Old Testament as Scripture.* London: SCM Press.

Christianson, E. S., 1998. *A Time To Tell: Narrative Strategies in Ecclesiastes.* JSOTSup 280. Sheffield: Sheffield Academic, 1998.

Cohen, A. (trans.), 1939. "Ecclesiastes", in *Midrash Rabbah. Ruth. Ecclesiastes*, eds. H. Freedman et al. (Vol. 8; London: Soncino), i-318.

Crenshaw, J. L., 1974. Wisdom", in *Old Testament Form Criticism*, ed. J. Hayes (San Antonio: Trinity University Press), 225-64.

_____. 1980. "The Birth of Skepticism in Ancient Israel", in *The Divine Helmsman: Studies on God's Control of Human Events*, ed. J. L. Crenshaw et al. (New York: KTAV), 5-15.

_____. 1988. *Ecclesiastes: a commentary*. OTL. London: SCM.

Crüsemann, F., 1984. "The Unchangeable World: the 'crisis of wisdom' in Koheleth", in *God of the Lowly: Socio-Historical Interpretations of the Bible*, ed. W. Schottroff et al. (New York: Orbis Books), 57-77.

Danby, H. (trans.), 1933. *The Mishnah*. Oxford: Clarendon.

Delitzsch, F., 1891. *Commentary on the Song of Songs and Ecclesiastes*. Translated by M. G. Easton. Edinburgh: T. & T. Clark. [German original: *Biblischer Commentar über die poetischen Bücher des Alten Testaments*. 4. Band *Hoheslied und Koheleth*. Leipzig: Dörffler und Franke, 1875.]

Dell, K. J., 1991. *The Book of Job as Sceptical Literature*. BZAW 197. Berlin: de Gruyter.

_____. 1994. "Ecclesiastes as Wisdom: Consulting Early Interpreters", *VT* 44: 301-29.

Donner, H., and W. Röllig, 1966-1969. *Kanaanäische und aramäische Inschriften*. 2nd edn. Wiesbaden: Harrassowitz.

Driver, S. R., 1913. *An Introduction to the Literature of the Old Testament*. 9th edn. Edinburgh: T. & T. Clark.

Eakin, P. J., 1985. *Fictions in Autobiography: Studies in the Art of Self-Invention*. Princeton: Princeton University Press.

Einstein, A., 1962. *Ideas and Opinions*. New York: Crown Publishers.

Eissfeldt, O., 1964. *Einleitung in das Alte Testament*. 3rd edn. Tübingen: Mohr (Paul Siebeck). [ET: *The Old Testament: An Introduction, including the Apocrypha and Pseudepigrapha*. Translated by P. Ackroyd. Oxford: Basil Blackwell, 1965.]

Ellermeier, F., 1967. *Qohelet I/1. Untersuchungen zum Buche Qohelet*. Herzberg: Jungfer.

Elliger, K., and W. Rudolph, 1984. *Biblia Hebraica Stuttgartensia*. Stuttgart: Deutsche Bibelgesellschaft.

Emerton, J. A., 2005. "Lines 25-6 of the Moabite Stone and a Recently-Discovered Inscription", *VT* 55: 293-303.

Engnell, I., 1967. *Studies in Divine Kingship in the Ancient Near East*. Oxford: Blackwell.

Euringer, S., 1890. *Der Masorahtext des Koheleth*. Leipzig: Hinrich's.

Evans, C. D., 1983. "Naram-Sin and Jeroboam: The Archetypal Unheilsherrscher in Mesopotamian and Biblical Historiography", in *Scripture in Context II: More essays in the comparative method*, ed. W. W. Hallo et al. (Winona Lake: Eisenbrauns), 97-126.

Farber, W., 1997. Review of T. Longman, *Fictional Akkadian Autobiographies*, *JNES* 56 (4): 228-30.

Finkelstein, J. J., 1957. "The So-Called 'Old-Babylonian Kutha Legend'", *JCS* 11: 83-88.

_____. 1963. "Mesopotamian Historiography", in *Proceedings of the American Philosophical Society 107*. (As cited by Evans 1983, 99 n.8.)

Fisch, H., 1988. "Qohelet: A Hebrew Ironist", in H. Fisch, *Poetry with a Purpose. Biblical Poetics and Interpretation* (ISBL; Bloomington/Indianapolis: Indiana University Press), 158-78.

Fischer, A., 1991. "Beobachtungen zur Komposition von Kohelet 1,3-3,15", *ZAW* 103: 72-86.

_____. 1997. *Skepsis oder Furcht Gottes? Studien zur Komposition und Theologie des Buches Kohelet*. BZAW 247. Berlin: de Gruyter.

Fohrer, G., 1965. *Einleitung in das Alte Testament*. 10th edn. Heidelberg: Quelle & Meyer. [ET: *Introduction to the Old Testament*. Translated by D. Green. Nashville: Abingdon, 1968.]

Förstemann, K. E., and H. E. Bindseil (eds.), 1844-1848. *D. Martin Luther's Tischreden oder Colloquia, ... nach Aurifaber's erster Ausgabe... herausgegeben und erläutert*. 4 vols. Berlin: Gebauer'sche Buchhandlung.

Fox, M. V., 1977. "Frame-Narrative and Composition in the Book of Qohelet", *HUCA* 47: 83-106.

_____. 1989. *Qohelet and his Contradictions*. JSOTSup 71. Sheffield: Almond.

_____. 1998. "The Inner Structure of Qohelet's Thought", in *Qoheleth in the Context of Wisdom*, ed. A. Schoors (BETL 136; Leuven: Uitgerenj Peeters), 225-38.

_____. 1999. *A Time to Tear Down and a Time to Build Up. A Rereading of Ecclesiastes*. Grand Rapids/Cambridge: Eerdmans.

Fredericks, D. C., 1988. *Qoheleth's Language: Re-evaluating its Nature and Date*. ANETS 3. Lewiston: Edwin Mellen.

Gadd, C. J., 1958. "The Harran Inscriptions of Nabonidus", *AnSt* 8: 35-92.

Galling, K., 1932. "Koheleth-Studien", *ZAW* 50: 276-99.

_____. 1964. "Predigerbuch", in *RGG³*, 1580-83.

_____. 1969. "Der Prediger", in *Die Fünf Megilloth*. HAT I, 18. 2nd edn. Tübingen: Mohr.

Galling, K., and H. F. Campenhausen (eds.), 1957-1965. *Die Religion in Geschichte und Gegenwart*. 7 vols. 3rd edn. Tübingen: J. C. B. Mohr. [= *RGG³*]

Garrett, D., 1993. *Proverbs, Ecclesiastes, Song of Songs*. NAC. Nashville: Broadman.

Gese, H., 1963. "Die Krisis der Weisheit bei Kohelet", in *Les sagesses du Proche-Orient ancien: Colloque de Strasbourg 17-19 mai, 1962* (TCESSHRS; Paris: Presses Universitaires de France), 139-51.

Gibson, J. C. L., 1971-1982. *Textbook of Syrian Semitic Inscriptions*. 3 vols. Oxford: Clarendon.

_____. 1994. *Davidson's Introductory Hebrew Grammar ~ Syntax*. 4th edn. Edinburgh: T. & T. Clark.

Ginsberg, H. L., 1950. *Studies in Koheleth*. TSJTSA 17. New York: Jewish Theological Seminary of America.

_____. 1955. "The Structure and Contents of the Book of Koheleth", in *Wisdom in Israel and in the Ancient Near East*, ed. M. Noth et al. (SVT 3; Leiden: Brill), 138-49.

Ginsburg, C. D., 1861. *Coheleth, Commonly Called the Book of Ecclesiastes: Translated from the Original Hebrew, with a Commentary, Historical and Critical*. London: Longman, Green, Longman, and Roberts.

Good, E. M., 1965. *Irony in the Old Testament*. London: SPCK.

Gordis, R., 1939. "Quotations in Wisdom Literature", *JQR* 30: 123-47.

_____. 1943/44. "The Social Background of Wisdom Literature", *HUCA* 18: 77-118.

_____. 1949. "Quotations as a Literary Usage in Biblical, Oriental, and Rabbinic Literature", *HUCA* 22: 157-219.

_____. 1968. *Koheleth – The Man and His World*. 3rd edn. New York: Schocken Books.

Görg, M., 1977. "Komparatistische Untersuchungen an Ägyptischer und Israelitischer Literatur", in *Fragen an die altägyptische Literatur*, ed. Jan Assmann et al. (Wiesbaden: Ludwig Reichert), 197-215.

Grant, C. A., 2000. *"Chasing After the Wind". An Examination of the Social and Historical Background of the Book of Ecclesiastes*. Ph.D. diss., University of Cambridge.

Grayson, A. K., 1972-76. *Assyrian Royal Inscriptions*. 2 vols. Wiesbaden: Harrassowitz.

_____. 1975. *Babylonian Historical-Literary Texts*. Toronto: University of Toronto Press.

_____. 1980a. "Assyria and Babylonia", *Or* 49: 140-94.

_____. 1980b. "Histories and Historians of the Ancient Near East: Assyria and Babylonia", *Or* 49: 182-87.

_____. 1981. "Assyrian Royal Inscriptions: Literary Characteristics", in *Assyrian Royal Inscriptions: New Horizons in literary, ideological, and historical analysis*, ed. F. M. Fales (Rome: Istitute per L'Oriente), 35-48.

_____. 1987-1996. *The Royal Inscriptions of Mesopotamia. Assyrian Periods*. 3 vols. Toronto: University of Toronto Press.

Grayson, A. K., and W. G. Lambert, 1964. "Akkadian Prophecies", *JCS* 18: 8.

Greenfield, J. C., 1971. "Scripture and inscription: The literary and rhetorical element in some early Phoenician inscriptions", in *Near Eastern Studies in Honor of W. F. Albright*, ed. H. Goedicke (Baltimore: The Johns Hopkins Press), 253-68.

_____. 1991. "Doves' Dung and the Price of Food: The Topoi of II Kings 6:24-7:2", in *Storia e tradizioni di Israele. Scritti in onore di J. Alberto Soggin*, ed. D. Garrone et al. (Brescia: Paideia), 121-26.

Greenstein, E. L., 1995. "Autobiographies in Ancient Western Asia", in *CANE*, 2421-32.

Gressmann, H., 1925. *Israels Spruchweisheit im Zusammenhang der Weltliteratur*. KA 6. Berlin: Karl Curtius.

Gunkel, H., 1909. "Predigerbuch", in *RGG¹*, 1405-408.

Gurney, O. R., 1955. "The Sultantepe Tablets IV. The Cuthaean Legend of Naram-Sin", in *AnSt* 5: 93-113.

_____. 1956. "Corrections to Previous Articles", *AnSt* 6: 163-4.

Güterbock, H. G., 1934. "Die historische Tradition und ihre literarische Gestaltung bei Babyloniern und Hethitern bis 1200", *ZA* 42: 1-91.

Hallo, W. W., and W. K. Simpson, 1998. *The Ancient Near East: A History.* 2nd edn. New York: Harcourt Brace.

Hallo, W. W., and K. L. Younger Jr. (eds.), 1997-2000. *The Context of Scripture.* 3 vols. Leiden: Brill.

Haupt, P., 1905. *The Book of Ecclesiastes.* Baltimore: Johns Hopkins.

Hawkins, J. D., 1995. "Karkamish and Karatepe: Neo-Hittite City-States in North Syria", in *CANE*, 1295-307.

_____. 1986. "Royal Statements of Ideal Prices: Assyrian, Babylonian, and Hittite", in *Ancient Anatolia, Aspects of Change and Cultural Development. Essays in Honor of Machteld J. Mellink,* ed. J. V. Canby et al. (Madison: University of Wisconsin), 93-106.

Heaton, E. W., 1974. *Solomon's New Men.* London: Thames and Hudson.

Heim, K. M., 2001. *Like Grapes of Gold Set in Silver. An Interpretation of Proverbial Clusters in Proverbs 10:1-22:16.* BZAW 273. Berlin: de Gruyter.

Hengel, M., 1974. *Judaism and Hellenism.* Translated by J. Bowden. 2 vols. London: SCM. [German original: *Judentum und Hellenismus.* WUNT 10. 2nd edn. Tübingen: J. C. B. Mohr (Paul Siebeck), 1973.]

Hengstenberg, E. W., 1869. *Commentary on Ecclesiastes.* Translated by D. W. Simon. Clark's Foreign Theological Library. Vol. 6. 3rd series. Edinburgh: T. & T. Clark. [German original: *Der Prediger Salomo ausgelegt von E. W. Hengstenberg.* Berlin: Oehmigke, 1859.]

Hertzberg, H. W., 1963. *Der Prediger.* Gütersloh: Gerd Mohn.

Hitzig, F., 1847. *Die Sprüche Salomo's. Der Prediger Salomo's.* Leipzig: Weidmann.

Höffken, P., 1985. "Das EGO des Weisen", *TZ* 4: 121-35.

Hoffner Jr., H. A., 1970. "Remarks on the Hittite Version of the Naram-Sin Legend", *JCS* 23: 17-22.

Holm-Nielsen, S., 1974. "On the Interpretation of Qoheleth in Early Christianity", *VT* 24: 168-77.

Isaksson, B., 1987. *Studies in the Language of Qoheleth: With Special Emphasis on the Verbal System.* SSU 10. Stockholm: Almqvist & Wiksell.

Japhet, S., and R. Salters (eds.), 1985. *The Commentary of R. Samuel Ben Meir Rashbam on Qoheleth.* Jerusalem: Magnes.

Jarick, J., 1990. *Gregory Thaumaturgos' Paraphrase of Ecclesiastes.* SBLSCS 29. Atlanta: Scholars Press.

Jastrow Jr., M., 1919. *A Gentle Cynic: being a translation of the book of Koheleth, commonly known as Ecclesiastes, stripped of later additions, also its origin, growth, and interpretation.* Philadelphia: J. B. Lippincott Company.

Johnson, R. F., 1973. *A Form Critical Analysis of the Sayings in the Book of Ecclesiastes.* Ph.D. diss., Emory University.

Johnston, R., 1976. "Confessions of a 'Workaholic': A Reappraisal of Qoheleth", *CBQ* 38: 14-28.

Joüon, P., 1991. *A Grammar of Biblical Hebrew.* Translated and revised by T. Muraoka. 2 vols. Subsidia biblica 14/1-2. Rome: Editrice Pontifio Istituto Biblico.

Kaiser, O., 1982. "Judentum und Hellenismus", *VF* 27: 69-73.

_____. 1985. "Fate, Suffering and God: The Crisis of Belief in a Moral World Order in the Book of Ecclesiastes", *OTE* 4: 1-13.

_____. 1995. "Qoheleth", in *Wisdom in Ancient Israel: Essays in Honour of J. A. Emerton,* ed. J. Day et al. (Cambridge: Cambridge University Press), 30-42.

Kalugila, L., 1980. *The Wise King: Studies in Royal Wisdom as Divine Revelation in the Old Testament and its Environment.* ConBOT 15. Uppsala: CWK Gleerup.

Kamano, N., 2002. *Cosmology and Character: Qoheleth's Pedagogy from a Rhetorical-Critical Perspective.* BZAW 312. Berlin: de Gruyter.

Kautzsch, E. (ed.), 1910. *Gesenius' Hebrew Grammar*. 2nd edn. [=28th German edn.] Translated by A. E. Cowley. Oxford: Clarendon.

Kitchen, K. A., 1977/8. "Proverbs and Wisdom Books of the Ancient Near East: The Factual History of a Literary Form", *TB* 28: 69-114.

_____. 1979. "The Basic Literary Forms and Formulations of Ancient Instructional Writings in Egypt and Western Asia", in *Studien zu Altägyptischen Lebenslehren*, ed. E. Hornung et al. (OBO 28; Freiburg, Schweiz: Universitätsverlag; Göttingen: Vandenhoeck & Ruprecht), 235-82.

Klein, C., 1994. *Kohelet und die Weisheit Israel. Eine formgeschichtliche Studie*. Stuttgart/Berlin/Köln: W. Kohlhammer.

Knobel, P., 1991. "The Targum of Qohelet", in *The Aramaic Bible*, ed. K. Cathcart et al. (Vol. 15; Edinburgh: T. & T. Clark).

Koehler, L., W. Baumgartner, and J. J. Stamm, 1995. *Hebräisches und aramäisches Lexikon zum Alten Testament*. 2 vols. 3rd edn. Leiden: Brill. [ET: *HALOT*]

_____. 1994-1999. *The Hebrew and Aramaic Lexicon of the Old Testament*. Translated and edited under the supervision of M. E. J. Richardson. 4 vols. Leiden: Brill. [= 3rd German edn. *HAL*]

Kroeber, R., 1963. *Der Prediger*. SQAW 13. Berlin: Akademie.

Krüger, T., 2004. *Qoheleth: A Commentary*. Hermeneia. Minneapolis: Fortress.

Lambert, W. G., 1960. "Gilgameš in Religious, Historical and Omen Texts and the Historicity of Gilgameš", in *Gilgameš et sa légende*, ed. P. Garelli (CRRAI 7, CGFTD 1; Paris: Imprimerie Nationale & Librarie C. Klincksieck), 39-56.

_____. 1965. *Cuneiform Texts from Babylonian Tablets in the British Museum*. Vol. XLVI. London: Trustees of the British Museum. Pl. 45. no. 46.

Lauha, A., 1955. "Die Krise des religiösen Glaubens bei Kohelet", in *Wisdom in Israel and in the Ancient Near East*, ed. M. Noth et al. (SVT 3; Leiden: Brill), 83-91.

_____. 1978. *Kohelet*. BKAT 19. Neukirchen-Vluyn: Neukirchener.

_____. 1981. "Kohelets Verhältnis zur Geschichte", in *Die Botschaft und die Boten: Festschrift für Hans Walter Wolff zum 70.*

Geburtstag, ed. Jörg Jeremias et al. (Neukirchen- Vluyn: Neukirchener), 393-401.

Leeuwen, R. C. van, 1961. "Proverbs 30:21-23 and the Biblical World Upside Down", *JBL* 105: 599-610.

_____. 1988. *Context and Meaning in Proverbs 25-27.* SBLDS 96. Atlanta: Scholars Press.

Leiman, S. Z., 1976. *The Canonization of Hebrew Scripture: The Talmudic and Midrashic Evidence.* Hamden, CT: Archon Books.

Lemaire, A., 1995. "Wisdom in Solomonic Historiography", in *Wisdom in Ancient Israel: Essays in Honour of J. A. Emerton,* ed. J. Day et al. (Cambridge: Cambridge University Press), 106-18.

Levine, E. (ed.), 1978. *The Aramaic Version of Qohelet.* New York: Sepher-Hermon Press.

_____. 1990. "Qoheleth's Fool: A Composite Portrait", in *On Humour and the Comic in the Hebrew Bible,* ed. Y. T. Radday et al. (Sheffield: Almond Press), 277-94.

Levy, M. L., 1912. *Das Buch Qohelet.* Leipzig: Hinrich's.

Lewis, B., 1980. *The Sargon Legend.* ASOR DS4. Cambridge, Mass.: ASOR.

Lichtheim, M., 1973-1980. *Ancient Egyptian Literature: A Book of Readings.* 3 vols. Berkeley: University of California Press.

_____. 1979. "Observations on Papyrus Insinger", in *Studien zu altägyptischen Lebenslehren,* ed. E. Hornung et al. (OBO 28; Freiburg, Schweiz: Universitätsverlag; Göttingen: Vandenhoeck & Ruprecht), 283-305.

_____. 1983. *Late Egyptian Wisdom Literature in the International Context: a Study of Demotic Instructions.* OBO 52. Freiburg: Universitätsverlag.

_____. 1988. *Ancient Egyptian Autobiographies Chiefly of the Middle Kingdom: a study and an anthology.* OBO 84. Göttingen: Vandenhoeck & Ruprecht. Freiburg, Schweiz: Universitätsverlag.

_____. 1992. *Maat in Egyptian Autobiographies and Related Studies.* OBO 120. Göttingen: Vandenhoeck & Ruprecht.

_____. 1996. "Didactic Literature", in *Ancient Egyptian Literature: History and Forms,* ed. A. Loprieno (Leiden/New York/Köln: Brill), 243-62.

Lipiński, E., 1977. "North-West Semitic Inscriptions", *OLP* 8: 81-117.

Liverani, M., 1979. "The Ideology of the Assyrian Empire", in *Power and Propaganda. A Symposium on Ancient Empires*, ed. M. T. Larsen (MCSA 7; Copenhagen: Akademisk Forlag), 297-318.

_____. 1995. "The Deeds of Ancient Mesopotamian Kings", in *CANE*, 2353-66.

Loader, J. A., 1979. *Polar Structures in the Book of Qohelet*. BZAW 152. Berlin: de Gruyter.

_____. 1986. *Ecclesiastes. A Practical Commentary*. Translated by J. Vriend. Text and Interpretation. Michigan: Eerdmans. [Dutch original: *Prediker: Een praktische bijbelverklaring*. Tekst en Toelichting. Kampen: Uitgeversmaatschappij J. H. Kok, 1984.]

Lohfink, N., 1982. "melek, šallît und môšēl bei Kohelet und die Abfassungszeit des Buches", *Bib* 62: 535-43.

_____. 2003. *Qoheleth: A Continental Commentary*. Translated by S. McEvenue. Minneapolis: Fortress. [German original: *Kohelet*. NEB. Würzburg: Echter, 1980.]

Longman III, T., 1991. *Fictional Akkadian Autobiography: a generic and comparative study*. Winona Lake: Eisenbrauns.

_____. 1998. *The Book of Ecclesiastes*. NICOT. Grand Rapids: Eerdmans.

Loretz, O., 1963. "Zur Darbietungsform der 'Ich-Erzählung' im Buche Qohelet", *CBQ* 25: 46-59.

_____. 1964. *Qohelet und der Alte Orient. Untersuchungen zu Stil und theologischer Thematik des Buches Qohelet*. Freiburg: Herder.

Lowth, R., 1815. *Lectures on the Sacred Poetry of the Hebrews*. Boston: Buckingham.

Luckenbill, D. D., 1924. *The Annals of Sennacherib*. Chicago: The University of Chicago Press.

_____. 1926-1927. *Ancient Records of Assyria and Babylonia*. 2 vols. Chicago: The University of Chicago Press.

Luther, M., 1972. "Notes on Ecclesiastes", in *Luther's Works*, ed. J. Pelikan (Vol. XV; St Louis: Concordia), 1-187.

Machinist, P.,   1995.   "Fate, miqreh, and Reason: Some
    Reflections on Qohelet and Biblical Thought", in *Solving
    Riddles and Untying Knots: Biblical, Epigraphic, and Semitic
    Studies in Honor of Jonas C. Greenfield*, ed. Z. Zevit et al.
    (Winona Lake: Eisenbrauns), 159-76.
Malamat, A., 1988. "The Kingdom of Judah Between Egypt and
    Babylon: A   Small   State   Within   A   Great   Power
    Confrontation", in *Text and Context. Old Testament and Semitic
    Studies for F. C. Fensham*, ed. W. T. Claassen (JSOTSup 48;
    Sheffield: JSOT Press), 117-129.
McCarter, P. K.,   2000.   "The Sarcophagus Inscription of
    'Eshmun'azor, King of Sidon", in *COS* 2.57.
McDonald, J., 1976. "The Status and Role of the na'ar in Israelite
    Society", *JNES* 35: 147-170.
McKane, W.,   1979.   "Functions of Language and Objectives of
    Discourse according to Proverbs, 10-30", in *La Sagesse de
    l'Ancient Testament*, ed. M. Gilbert (BETL 51; Gembloux:
    Duculot), 166-85.
McNeile, A. H., 1904. *An Introduction to Ecclesiastes*. Cambridge:
    Cambridge University Press.
Meade, D., 1986. *Pseudonymity and Canon*. WUNT 39. Tübingen:
    Mohr.
Messerschmidt, L., 1911. *Keilschrifttexte aus Assur, historischen
    Inhalts*. Vol. 1. WVDOG 16. Leipzig: J. C. Hinrichs.
Michel, D., 1988. *Qohelet*. EF 258. Darmstadt: Wissenschaftliche
    Buchgesellschaft.
_____. 1989. *Untersuchungen zur Eigenart des Buches Qohelet*.
    BZAW 183. Berlin: de Gruyter.
Migne, J. P. (ed.),   1845.   *Patrologiae cursus completus.   Sancti
    Eusebii Hieronymi stridonensis presbyteri Opera Omnia*. Vol. 23.
    Paris: Vrayet.
Millard, A. R., 1972. "The Practice of Writing in Ancient Israel",
    BA 35: 98-111.
Misch, G., 1950. *A History of Autobiography in Antiquity*.
    Translated in collaboration with the author by E. W. Dickes.
    Vol. 1, 2 parts. ILSSR. London: Routledge & Kegan Paul.
    [German   original: *Geschichte   der   Autobiographie*.
    Leipzig/Berlin: B. G. Teubner, 1907.]

Müller, H. –P., 1968. "Wie sprach Qohälät von Gott?", *VT* 18: 507-21.

_____. 1978. "Neige der althebräischen 'Weisheit.' Zum Denken Qohäläts", *ZAW* 90: 238-64.

Murphy, R. E., 1981. "Qohelet's 'Quarrel' with the Father", in *From Faith to Faith: Essays in Honor of Donald E. Miller*, ed. D. Y. Hadidian (Pittsburg: Pickwick), 235-45.

_____. 1982. "Qoheleth Interpreted: The Bearing of the Past on the Present", *VT* 32: 331-37.

_____. 1990. *The Tree of Life. An Exploration of Biblical Wisdom Literature*. New York: Bantam Doubleday Dell.

_____. 1992. *Ecclesiastes*. WBC 23A. Dallas: Word Books.

Newsome, C., 1995. "Job and Ecclesiastes", in *Old Testament Interpretation: Past, Present and Future Essays in Honor of Gene M. Tucker*, ed. J. L. Mays et al. (Nashville: Abingdon Press, Edinburgh: T. & T. Clark), 177-94.

Nowack, W., 1883. *Der Prediger Salomo*. Leipzig: Hirzel.

Ogden, G., 1987. *Qoheleth. Readings – A New Biblical Commentary*. Sheffield: JSOT Press.

Olmstead, A. T. E., 1916. *Assyrian Historiography: A Source Study*. UMS.SS Vol. 3, No.1. Missouri: University of Missouri.

Olney, J., 1972. *Metaphors of Self: The Meaning of Autobiography*. Princeton: Princeton University Press.

Oppenheim, A. L., 1964. *Ancient Mesopotamia: Portrait of a Dead Civilization*. Chicago: The University of Chicago Press.

Pardee, D., 1978. "Letters from Tel Arad", *UF* 10: 289-336.

_____. 2002. "Arad 88: A Fragment of a Copy of a Royal Proclamation", in *COS* 3:43M.

Pardee, D., S. D. Sperling, J. D. Whitehead, and P. E. Dion, 1982. *Handbook of Ancient Hebrew Letters*. SBLSBS 15. California: Scholars Press.

Parker, S. B., 1997. *Stories in Scripture and Inscriptions. Comparative Studies on Narratives in Northwest Semitic Inscriptions and the Hebrew Bible*. New York: Oxford University Press.

Parkinson, R. B., 1996. "Types of Literature in the Middle Kingdom", in *Ancient Egyptian Literature: History and Forms*, ed. A. Loprieno (Leiden: Brill), 297-312.

_____. 2002. *Poetry and Culture in Middle Kingdom Egypt: A Dark Side to Perfection*. APEANES. London: Continuum.

Pascal, R., 1960. *Design and Truth in Autobiography*. Cambridge: Harvard University Press.

Perdue, L., 1994. *Wisdom and Creation: The Theology of Wisdom Literature*. Nashville: Abingdon.

_____. 2003. "Wisdom and Apocalyptic: The Case of Qoheleth", in *Wisdom and Apocalypticism in the Dead Sea Scrolls and in the Biblical Tradition*, ed. García Martínez (BETL 168; Leuven: Leuven University Press), 231-59.

Perry, T. A., 1993. *Dialogues with Kohelet: The Book of Ecclesiastes: translation and commentary*. University Park, PA: Pennsylvania State University.

Plöger, O., 1984. *Sprüche Salomos (Proverbia)*. BKAT 17. Neukirchen-Vluyn: Neukirchener.

Plumptre, E. H., 1881. *Ecclesiastes, or, the Preacher: with notes, and introduction*. CBSC. Cambridge: Cambridge University Press.

Podechard, E., 1912. *L'Ecclésiaste*. EB. Paris: Librairie Victor Lecoffre.

Polk, T., 1976. "The Wisdom of Irony: A Study of Hebel and its Relation to Joy and the Fear of God in Ecclesiastes", *SBTh* 6: 3-17.

Pritchard, J. B. (ed.), 1969. *Ancient Near Eastern Texts Relating to the Old Testament*. 3rd edn. Princeton: Princeton University Press.

Rad, G. von, 1970. *Weisheit in Israel*. Neukirchen-Vluyn: Neukirchener. [ET: *Wisdom in Israel*. Translated by J. D. Martin. London: SCM, 1972.]

Rainey, A. F., 1977. "Three Additional Hebrew Ostraca from Tel Arad", *Tel Aviv* 4: 97-104.

Reade, J., 1981. "Neo-Assyrian Monuments in their Historical Context", in *Assyrian Royal Inscriptions: New Horizons in Literary, Ideological, and Historical Analysis*, ed. F. M. Fales (Rome: Istitute per L'Oriente), 143-168.

Röllig, W., 1992. "Asia Minor as a Bridge between East and West: The Role of the Phoenicians and Arameans in the Transfer of Culture", in *Greece between East and West: 10th-8th Centuries B.C.*, ed. G. Kopcke et al. (Mainz, Rhine: Philip von Zabern), 93-102.

Rousseau, F., 1981. "Structure de Qohelet i 4-11 et plan du livre", *VT* 31: 200-17.

Salyer, G. D., 2001. *Vain Rhetoric: Private Insight and Public Debate in Ecclesiastes*. JSOTSup 327. Sheffield: Sheffield Academic.

Sandberg, R. N., 1999. *Rabbinic Views on Qohelet*. MBPS 57. Lewiston: Edwin Mellen.

Sasson, J. (ed.), 1995. *Civilizations of the Ancient Near East*. 4 vols. New York: Simon & Schuster Macmillan.

Scheel, O., L. Zscharnack and H. Gunkel (eds.), 1909-1914. *Die Religion in Geschichte und Gegenwart*. 5 vols. Tübingen: J. C. B. Mohr. [=*RGG¹*]

Schmid, H. H., 1966. *Wesen und Geschichte des Weisheit: Eine Untersuchung zur altorientalischen und israelitischen Weisheisliteratur*. BZAW 101. Berlin: de Gruyter.

Schoors, A., 1992. *The Preacher Sought to Find Pleasing Words: A Study of the Language of Qoheleth*. OLA 41. Leuven: Uitgeverij Peeters.

_____. 1996. "The Verb ראה in the Book of Qoheleth", in *„Jedes Ding hat seine Zeit..."* *Studien zur israelitischen und altorientalischen Weisheit*, ed. A. A. Diesel et al. (BZAW 241; Berlin: de Gruyter), 227-42.

_____. 1998. "Words Typical of Qohelet", in *Qohelet in the Context of Wisdom*, ed. A. Schoors (Leuven: Uitgeverij Peeters), 17-40 .

Schroeder, O., 1922. *Keilschrifttexte aus Assur, historischen Inhalts*. Vol. 2. WVDOG 37. Leipzig: J. C. Hinrichs.

Schunck, K. D., 1959. "Drei Seleukiden im Buche Kohelet?", *VT* 9: 192-201.

Schwienhorst-Schönberger, L., 1994. *„Nicht im Menschen gründet das Glück": (Koh 2,24). Kohelet im Spannungsfeld jüdischer Weisheit und hellenistischer Philosophie*. HBS 2. Freiburg: Herder.

Scott, R. B. Y., 1965. *Proverbs. Ecclesiastes*. AB 18. Garden City, New York: Doubleday.

Seow, C. L., 1995. "Qohelet's Autobiography", in *Fortunate the Eyes that See: Essays in Honor of David Noel Freedman*, ed. A. Beck et al. (Grand Rapids: Eerdmans), 275-87.

_____. 1996. "Linguistic Evidence and the Dating of Qohelet", *JBL* 115: 643-66.

_____. 1997. *Ecclesiastes*. AB 18C. New York: Doubleday.

Seux, M.-J., 1967. *Épithètes royals akkadiennes et sumériennes*. Paris: Letouzey et Ané.

Sheppard, G. T., 1977. "The Epilogue to Qoheleth as Theological Commentary", *CBQ* 39: 182-189.

Siegfried, C. G., 1898. *Prediger und Hoheslied*. HKAT 2:3,2. Göttingen: Vandenhoeck & Ruprecht.

Silverman, D. P., 1995. "The Nature of Egyptian Kingship", in *Ancient Egyptian Kingship*, ed. David O'Connor et al. (Leiden/New York/Köln: Brill), 49-94.

Simon, M. (trans.), 1938. "Megillah", in *The Babylonian Talmud. Seder Mo'ed*, ed. I. Epstein (Vol. 4; London: Soncino), i-232.

Smalley, B., 1986. *Medieval Exegesis of Wisdom Literature*, ed. R. E. Murphy (Atlanta: Scholars Press).

Smelik, K. A. D., 1991. *Writings from Ancient Israel. A Handbook of Religious and Historical Documents*. Translated by G. I. Davies. Edinburgh: T. & T. Clark. [Dutch original: *Behouden Schrift: historische documenten uit het Oude Israël*. Baarn: Uitgeverij Ten Have, 1984.]

Spengemann, W. C., 1980. *The Forms of Autobiography: Episodes in the History of a Literary Genre*. New Haven: Yale University Press.

Starobinski, J., 1971. "The Style of Autobiography", in *Literary Style: A Symposium*, ed. S. Chatman (London: Oxford University Press), 285-96.

Streck, M., 1916. *Assurbanipal und die letzten assyrischen Könige bis zum Untergange Niniveh's*. VAB 7. 3 vols. Leipzig: Hinrichs'sche Buchhandlung.

Sturrock, J., 1993. *The Language of Autobiography: Studies in the First Person Singular*. Cambridge: Cambridge University Press.

Tadmor, H., 1981. "History and Ideology in the Assyrian Royal Inscriptions", in *Assyrian Royal Inscriptions: New Horizons in literary, ideological, and historical analysis*, ed. F. M. Fales (Rome: Istitute per L'Oriente), 35-48.

_____. 1983. "Autobiographical Apology in the Royal Assyrian Literature", in *History, Historiography and Interpretation*, ed. H. Tadmor et al. (Jerusalem: Magnes), 36-57.

Thomas, D. W., 1949. "A Note on בְּמַדְּעֲךָ in Ecclesiastes X 20", *JTS* 50: 177

Vinel, F., 1998. "Le texte grec de l'Ecclésiaste et ses caractéristiques. Une relecture critique de l'histoire de la royauté", in *Qohelet in the Context of Wisdom*, ed. A. Schoors (BETL 136; Leuven: Uitgeverij Peeters), 283-302.

Waltke, B., and M. O'Connor, 1990. *An Introduction to Biblical Hebrew Syntax*. Winona Lake: Eisenbrauns.

Weber, O., 1907. *Die Literatur der Babylonier und Assyrer*. Leipzig: Hinrich's.

Weintraub, K. J., 1978. *The Value of the Individual: Self and Circumstance in Autobiography*. Chicago: University of Chicago Press.

Westenholz, J. A., 1984. "Heroes of Akkad", in *Studies in Literature from the Ancient Near East by members of the American Oriental Society dedicated to Samuel Noah Kramer*, ed. Jack M. Sasson (New Haven: American Oriental Society), 327-36.

_____. 1997. *Legends of the Kings of Akkade*. MC 7. Winona Lake: Eisenbrauns.

Whitley, C. F., 1979. *Koheleth: His Language and Thought*. BZAW 148. Berlin: de Gruyter.

Whybray, R. N., 1978. "Qoheleth the Immoralist (Qoh 7:16-17)", in *Israelite Wisdom*, ed. J. G. Gammie et al. (Missoula: Scholars Press), 191-204.

_____. 1981. "The Identification and Use of Quotations in Qoheleth", in *Congress Volume: Vienna 1980*, ed. J. A. Emerton (SVT 32; Leiden: Brill), 435-51.

_____. 1989. *Ecclesiastes*. NCBC. London: Marshall, Morgan & Scott.

_____. 1998. "Qoheleth as a Theologian", in *Qoheleth in the Context of Wisdom*, ed. A. Schoors (BETL 136; Leuven: Uitgerenj Peeters), 239-66.

Wildeboer, D. G., 1898. "Der Prediger", in *Die Fünf Megillot*. KHC 17. (Freiburg: Mohr), 109-68.

Witzenrath, H. H., 1979. *Süß ist das Licht...: Eine literaturwissenschaftliche Untersuchung zu Koh 11,7 – 12,7*. ATAT 11. St Ottilien: EOS Verlag.

Wright, A. G., 1968. "The Riddle of the Sphinx: The Structure of the Book of Qoheleth", *CBQ* 30: 313-334.

Wright, C. H. H., 1883. *The Book of Koheleth*. *Donnellan Lectures 1880-1881*. London: Hodder and Stoughton.

Wright, J. S., 1946. "The Interpretation of Ecclesiastes", *EQ* 18: 18-34.

Yadin, Y., 1976. "The Historical Significance of Inscription 88 from Arad: A Suggestion", *IEJ* 26: 9-14.

Younger Jr., K. L., 1990. "The Figurative Aspect and the Contextual Method in the Evaluation of the Solomonic Empire (1 Kings 1-11)", in *The Bible in Three Dimensions. Essays in Celebration of Forty Years of Biblical Studies in the University of Sheffield*, ed. D. J. A. Clines et al. (JSOTSup 87; Sheffield: Sheffield Academic).

_____. 2000. "The Panamuwa Inscription", in *COS* 2.37.

Zimmerli, W., 1962. *Das Buch Predigers Salomo*. ATD 16/1. Göttingen:Vandenhoeck & Ruprecht.

_____. 1964. "The Place and Limit of the Wisdom in the Framework of the Old Testament Theology", *SJT* 17: 146-158.

_____. 1974. "Das Buch Kohelet – Traktat oder Sentenzensammlung?", *VT* 24: 221-30.

Zimmerman, F., 1973. *The Inner World of Qohelet*. New York: KTAV.

Zimmerman, O. J., 1959. *Saint Gregory the Great: Dialogues*. FC 39. New York: Fathers of the Church.

Index of Biblical and Apocryphal References